# READY NOTES

for use with

# MANAGERIAL ACCOUNTING

Eighth Edition

**Ray H. Garrison**
**Eric W. Noreen**

Prepared by

**Jon A. Booker**
**Charles W. Caldwell**
**Susan C. Galbreath**
**Richard S. Rand**
*All of Tennessee Technological University*

**IRWIN**
Chicago • Bogotá • Boston • Buenos Aires • Caracas
London • Madrid • Mexico City • Sydney • Toronto

*Printed in the United States of America.*

ISBN 0–256–16943–8

2 3 4 5 6 7 8 9 0 EB 3 2 1 0 9 8 7 6

WELCOME TO *RICHARD D. IRWIN'S*

# READY NOTES

**to accompany**

## Managerial Accounting

**Eighth Edition**
**by Garrison and Noreen**

Your life just got easier! This booklet includes *Ready Notes* to accompany Managerial Accounting, eighth edition by Garrison and Noreen. *Ready Notes* was designed as a classroom supplement to accompany *Ready Shows*. More importantly, *Ready Notes* was developed for you, the student.

Somewhere in your educational experience, you have undoubtably encountered a common dilemma facing many students; the feeling of helplessness that comes from trying to write down everything your instructor says and at the same time actually paying attention to what is being taught. *Ready Notes* addresses this problem by providing pre-prepared lecture outlines to accompany the *Ready Shows* your instructor will be using in class. Rather than spending time copying material that is already in the book, you will be able to focus on the most important aspects of what your instructor is actually saying. You will still be expected to take notes, but the nature of those notes will change.

Each page in *Ready Notes* includes reproductions of the actual projected screens that you will be seeing in class. The *Ready Notes* booklet includes the information for many of the examples that your instructor will be presenting in class. Also, throughout the booklet, appropriate worksheets have been included for you to tear out and use to complete in-class exercises and problems.

It is your responsibility to attend class regularly and to be prepared for class. However, used properly, *Ready Notes* will help you to achieve your goals for this course. Good luck and good accounting!

## CONTENTS

MANAGERIAL

GARRISON

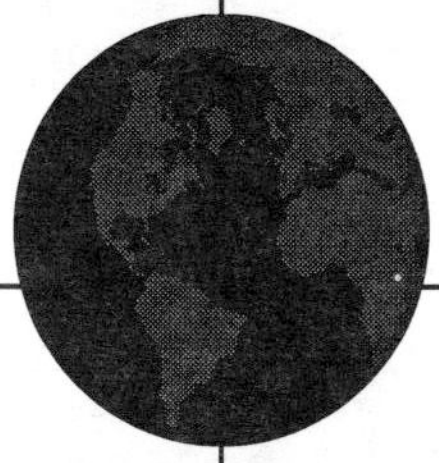

Eighth Edition

ACCOUNTING

NOREEN

---

1

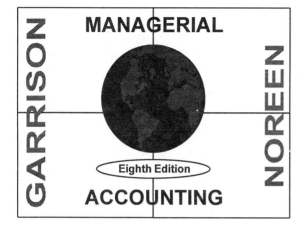

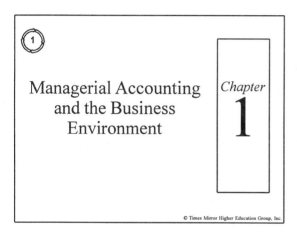

# Managerial Accounting and the Business Environment

*Chapter*

1



---

1

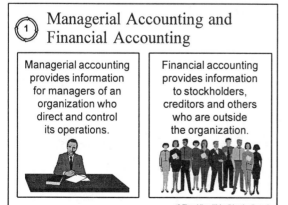

## Managerial Accounting and Financial Accounting

Managerial accounting provides information for managers of an organization who direct and control its operations.

Financial accounting provides information to stockholders, creditors and others who are outside the organization.

## 1 Work of Management

- Planning
- Directing and Motivating
- Controlling

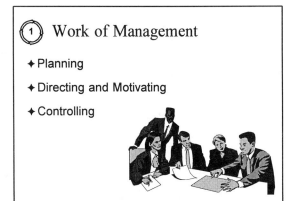

## 1 Planning and Control Cycle

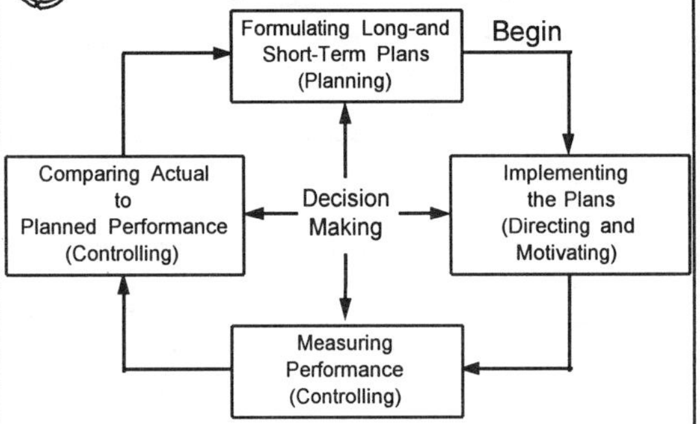




## 1 Differences Between Financial and Managerial Accounting

| | Financial Accounting | Managerial Accounting |
|---|---|---|
| 1. Users | External persons who make financial decisions | Managers who plan for and control an organization |
| 2. Time focus | Historical perspective | Future emphasis |
| 3. Verifiability versus relevance | Emphasis on verifiability | Emphasis on relevance for planning and control |
| 4. Precision versus timeliness | Emphasis on precision | Emphasis on timeliness |
| 5. Subject | Primary focus is on the whole organization | Focuses on specific projects and processes |
| 6. Requirements | Must follow GAAP and prescribed formats | Need not follow GAAP or any prescribed format |

## 1 Expanding Role of Managerial Accounting

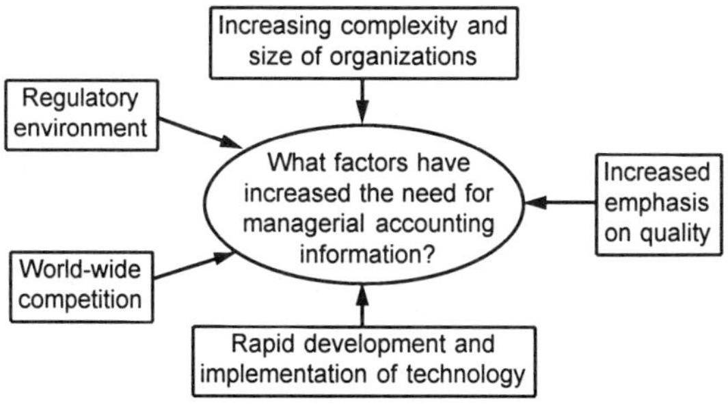




## 1 The Changing Business Environment

**How has the business environment changed in the past twenty years?**

**A more competitive environment emphasizing:**

- ❶ **Higher quality products**
- ❷ **Lower prices and costs**
- ❸ **Increased production**
- ❹ **Meeting and anticipating customer needs**



## 1 The Changing Business Environment

**What new tools or approaches do managers use?**

**Just-In-Time**

**Total Quality Management**

**Process Reengineering**

**Automation**

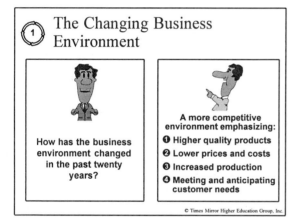

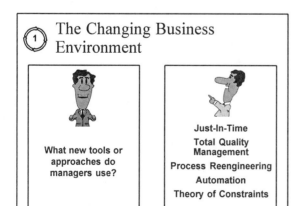

**Theory of Constraints**

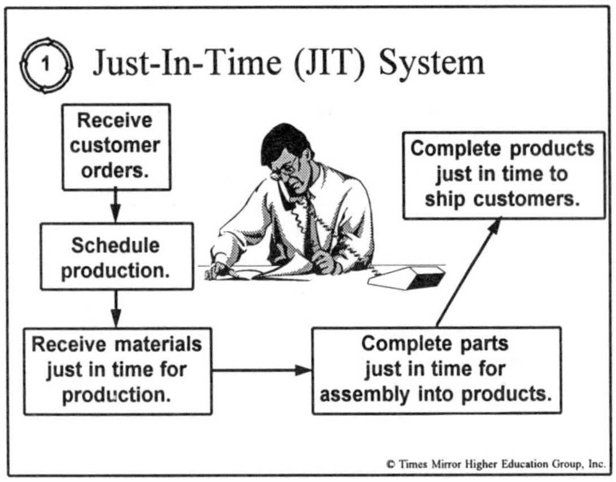
1
Just-In-Time (JIT) System
Receive customer orders.
Schedule production.
Receive materials just in time for production.
Complete parts just in time for assembly into products.
Complete products just in time to ship customers.
© Times Mirror Higher Education Group, Inc.

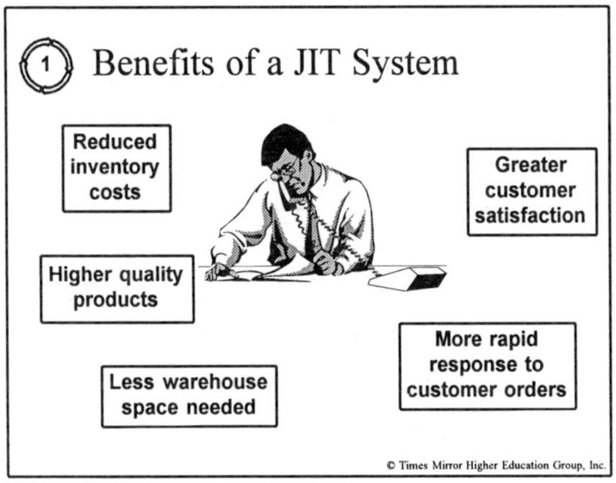
1
Benefits of a JIT System
Reduced inventory costs
Higher quality products
Less warehouse space needed
Greater customer satisfaction
More rapid response to customer orders
© Times Mirror Higher Education Group, Inc.

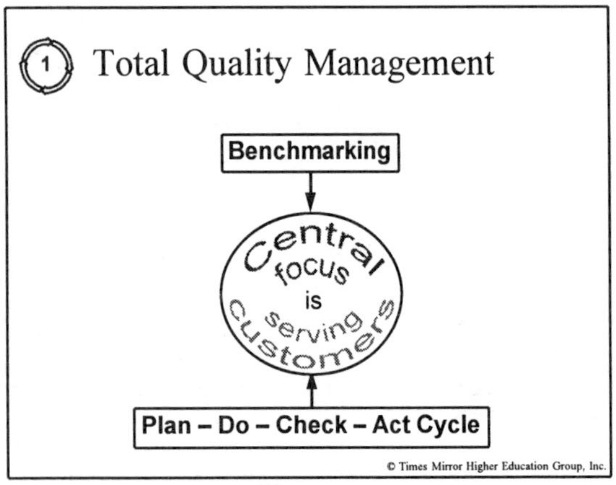
1
Total Quality Management
Benchmarking
Central focus is serving customers
Plan – Do – Check – Act Cycle
© Times Mirror Higher Education Group, Inc.

## Plan-Do-Check-Act Cycle

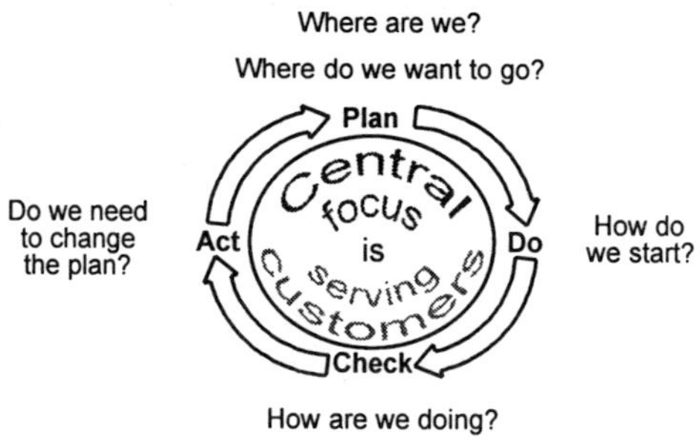




## Process Reengineering

❶A business process is diagrammed in detail.

❷Every step in the business process must be justified.

❸The process is redesigned to include only those steps that make our product more valuable.

## Automation

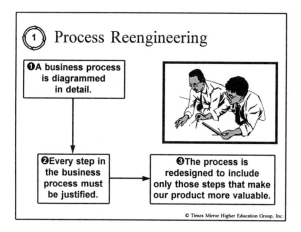

- Automation frequently involves replacing people with machines.
- Benefits of automation:
  - Reduces labor costs.
  - Reduces defects.
  - Increases output.

## Theory of Constraints

A sequential process of identifying and removing constraints in a system.

Restrictions or barriers that impede progress toward an objective

## International Competition

Meeting world-class competition demands a world-class management accounting system.

Managers must make decisions to plan, direct, and control a world-class organization.

## Organizations and their Objectives

An organization is a group of people united for a common purpose.

## 1 Organizational Structure

Corporate Organization Chart

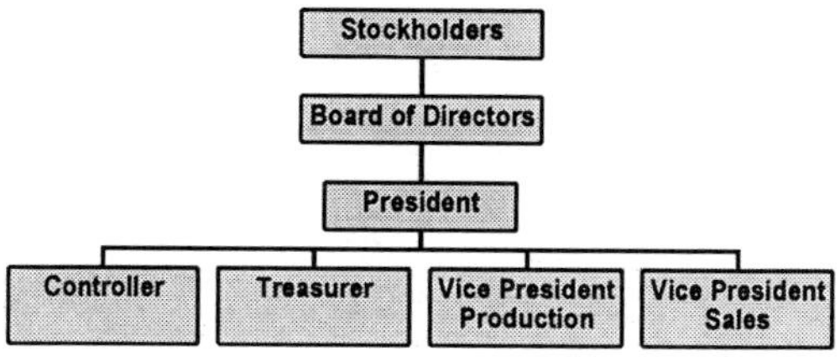




## 1 Decentralization

Corporate Organization Chart

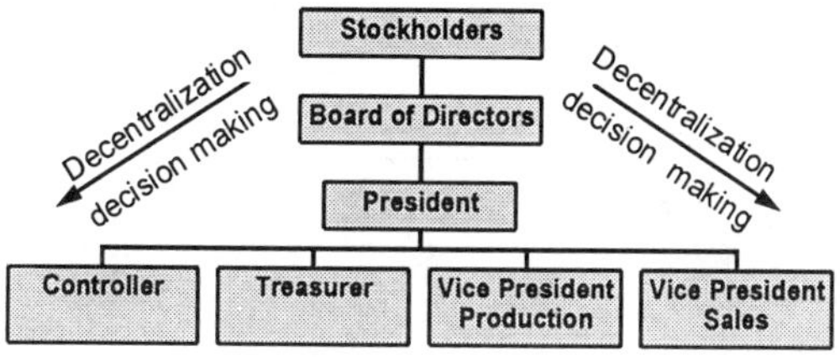




## 1 Line and Staff Relationships

- A line position is directly related to achievement of the basic objectives of an organization.
  - Example: A production supervisor in a manufacturing plant.

- A staff position supports and assists line positions.
  - Example: A cost accountant in the manufacturing plant.

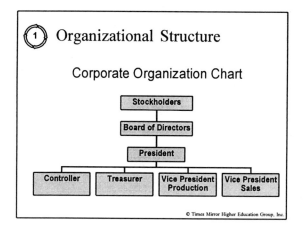

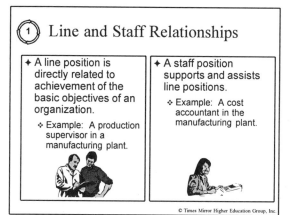

## ① The Controller

- The chief accountant in an organization with responsibility for:
  - Financial planning and analysis.
  - Cost control.
  - Financial reporting.
  - Accounting information systems.

## ① Professional Ethics

- Ethics are . . .
  1. Principles that determine the rightness or wrongness of particular acts or activities.
  2. Accepted standards of good behavior that govern the conduct of an individual or a profession.

## ① Professional Ethics

Ethical business practices build trust and promote loyal, productive relationships with customers, employees and suppliers.

Many companies have written codes of ethics which serve as guides for employees to follow.

## Importance of Ethics in Accounting

Users must be able to trust information provided by accountants.

Management accountants are governed by a code of ethics issued by the Institute of Management Accountants (IMA).

## IMA Code of Ethics for Management Accountants

Competence

Confidentiality

Integrity

Objectivity

Resolution of Ethical Conflict

## IMA Code of Ethics for Management Accountants

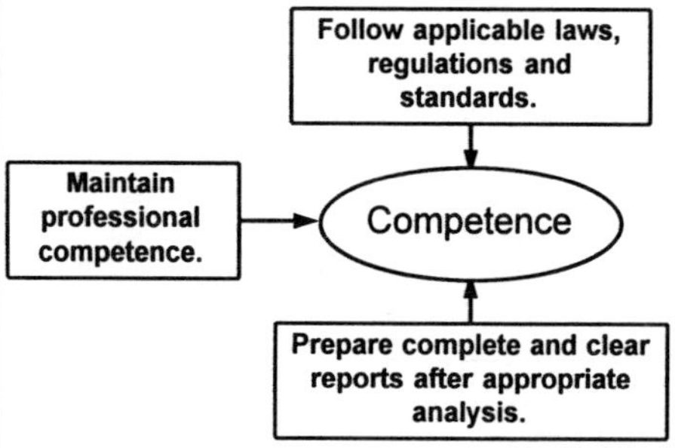
Follow applicable laws, regulations and standards.
Maintain professional competence.
Competence
Prepare complete and clear reports after appropriate analysis.

## IMA Code of Ethics for Management Accountants

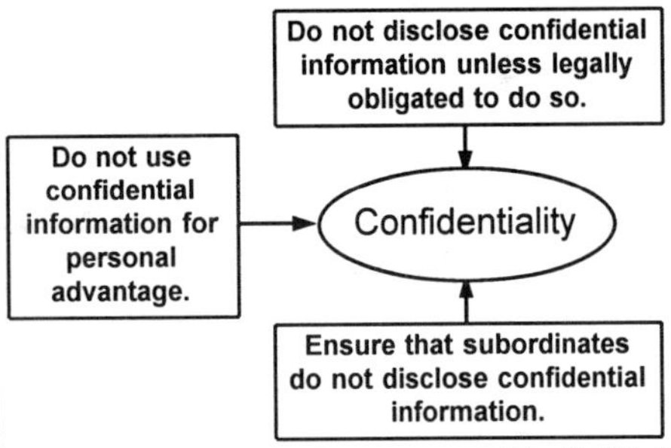




## IMA Code of Ethics for Management Accountants

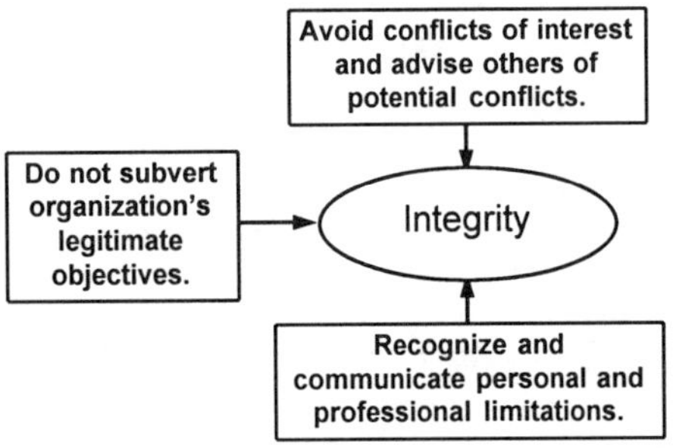




## IMA Code of Ethics for Management Accountants

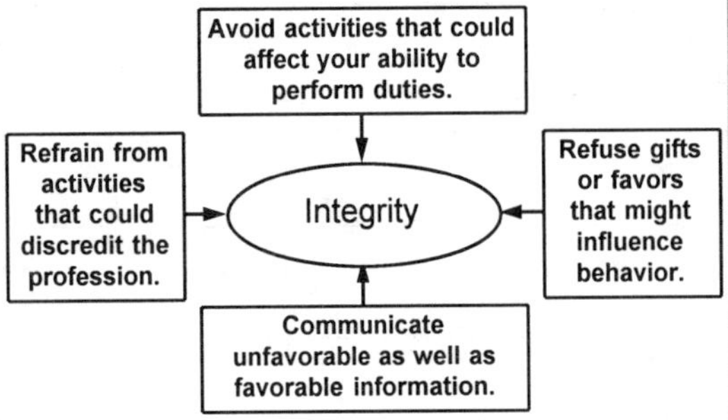

## IMA Code of Ethics for Management Accountants

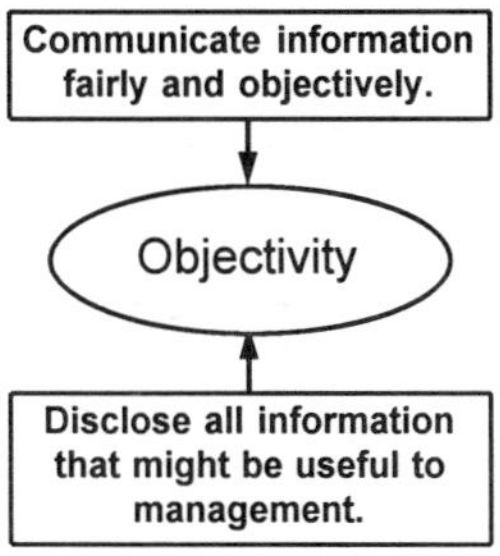

Communicate information fairly and objectively.
Objectivity
Disclose all information that might be useful to management.

## IMA Code of Ethics for Management Accountants

### Resolution of Ethical Conflict

❶Follow established policies of your organization.

❷If unresolved or if policy does not exist:

- Clarify relevant concepts in a confidential discussion with an objective advisor to explore possible courses of action.
- Discuss problem with immediate supervisor.



## IMA Code of Ethics for Management Accountants

### Resolution of Ethical Conflict

❸If immediate supervisor is involved in the unethical behavior, discuss at the next level.

❹If problem is not resolved, the last resort is to resign.

❺Generally, do not communicate ethical conflicts to outsiders.

1 End of Chapter 1

GARRISON

# MANAGERIAL ACCOUNTING

Eighth Edition

NOREEN

---

2

# Cost Terms, Concepts, and Classifications

*Chapter* 2



---

2

## Comparing Merchandising and Manufacturing Activities

**Merchandisers . . .**

- Buy finished goods.
- Sell finished goods.

**Manufacturers . . .**

- Buy raw materials.
- Produce and sell finished goods.

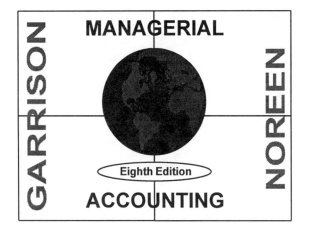

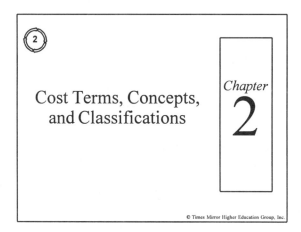

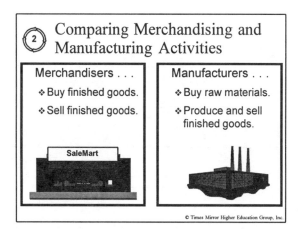

## 2 Manufacturing Cost Concepts

Our focus changes from financial statement costs to product costs

**Financial Accounting**

Cost is a measure of resources used or given up to achieve a stated purpose.

**Managerial Accounting**

Product costs are the costs a company assigns to units produced.



## 2 Classifications of Product Costs in Manufacturing Companies

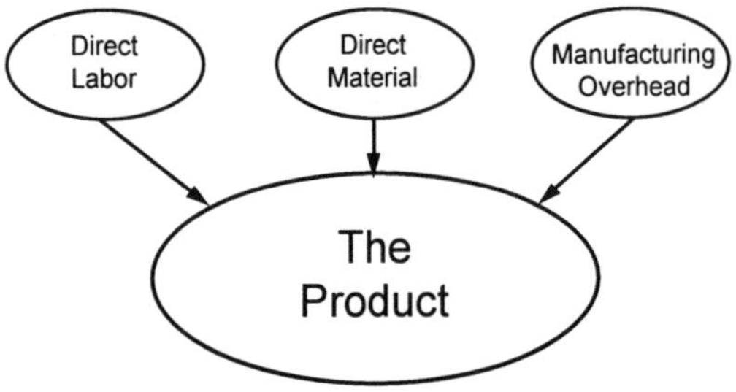




## 2 Direct Materials

Those materials that are an integral part of the product and that can be conveniently traced directly to the product.

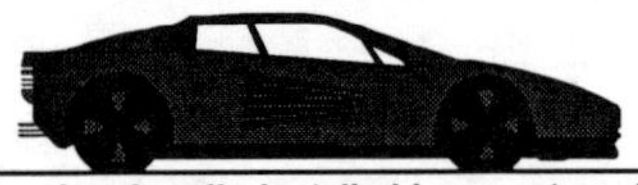

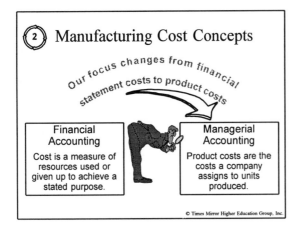

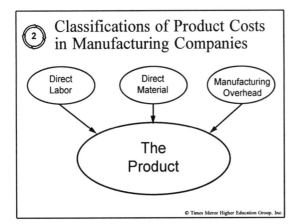

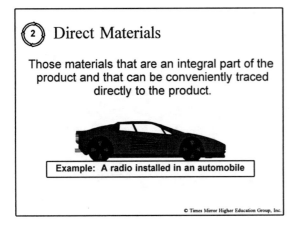

**Example: A radio installed in an automobile**

## ② Direct Labor

Wages paid to employees who convert direct materials into finished products.

Direct labor costs can be physically and conveniently traced to products.

**Example: Wages paid to automobile assembly workers**



## ② Manufacturing Overhead

Manufacturing costs that cannot be traced directly to specific units produced.

**Examples: Indirect labor and indirect material**

**Indirect labor is wages paid to employees who are not directly involved in production work. Examples: maintenance workers, janitors and security guards.**

**Indirect materials are used to support the production process. Examples: lubricants and cleaning supplies used in the automobile assembly plant.**



## ② Manufacturing Overhead

Manufacturing costs that cannot be traced directly to specific units produced.

**Examples: Indirect labor and indirect material**

**All manufacturing costs except direct material and direct labor must be manufacturing overhead!**

## Classifications of Costs in Manufacturing Companies

Manufacturing costs are often combined as follows:

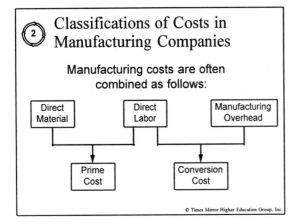

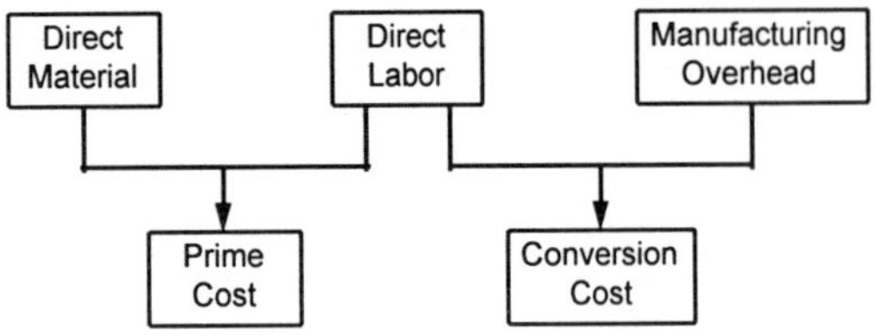




## Cost Classifications on Financial Statements – Balance Sheet

| Merchandiser | Manufacturer |
|---|---|
| Current Assets | Current Assets |
| ❖ Cash | ❖ Cash |
| ❖ Receivables | ❖ Receivables |
| ❖ Prepaid Expenses | ❖ Prepaid Expenses |
| ❖ Merchandise Inventory | ❖ Inventories |
| | Raw Materials |
| | Work in Process |
| | Finished Goods |



## Inventory Relationships

Costs of raw materials are transferred to work in process as materials are used.

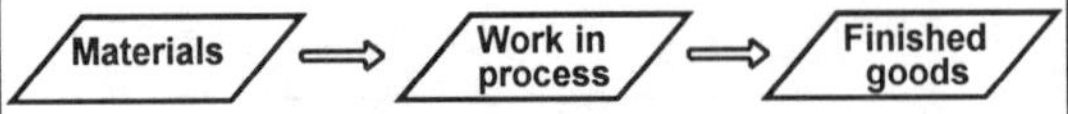


As units are completed, costs of completed units are transferred to finished goods.

## Flows of Resources Through the Inventories

**Inventory**

Beginning inventory
+ Additions to inventory
= Inventory available for use or sale
- Ending inventory
= Goods transferred out or sold

**The inflow/outflow model used for raw materials, work in process, and finished goods is the same regardless of inventory account.**



## The Income Statement

Cost of goods sold for manufacturers differs only slightly from cost of goods sold for merchandisers.

**Merchandising Company**

| Cost of goods sold: | |
|---|---|
| Beg. merchandise inventory | $ 14,200 |
| + Purchases | 234,150 |
| Goods available for sale | $ 248,350 |
| - Ending merchandise inventory | (12,100) |
| = Cost of goods sold | $ 236,250 |

**Manufacturing Company**

| Cost of goods sold: | |
|---|---|
| Beg. finished goods inv. | $ 14,200 |
| + Cost of goods manufactured | 234,150 |
| Goods available for sale | $ 248,350 |
| - Ending finished goods inventory | (12,100) |
| = Cost of goods sold | $ 236,250 |



## Manufacturing Cost Flows

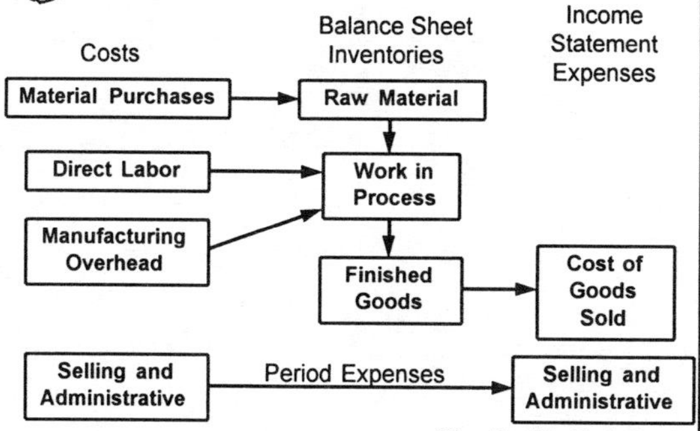

## 2 Flows of Resources Through the Inventories

**Raw Materials**

Beginning raw materials inventory
\+ Raw materials purchased
= Raw materials available for use in production
– Ending raw materials inventory
= Raw materials used in production

**Manufacturing Costs**

Direct materials
\+ Direct labor
\+ Mfg. overhead
= Manufacturing costs for the period

**Work In Process**

Beginning work in process inventory
\+ Manufacturing costs for the period
= Total work in process for the period
– Ending work in process inventory
= Cost of goods manufactured.



## 2 Flows of Resources Through the Inventories

**Work In Process**

Beginning work in process inventory
\+ Manufacturing costs for the period
= Total work in process for the period
– Ending work in process inventory
= Cost of goods manufactured

**Finished Goods**

Beginning finished goods inventory
\+ Cost of goods manufactured
= Cost of goods available for sale
– Ending finished goods inventory
= Cost of goods sold



## 2 Schedule of Cost of Goods Manufactured

Direct materials
\+ Direct labor
\+ Manufacturing overhead
= Total manufacturing costs
\+ Beginning work in process
= Total costs to account for
– Ending work in process
= Cost of goods manufactured

2

# Schedule of Cost of Goods Manufactured

| GRAHAM MANUFACTURING<br>Schedule of Cost of Goods Manufactured | |
|---|---|
| Cost of direct materials used in production | $ 410,000 |
| Direct labor | 60,000 |
| Total manufacturing overhead costs | 350,000 |
| Total manufacturing costs for the period | 820,000 |
| Add: Beginning work in process inventory | 90,000 |
| Total work in process during the period | 910,000 |
| Deduct: Ending work in process inventory | 60,000 |
| Cost of goods manufactured | $ 850,000 |



2

| Computation of Cost of Direct Material Used | |
|---|---|
| Beginning raw materials inventory | $ 70,000 |
| Add: Purchases of raw materials | 390,000 |
| Cost of raw materials available for use | 460,000 |
| Deduct: Ending raw materials inventory | 50,000 |
| Cost of direct materials used in production | $ 410,000 |

| Schedule of Cost of Goods Manufactured | |
|---|---|
| Cost of direct materials used in production | $ 410,000 |
| Direct labor | 60,000 |
| Total manufacturing overhead costs | 350,000 |
| Total manufacturing costs for the period | 820,000 |
| Add: Beginning work in process inventory | 90,000 |
| Total work in process during the period | 910,000 |
| Deduct: Ending work in process inventory | 60,000 |
| Cost of goods manufactured | $ 850,000 |



2

# Sche
Man

| Computation of Total Manufacturing Overhead | |
|---|---|
| Insurance, factory | $ 6,000 |
| Indirect labor | 100,000 |
| Machine rental | 50,000 |
| Utilities, factory | 75,000 |
| Supplies | 21,000 |
| Depreciation, factory | 90,000 |
| Property taxes, factory | 8,000 |
| Total manufacturing overhead costs | $ 350,000 |

| Sch | |
|---|---|
| Cost of direct | |
| Direct labor | 60,000 |
| Total manufacturing overhead costs | 350,000 |
| Total manufacturing costs for the period | 820,000 |
| Add: Beginning work in process inventory | 90,000 |
| Total work in process during the period | 910,000 |
| Deduct: Ending work in process inventory | 60,000 |
| Cost of goods manufactured | $ 850,000 |

## Income Statement for a Manufacturer

GRAHAM MANUFACTURING
Partial Income Statement
For the Year Ended December 31, 19XX

| | | |
|---|---|---|
| Sales revenue | | $ 1,500,000 |
| Cost of goods sold: | | |
| Beginning finished goods inventory | $ 125,000 | |
| Add: Cost of goods manufactured | 850,000 | |
| Cost of finished goods available for sale | 975,000 | |
| Deduct: Ending finished goods inventory | 175,000 | |
| Cost of goods sold | | 800,000 |
| Gross margin | | $ 700,000 |



## In
## M

GRAHAM MANUFACTURING
Schedule of Cost of Goods Manufactured

| | |
|---|---|
| Cost of direct materials used in production | $ 410,000 |
| Direct labor | 60,000 |
| Total manufacturing overhead costs | 350,000 |
| Total manufacturing costs for the period | 820,000 |
| Add: Beginning work in process inventory | 90,000 |
| Total work in process during the period | 910,000 |
| Deduct: Ending work in process inventory | 60,000 |
| Cost of goods manufactured | $ 850,000 |

| | | |
|---|---|---|
| Sales revenue | | $ 1,500,000 |
| Cost of goods sold: | | |
| Beginning finished goods inventory | $ 125,000 | |
| Add: Cost of goods manufactured | 850,000 | |
| Cost of finished goods available for sale | 975,000 | |
| Deduct: Ending finished goods inventory | 175,000 | |
| Cost of goods sold | | 800,000 |
| Gross margin | | $ 700,000 |

© Times Mirror Higher Education Group, Inc.

## Resource Flows Question 1

Beginning raw materials inventory was $32,000. During the month, $276,000 of raw material was purchased. A count at the end of the month revealed that $28,000 of raw material was still present. What is the cost of direct material used?

a. $276,000
b. $272,000
c. $280,000
d. $ 2,000

© Times Mirror Higher Education Group, Inc.

## 2 Resource Flows Question 2

Direct materials used in production totaled $280,000. Direct Labor was $375,000 and factory overhead was $180,000. What were total manufacturing costs incurred for the month?

a. $555,000
b. $835,000
c. $655,000
d. Cannot be determined.



## 2 Resource Flows Question 3

Beginning work in process was $125,000. Manufacturing costs incurred for the month were $835,000. There were $200,000 of partially finished goods remaining in work in process inventory at the end of the month. What was the cost of goods manufactured during the month?

a. $1,160,000
b. $ 910,000
c. $ 760,000
d. Cannot be determined.



## 2 Cost Classifications for Predicting Cost Behavior

- Cost behavior means how a cost will react to changes in the level of business activity.
  - Total variable costs change when activity changes.
  - Total fixed costs remain unchanged when activity changes.

## Total Variable Cost Example

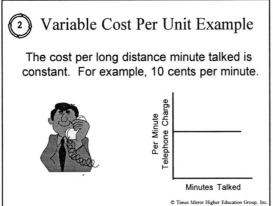

Your total long distance telephone bill is based on how many minutes you talk.

## Variable Cost Per Unit Example

The cost per long distance minute talked is constant. For example, 10 cents per minute.

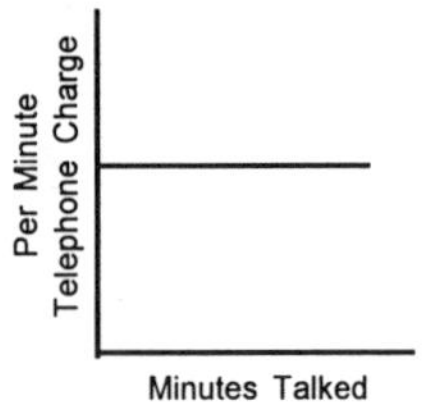




## Total Fixed Cost Example

Your monthly basic telephone bill probably does not change when you make more local calls.

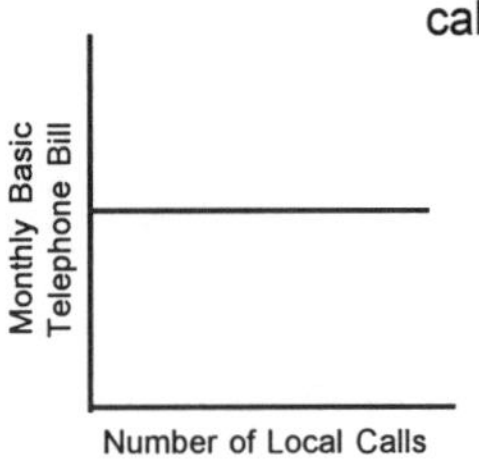

## Fixed Cost Per Unit Example

The average cost per local call decreases as more local calls are made.

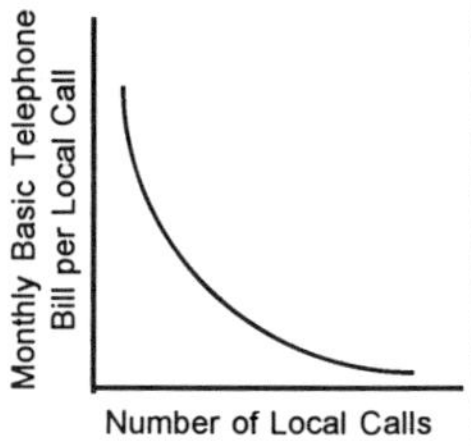




## Cost Classifications for Predicting Cost Behavior

**Summary of Variable and Fixed Cost Behavior**

| Cost | In Total | Per Unit |
|---|---|---|
| Variable | Total variable cost changes as activity level changes. | Variable cost per unit remains the same over wide ranges of activity. |
| Fixed | Total fixed cost remains the same even when the activity level changes. | Fixed cost per unit goes down as activity level goes up. |



## Cost Behavior Question 1

Fixed costs are usually characterized by:

a. Unit costs that remain constant.

b. Total costs that increase as activity decreases.

c. Total costs that increase as activity increases.

d. Total costs that remain constant.

## Cost Behavior Question 2

Variable costs are usually characterized by:

a. Unit costs that decrease as activity increases.
b. Total costs that increase as activity decreases.
c. Total costs that increase as activity increases.
d. Total costs that remain constant.



## Direct Costs and Indirect Costs

**Direct costs**

- Costs that can be easily and conveniently traced to a unit of product or other cost objective.
- Examples: direct material and direct labor

**Indirect costs**

- Costs that must be allocated in order to be assigned to a unit of product or other cost objective.
- Example: manufacturing overhead

## Differential Costs and Revenues

Costs and revenues that differ among alternatives.

**Example: You have a job paying $1,500 per month in your hometown. You have a job offer in a neighboring city that pays $2,000 per month. The commuting cost to the city is $300 per month.**

**What is your differential revenue?**

## ② Differential Costs and Revenues

Costs and revenues that differ among alternatives.

**Example: You have a job paying $1,500 per month in your hometown. You have a job offer in a neighboring city that pays $2,000 per month. The commuting cost to the city is $300 per month.**

**What is your differential cost?**



## ② Opportunity Costs

- The potential benefit that is given up when one alternative is selected over another.
  - Example: If you were not attending college, you could be earning $15,000 per year. Your opportunity cost of attending college for one year is $15,000.

## ② Sunk Costs

All costs incurred in the past that cannot be changed by any decision made now or in the future.

Sunk costs should not be considered in decisions.

- Example: You bought an automobile that cost $10,000 two years ago. The $10,000 cost is sunk because whether you drive it, park it, trade it, or sell it, you cannot change the $10,000 cost.

End of Chapter 2

GARRISON

MANAGERIAL

Eighth Edition

ACCOUNTING

NOREEN

---

3

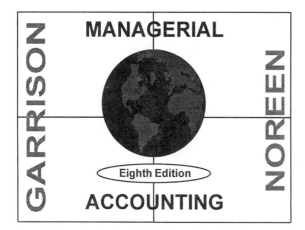

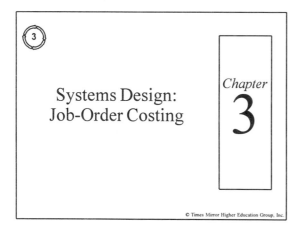

Systems Design:
Job-Order Costing

*Chapter*
3

---

## The Need for Product Cost Data

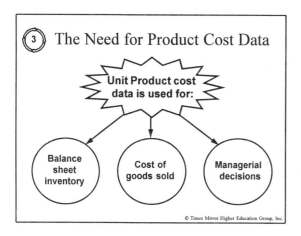

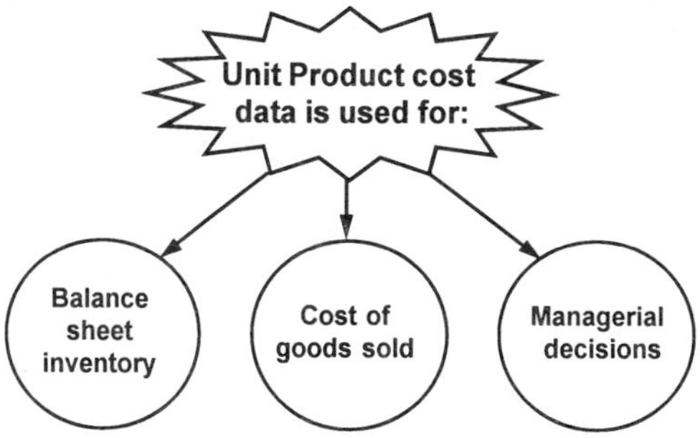
Unit Product cost
data is used for:
Balance sheet inventory
Cost of goods sold
Managerial decisions

## Types of Costing Systems Used to Determine Product Costs

Process Costing | Job-order Costing

- Used for production of small, identical, low cost items.
- Mass produced in automated continuous production process.
- Costs cannot be directly traced to each unit of product.



## Types of Costing Systems Used to Determine Product Costs

Process Costing | Job-order Costing

Typical process cost applications:

- Petrochemical refinery
- Paint manufacturer
- Paper mill

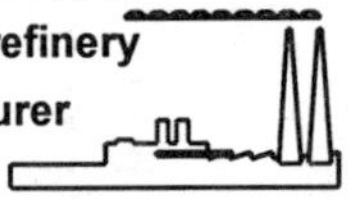



## Types of Costing Systems Used to Determine Product Costs

Process Costing | Job-order Costing

- Used for production of large, unique, high-cost items.
- Built to order rather than mass produced.
- Many costs can be directly traced to each job.

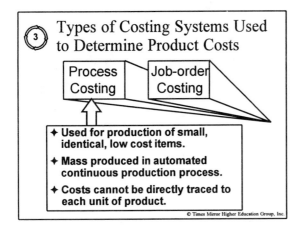

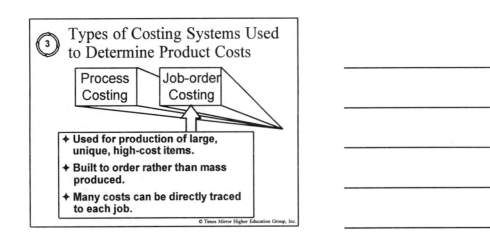

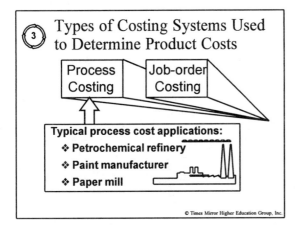

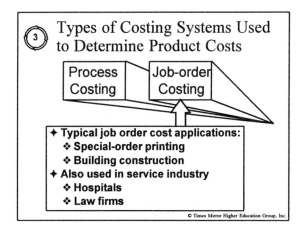

## Types of Costing Systems Used to Determine Product Costs

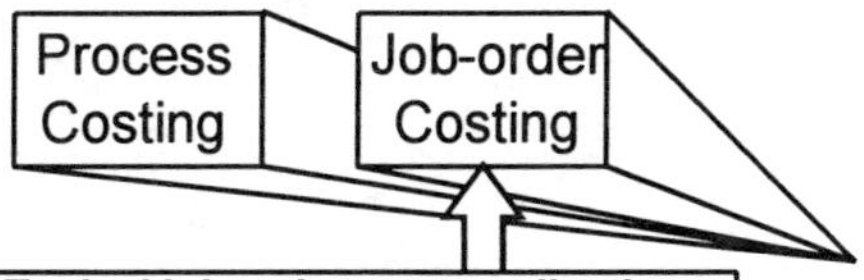


- Typical job order cost applications:
  - Special-order printing
  - Building construction
- Also used in service industry
  - Hospitals
  - Law firms



## Job-Order Costing

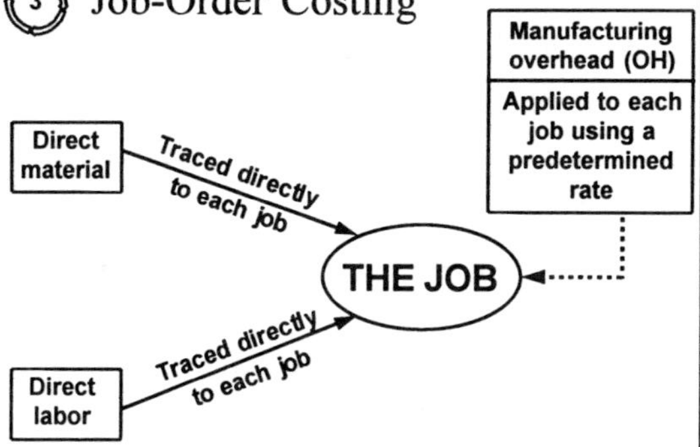

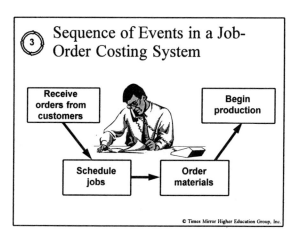

## Sequence of Events in a Job-Order Costing System

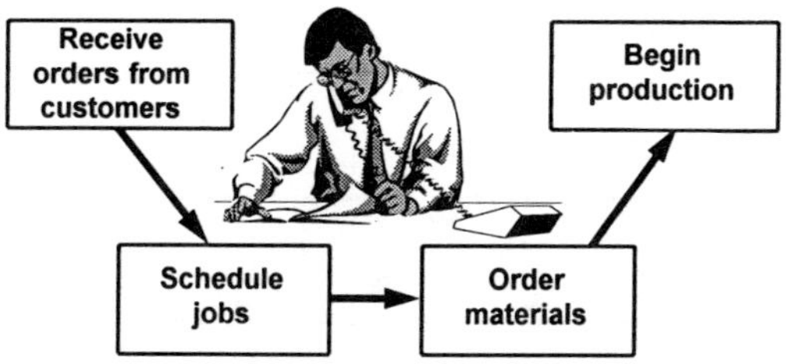

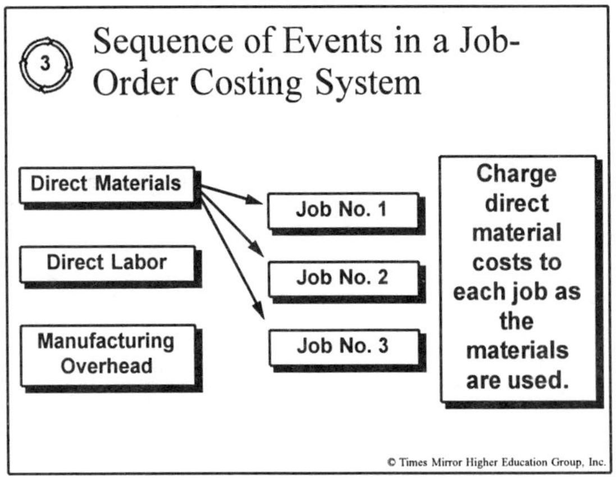
3
Sequence of Events in a Job-Order Costing System
Direct Materials
Direct Labor
Manufacturing Overhead
Job No. 1
Job No. 2
Job No. 3
Charge direct material costs to each job as the materials are used.
© Times Mirror Higher Education Group, Inc.

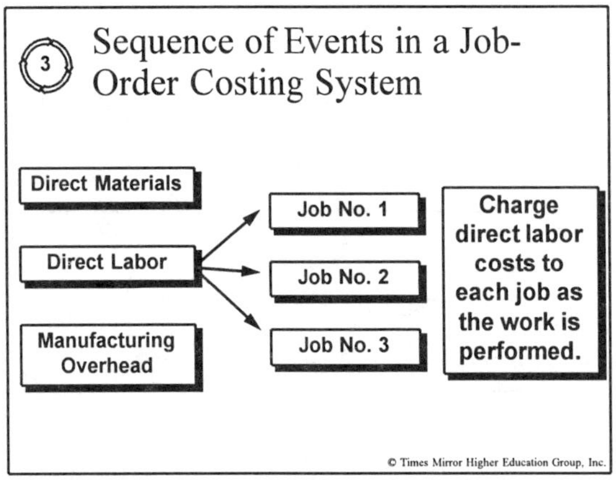
3
Sequence of Events in a Job-Order Costing System
Direct Materials
Direct Labor
Manufacturing Overhead
Job No. 1
Job No. 2
Job No. 3
Charge direct labor costs to each job as the work is performed.
© Times Mirror Higher Education Group, Inc.

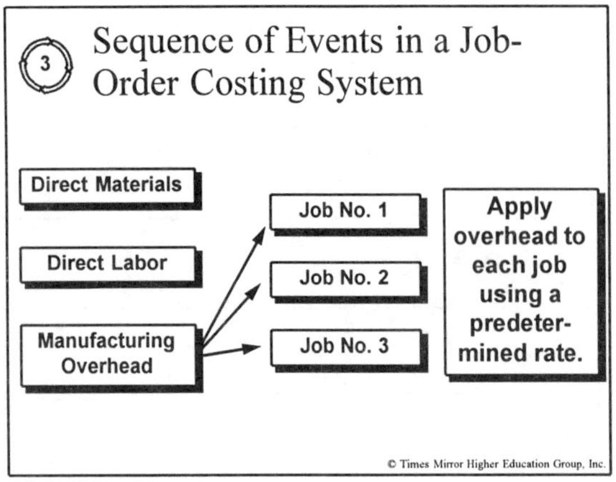
3
Sequence of Events in a Job-Order Costing System
Direct Materials
Direct Labor
Manufacturing Overhead
Job No. 1
Job No. 2
Job No. 3
Apply overhead to each job using a predetermined rate.
© Times Mirror Higher Education Group, Inc.

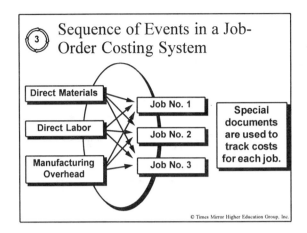

## 3 Sequence of Events in a Job-Order Costing System

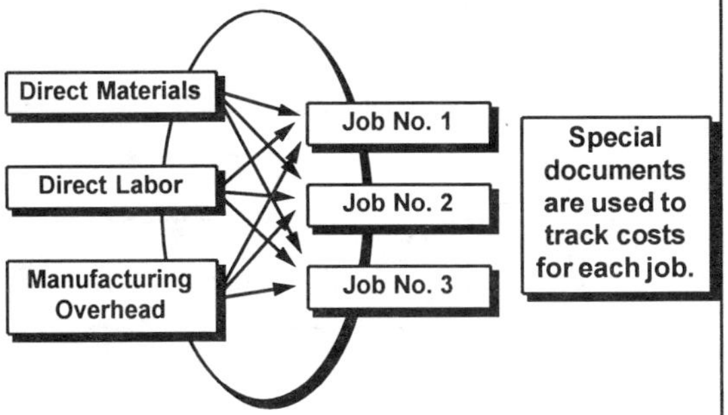




## 3 Job-Order Cost Accounting

The primary document for tracking the costs associated with a given job is the job cost sheet.

Let's investigate



## 3 Job-Order Cost Accounting

**PearCo Job Cost Sheet**

Job Number A - 143 Date Initiated 3-4-X7
Date Completed
Department B3 Units Completed
Item Wooden cargo crate

| Direct Materials | | Direct Labor | | | Manufacturing Overhead | | |
|---|---|---|---|---|---|---|---|
| Req. No. | Amount | Ticket | Hours | Amount | Hours | Rate | Amount |
| | | | | | | | |

| Cost Summary | | Units Shipped | | |
|---|---|---|---|---|
| | | Date | Number | Balance |
| Direct Materials | | | | |
| Direct Labor | | | | |
| Manufacturing Overhead | | | | |
| Total Cost | | | | |
| Unit Cost | | | | |

## 3 Materials Requisition Form

**PearCo Materials Requisition Form**

Requisition No. X7 - 6890    Date 3-4-X7
Job No. A - 143
Department B3

| Description | Quantity | Unit Cost | Total Cost |
|---|---|---|---|
| 2 x 4, 12 feet | 12 | $ 3.00 | $ 36.00 |
| 1 x 6, 12 feet | 20 | 4.00 | 80.00 |
| | | | $ 116.00 |

Authorized Signature *Will E. Delite*



## 3 Job-Order Cost Accounting

**PearCo Job Cost Sheet**

Job Number A - 143    Date Initiated 3-4-X7
Date Completed
Department B3    Units Completed
Item Wooden cargo crate

| Direct Materials | | Direct Labor | | | Manufacturing Overhead | | |
|---|---|---|---|---|---|---|---|
| Req. No. | Amount | Ticket | Hours | Amount | Hours | Rate | Amount |
| X7-6890 | $ 116 | | | | | | |

| Cost Summary | | Units Shipped | | |
|---|---|---|---|---|
| | | Date | Number | Balance |
| Direct Materials | $ 116 | | | |
| Direct Labor | | | | |
| Manufacturing Overhead | | | | |
| Total Cost | | | | |
| Unit Cost | | | | |



## 3 Employee Time Ticket

**PearCo Employee Time Ticket**

Time Ticket No. 36    Date 3-5-X7
Employee I. M. Skilled    Station 42

| Starting Time | Ending Time | Hours Completed | Hourly Rate | Amount | Job No. |
|---|---|---|---|---|---|
| 0800 | 1600 | 8.00 | $ 11.00 | $ 88.00 | A-143 |
| Totals | | 8.00 | $ 11.00 | $ 88.00 | A-143 |

Supervisor [illegible]

## 3 Job-Order Cost Accounting

**PearCo Job Cost Sheet**

Job Number A - 143 | Date Initiated 3-4-X7
Date Completed
Department B3 | Units Completed
Item Wooden cargo crate

| Direct Materials | | Direct Labor | | | Manufacturing Overhead | | |
|---|---|---|---|---|---|---|---|
| Req. No. | Amount | Ticket | Hours | Amount | Hours | Rate | Amount |
| X7-6890 | $ 116 | 36 | 8 | $ 88 | | | |

| Cost Summary | | Units Shipped | | |
|---|---|---|---|---|
| | | Date | Number | Balance |
| Direct Materials | $ 116 | | | |
| Direct Labor | $ 88 | | | |
| Manufacturing Overhead | | | | |
| Total Cost | | | | |
| Unit Cost | | | | |



## 3 Job-Order Cost Accounting

**PearCo Job Cost Sheet**

Job Number A - 143 | Date Initiated 3-4-X7
Date Completed 3-5-X7
Department B3 | Units Completed 2
Item Wooden cargo crate

| Direct Materials | | Direct Labor | | | Manufacturing Overhead | | |
|---|---|---|---|---|---|---|---|
| Req. No. | Amount | Ticket | Hours | Amount | Hours | Rate | Amount |
| X7-6890 | $ 116 | 36 | 8 | $ 88 | 8 | $ 4 | $ 32 |

| Cost Summary | | Units Shipped | | |
|---|---|---|---|---|
| | | Date | Number | Balance |
| Direct Materials | $ 116 | | | |
| Direct Labor | $ 88 | | | |
| Manufacturing Overhead | $ 32 | | | |
| Total Cost | $ 236 | | | |
| Unit Cost | $ 118 | | | |



## 3 Application of Manufacturing Overhead

The predetermined overhead rate (POHR) used to apply overhead to jobs is determined before the period begins.

$$\text{POHR} = \frac{\text{Estimated total manufacturing overhead cost for the coming period}}{\text{Estimated total units in the activity base for the coming period}}$$

**The activity base used in the denominator is called the allocation base.**

## 3 Application of Manufacturing Overhead

- The allocation base should be a cost driver – it should be the cause of the overhead.
- Some examples of cost drivers include:
  - Units produced.
  - Direct labor hours
  - Machine hours.

**Overhead applied = POHR × Actual activity**

**Recall the wooden crate example where:**

**Overhead applied = $4 per DLH × 8 DLH = $32**



## 3 The Need for a Predetermined Manufacturing Overhead Rate

Using a predetermined rate makes it possible to estimate total job costs sooner.

Actual overhead for the period is not known until the end of the period.



## 3 Overhead Application Example

PearCo applies overhead based on direct labor hours. Total estimated overhead for the year is $640,000. Total estimated labor cost is $1,400,000 and total estimated labor hours are 160,000.
What is PearCo's predetermined overhead rate?

# Overhead Application Example

**PearCo Job Cost Sheet**

Job Number X - 32
Date Initiated 3-9-X7
Date Completed 3-11-X7
Department B3
Units Completed 6
Item Wooden cargo crate

| Direct Materials | | Direct Labor | | | Manufacturing Overhead | | |
|---|---|---|---|---|---|---|---|
| Req. No. | Amount | Ticket | Hours | Amount | Hours | Rate | Amount |
| X7-7456 | $ 240 | 23 | 26 | $ 286 | | | |

| Cost Summary | | Units Shipped | | |
|---|---|---|---|---|
| | | Date | Number | Balance |
| Direct Materials | $ 240 | | | |
| Direct | | | | |
| Manu | | | | |
| Total | | | | |
| Unit Cost | | | | |

What amount of overhead will PearCo apply to Job X-32?



# Job-Order Costing Document Flow Summary

The materials requisition indicates the cost of direct material to charge to jobs and the cost of indirect material to charge to overhead.

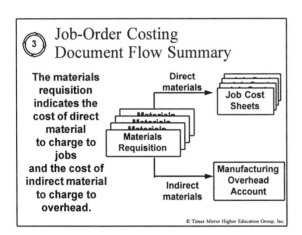

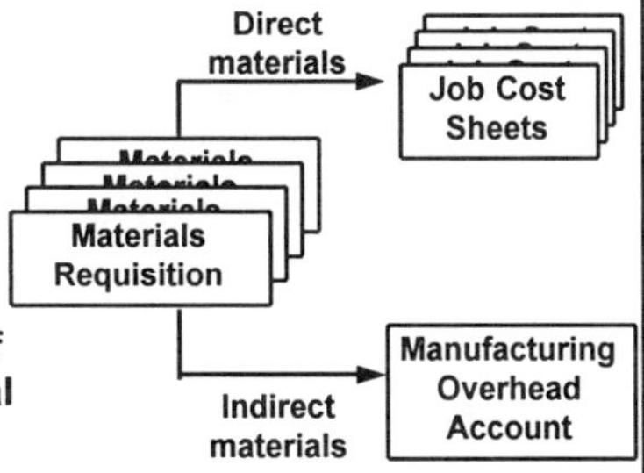




# Job-Order Costing Document Flow Summary

Employee time tickets indicate the cost of direct labor to charge to jobs and the cost of indirect labor to charge to overhead.

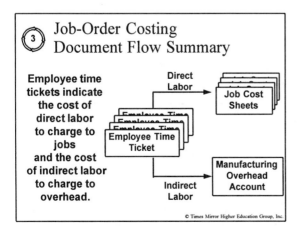

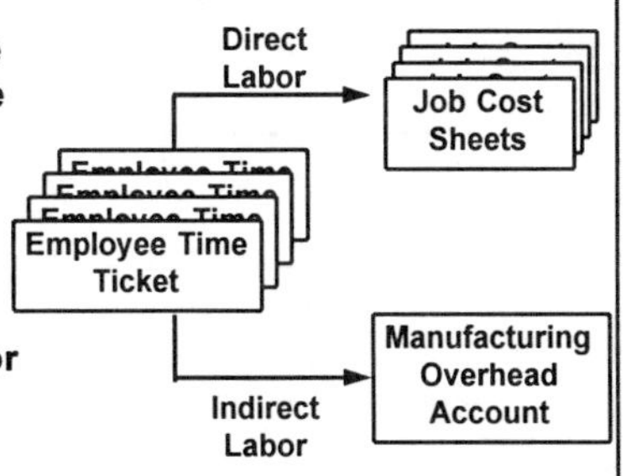

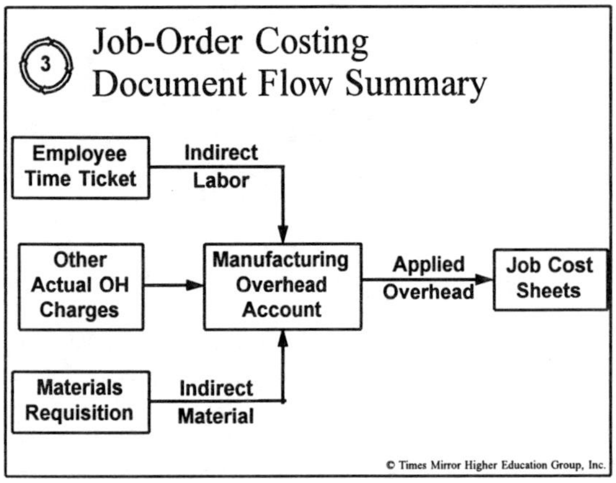
3
Job-Order Costing
Document Flow Summary
Employee Time Ticket
Indirect Labor
Other Actual OH Charges
Manufacturing Overhead Account
Applied Overhead
Job Cost Sheets
Materials Requisition
Indirect Material
© Times Mirror Higher Education Group, Inc.

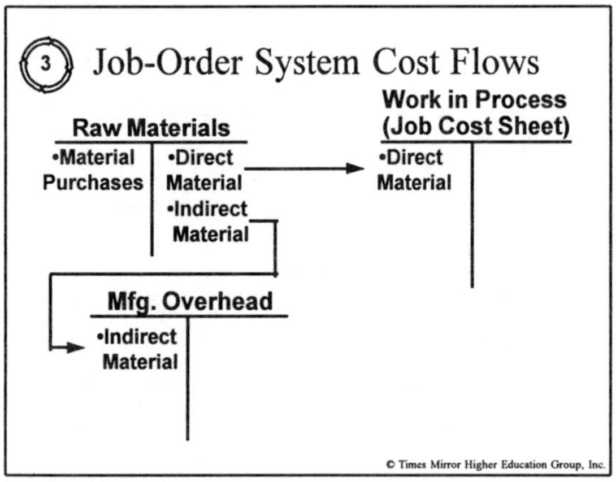
3
Job-Order System Cost Flows
Raw Materials
•Material Purchases
•Direct Material
•Indirect Material
Work in Process (Job Cost Sheet)
•Direct Material
Mfg. Overhead
•Indirect Material
© Times Mirror Higher Education Group, Inc.

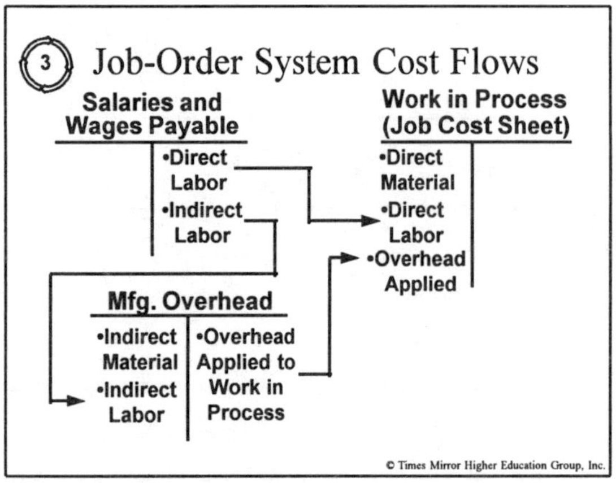
3
Job-Order System Cost Flows
Salaries and Wages Payable
•Direct Labor
•Indirect Labor
Work in Process (Job Cost Sheet)
•Direct Material
•Direct Labor
•Overhead Applied
Mfg. Overhead
•Indirect Material
•Indirect Labor
•Overhead Applied to Work in Process
© Times Mirror Higher Education Group, Inc.

## Job-Order System Cost Flows

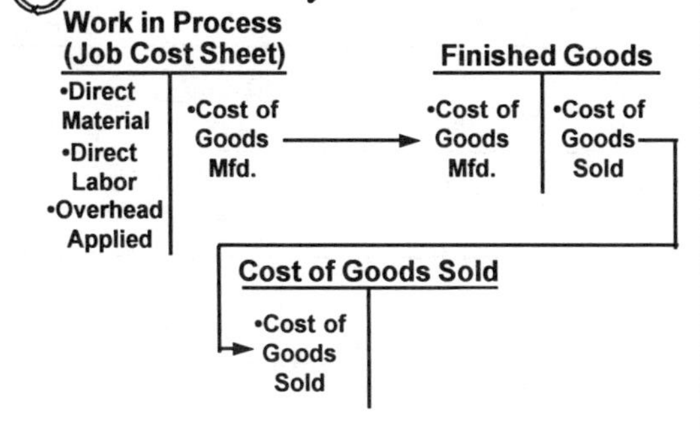




## Overhead Application Example

PearCo's actual overhead for the year was $650,000 and a total 170,000 direct labor hours were worked.

Using PearCo's predetermined overhead rate of $4.00 per direct labor hour, how much overhead was applied to all of PearCo's jobs during the year?

## Overapplied and Underapplied Manufacturing Overhead

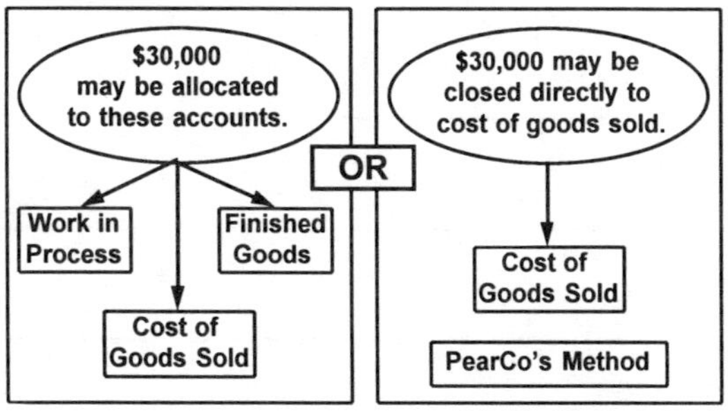

## 3 Overapplied and Underapplied Manufacturing Overhead

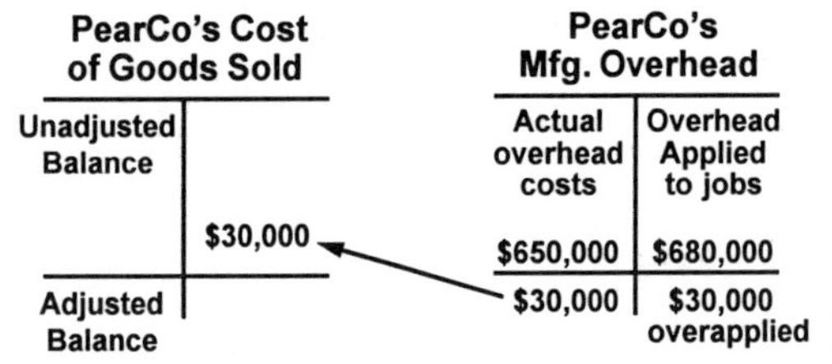




## 3 Overapplied and Underapplied Manufacturing Overhead - Summary

| If Manufacturing Overhead is . . . | Alternative 1<br>Allocation | Alternative 2<br>Close to Cost of Goods Sold |
|---|---|---|
| UNDERAPPLIED<br>(Applied OH is less than actual OH) | INCREASE<br>Work in Process<br>Finished Goods<br>Cost of Goods Sold | INCREASE<br>Cost of Goods Sold |
| OVERAPPLIED<br>(Applied OH is greater than actual OH) | DECREASE<br>Work in Process<br>Finished Goods<br>Cost of Goods Sold | DECREASE<br>Cost of Goods Sold |



## 3 Overhead Application Question 1

Tiger, Inc. had actual manufacturing overhead costs of $1,210,000 and a predetermined overhead rate of $4.00 per machine hour. Tiger, Inc. worked 290,000 machine hours during the period. Tiger's manufacturing overhead is

a. $50,000 overapplied.
b. $50,000 underapplied.
c. $60,000 overapplied.
d. $60,000 underapplied.

## ③ Overhead Application Question 2

Assume that Tiger's overhead was $60,000 underapplied. This amount would result in an adjustment that would decrease cost of goods sold by $60,000.

a. True
b. False

## ③ Cost Flows – Material Purchases

Raw material purchases are recorded in an inventory account.

**GENERAL JOURNAL** Page 3

| Date | | Description | Post. Ref. | Debit | Credit |
|---|---|---|---|---|---|
| | | Raw Materials | | XXXXX | |
| | | Accounts Payable | | | XXXXX |
| | | | | | |
| | | | | | |
| | | | | | |



## ③ Cost Flows – Material Usage

Direct materials issued to a job increase Work in Process and decrease Raw Materials. Indirect materials used on a job are charged to Manufacturing Overhead and also decrease Raw Materials.

**GENERAL JOURNAL** Page 3

| Date | | Description | Post. Ref. | Debit | Credit |
|---|---|---|---|---|---|
| | | Work in Process | | XXXXX | |
| | | Manufacturing Overhead | | XXXXX | |
| | | Raw Materials | | | XXXXX |
| | | | | | |
| | | | | | |

## Cost Flows – Labor

The cost of direct labor incurred on a job increases Work in Process and the cost of indirect labor on a job increases Manufacturing Overhead.

GENERAL JOURNAL Page 3

| Date | | Description | Post. Ref. | Debit | Credit |
|---|---|---|---|---|---|
| | | Work in Process | | XXXXX | |
| | | Manufacturing Overhead | | XXXXX | |
| | | Salaries and Wages Payable | | | XXXXX |
| | | | | | |
| | | | | | |



## Cost Flows – Actual Overhead

In addition to indirect materials and indirect labor, other manufacturing overhead costs are charged to the Manufacturing Overhead account as they are incurred.

GENERAL JOURNAL Page 3

| Date | | Description | Post. Ref. | Debit | Credit |
|---|---|---|---|---|---|
| | | Manufacturing Overhead | | XXXXX | |
| | | Accounts Payable | | | XXXXX |
| | | Property Taxes Payable | | | XXXXX |
| | | Prepaid Insurance | | | XXXXX |
| | | Accumulated Depreciation | | | XXXXX |



## Cost Flows – Overhead Applied

Work in Process is increased when Manufacturing Overhead is applied to jobs.

GENERAL JOURNAL Page 3

| Date | | Description | Post. Ref. | Debit | Credit |
|---|---|---|---|---|---|
| | | Work in Process | | XXXXX | |
| | | Manufacturing Overhead | | | XXXXX |
| | | | | | |
| | | | | | |
| | | | | | |

## Cost Flows – Period Expenses

Nonmanufacturing costs (period expenses) are charged to expense as they are incurred.

GENERAL JOURNAL Page 3

| Date | | Description | Post. Ref. | Debit | Credit |
|---|---|---|---|---|---|
| | | Salaries Expense | | XXXXX | |
| | | Salaries and Wages Payable | | | XXXXX |
| | | | | | |
| | | Advertising Expense | | XXXXX | |
| | | Accounts Payable | | | XXXXX |



## Cost Flows – Cost of Goods Manufactured

As jobs are completed, the cost of goods manufactured is transferred to Finished Goods from Work in Process.

GENERAL JOURNAL Page 3

| Date | | Description | Post. Ref. | Debit | Credit |
|---|---|---|---|---|---|
| | | Finished Goods | | XXXXX | |
| | | Work in Process | | | XXXXX |
| | | | | | |
| | | | | | |
| | | | | | |



## Cost Flows – Sales

When finished goods are sold, two entries are required: (1) to record the sale; and (2) to record Cost of Goods Sold and reduce Finished Goods.

GENERAL JOURNAL Page 3

| Date | | Description | Post. Ref. | Debit | Credit |
|---|---|---|---|---|---|
| | | Accounts Receivable | | XXXXX | |
| | | Sales | | | XXXXX |
| | | | | | |
| | | Cost of Goods Sold | | XXXXX | |
| | | Finished Goods | | | XXXXX |

## End of Chapter 3

GARRISON

MANAGERIAL

Eighth Edition

ACCOUNTING

NOREEN

Chapter 4

Systems Design:
Process Costing

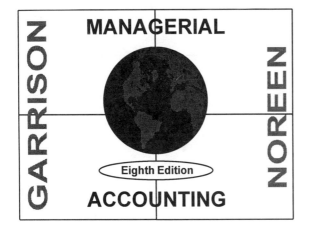

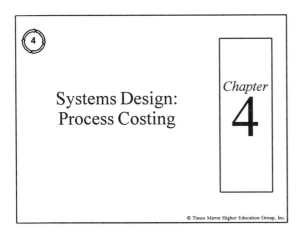

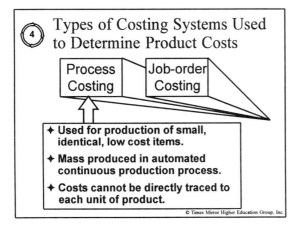

## Types of Costing Systems Used to Determine Product Costs

Process Costing | Job-order Costing

- **Used for production of small, identical, low cost items.**
- **Mass produced in automated continuous production process.**
- **Costs cannot be directly traced to each unit of product.**

## Types of Costing Systems Used to Determine Product Costs

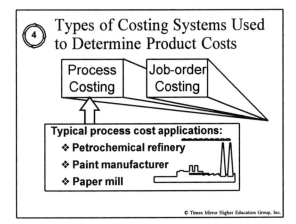

Process Costing | Job-order Costing

**Typical process cost applications:**

- **Petrochemical refinery**
- **Paint manufacturer**
- **Paper mill**

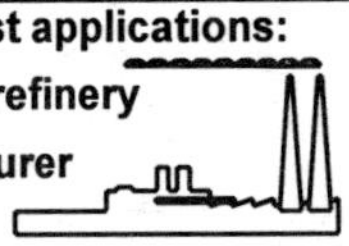



## Comparing Job-Order and Process Costing

| Job order costing | Process costing |
|---|---|
| Costs accumulated by the job. | Costs accumulated by department or process. |
| Work in process has a job cost sheet for each job. | Work in process has a production report for each batch of products. |
| Many unique, high cost jobs. | A few identical, low cost products. |
| Jobs built to customer order. | Units continuously produced for inventory in automated process. |



## Process Costing

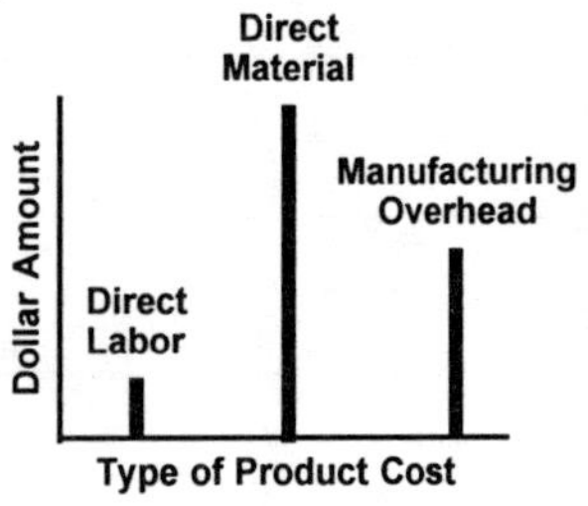


**Direct labor costs are usually small in comparison to other product costs in process cost systems. (high level of automation)**

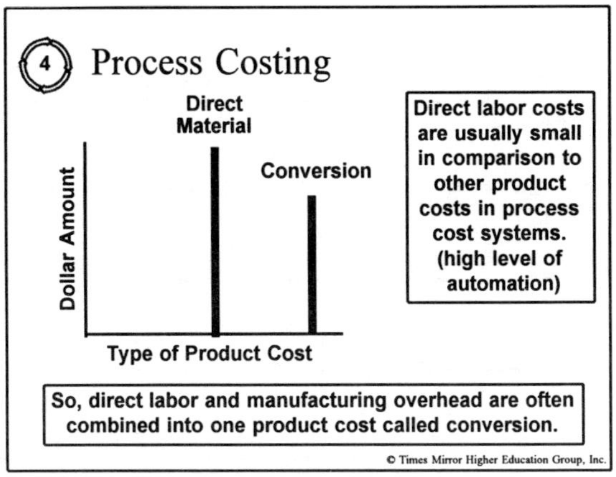
4
Process Costing
Direct Material
Conversion
Dollar Amount
Type of Product Cost
Direct labor costs are usually small in comparison to other product costs in process cost systems. (high level of automation)
So, direct labor and manufacturing overhead are often combined into one product cost called conversion.
© Times Mirror Higher Education Group, Inc.

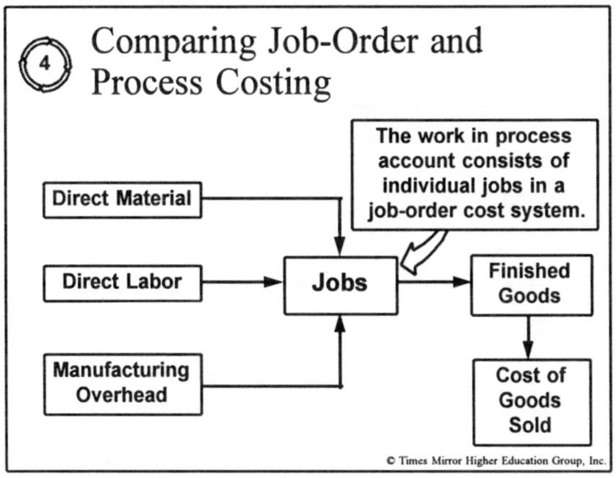
4
Comparing Job-Order and Process Costing
The work in process account consists of individual jobs in a job-order cost system.
Direct Material
Direct Labor
Jobs
Finished Goods
Manufacturing Overhead
Cost of Goods Sold
© Times Mirror Higher Education Group, Inc.

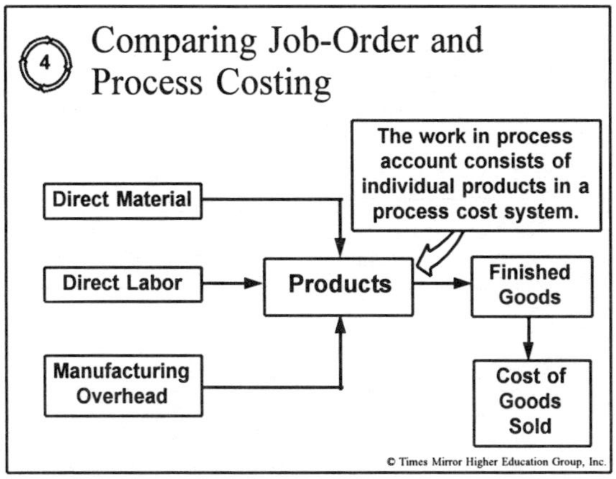
4
Comparing Job-Order and Process Costing
The work in process account consists of individual products in a process cost system.
Direct Material
Direct Labor
Products
Finished Goods
Manufacturing Overhead
Cost of Goods Sold
© Times Mirror Higher Education Group, Inc.

## 4 Comparing Job-Order and Process Costing

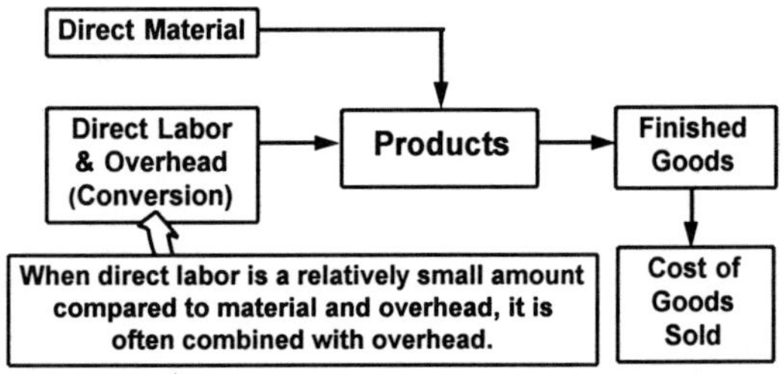




## 4 Job-Order and Process Costing Similarities

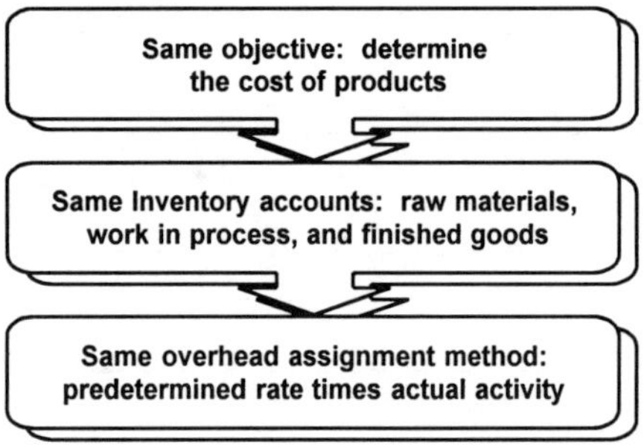




## 4 Process Cost Flows

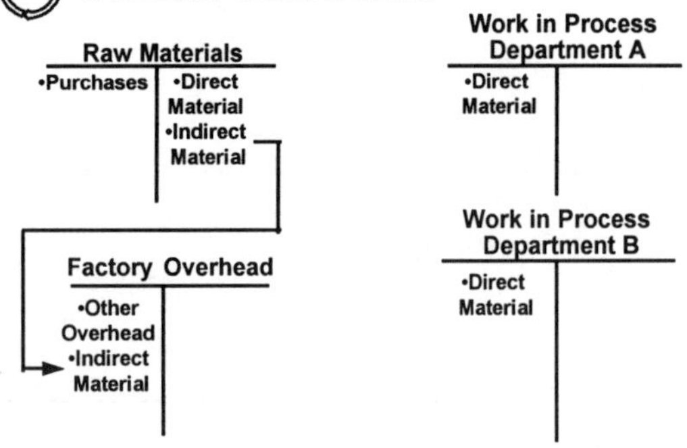

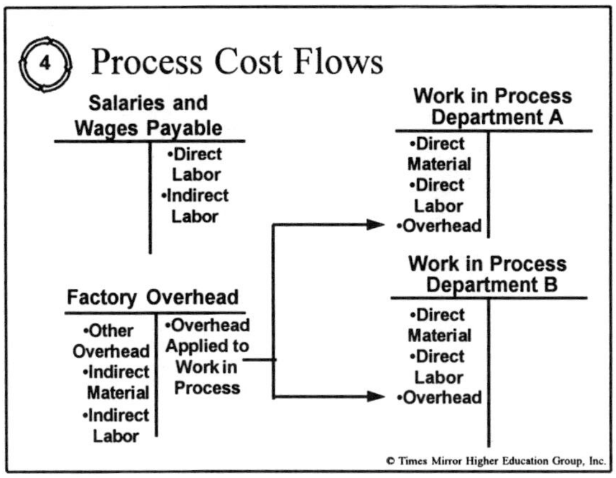
4
Process Cost Flows
Salaries and Wages Payable
•Direct Labor
•Indirect Labor
Factory Overhead
•Other Overhead
•Indirect Material
•Indirect Labor
•Overhead Applied to Work in Process
Work in Process Department A
•Direct Material
•Direct Labor
•Overhead
Work in Process Department B
•Direct Material
•Direct Labor
•Overhead
© Times Mirror Higher Education Group, Inc.

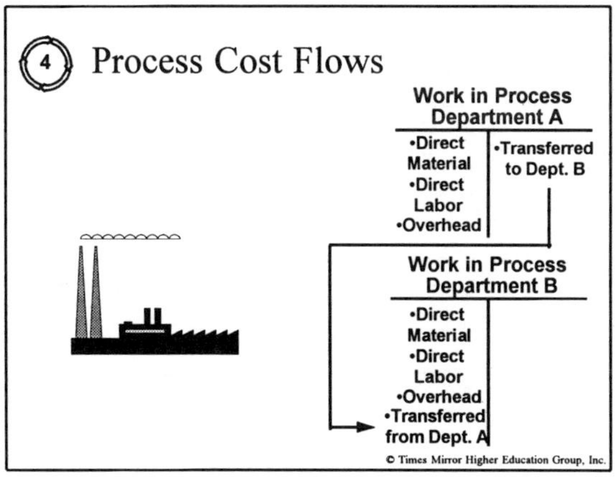
4
Process Cost Flows
Work in Process Department A
•Direct Material
•Direct Labor
•Overhead
•Transferred to Dept. B
Work in Process Department B
•Direct Material
•Direct Labor
•Overhead
•Transferred from Dept. A
© Times Mirror Higher Education Group, Inc.

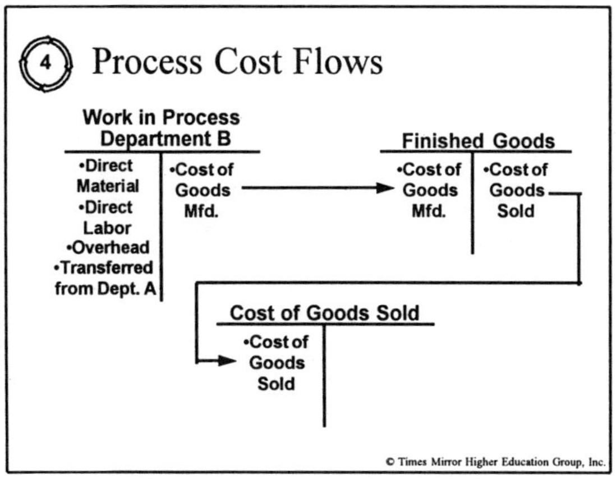
4
Process Cost Flows
Work in Process Department B
•Direct Material
•Direct Labor
•Overhead
•Transferred from Dept. A
•Cost of Goods Mfd.
Finished Goods
•Cost of Goods Mfd.
•Cost of Goods Sold
Cost of Goods Sold
•Cost of Goods Sold
© Times Mirror Higher Education Group, Inc.

## Calculating and Using Equivalent Units of Production

- Costs are accumulated for a period of time for products in work in process inventory.
- Products in work in process inventory at the beginning and end of the period are only partially complete.
- Equivalent units is a concept expressing these partially completed products as a smaller number of fully completed products.



## Equivalent Units Examples

**Two one-half completed products are equivalent to one completed product.**

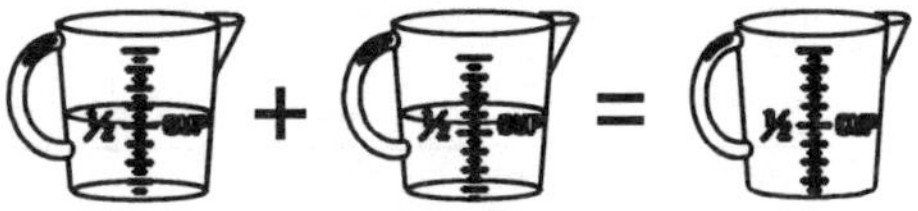

**So, 10,000 units 70 percent complete are equivalent to 7,000 complete units.**



## Equivalent Units Question 1

For the current period, Jones started 15,000 units and completed 10,000 units, leaving 5,000 units in process 30 percent complete. How many equivalent units of production did Jones have for the period?

a. 10,000
b. 11,500
c. 13,500
d. 15,000

## Calculating and Using Equivalent Units of Production

To calculate the cost per equivalent unit for the period:

$$\text{Cost per equivalent unit} = \frac{\text{Costs for the period}}{\text{Equivalent units for the period}}$$



## Equivalent Units Question 2

Now assume that Jones incurred $27,600 in production costs for the 11,500 equivalent units. What was Jones' cost per equivalent unit for the period?

a. $1.84
b. $2.40
c. $2.76
d. $2.90



## Equivalent Units of Production – Weighted Average Method

- The weighted average method . . .
  - Makes no distinction between work done in the prior period and work done in the current period.
  - Blends together units and costs from the prior period and the current period.

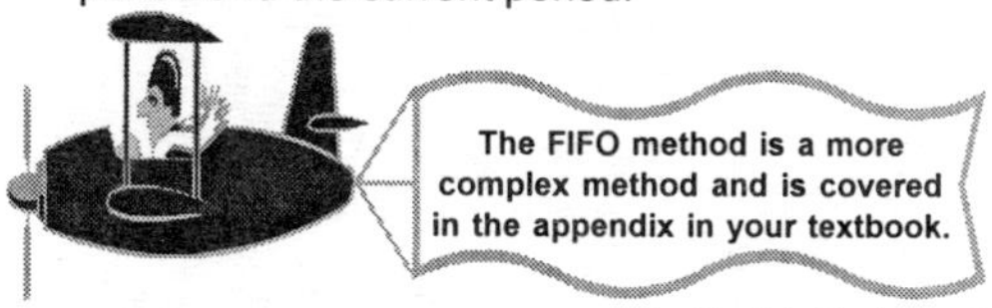
The FIFO method is a more complex method and is covered in the appendix in your textbook.

## (4) Weighted Average Example

Smith Company reported the following activity in Department A for the month of June:

| | | Percent Completed | |
|---|---|---|---|
| | Units | Materials | Conversion |
| Work in process, June 1 | 300 | 40% | 20% |
| Units started into production in June | 6,000 | | |
| Units completed and transferred out of Department A during June | 5,400 | | |
| Work in process, June 30 | 900 | 60% | 30% |



## (4) Weighted Average Example

Equivalent units are calculated as follows:

| | Materials | Conversion |
|---|---|---|
| Units completed and transferred out of Department A in June | ? | ? |
| Work in process, June 30: | | |
| | ? | |
| | | ? |
| Equivalent units of Production in Department A during June | ? | ? |



## (4) Weighted Average Example Materials

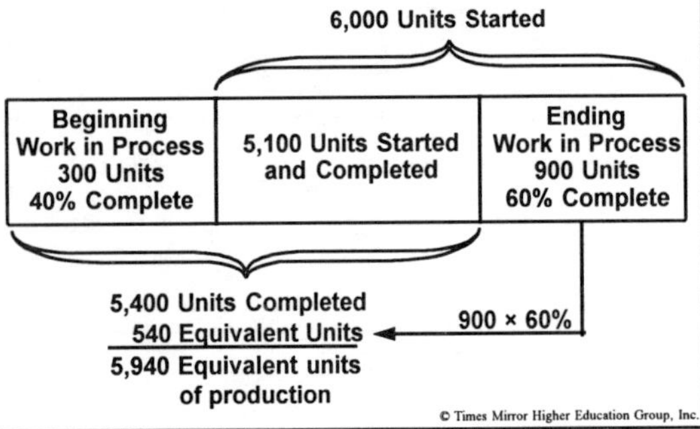

## Weighted Average Example Conversion

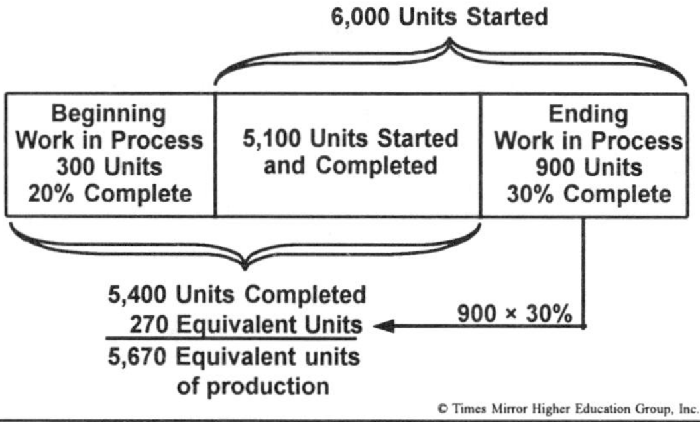




## Production Report

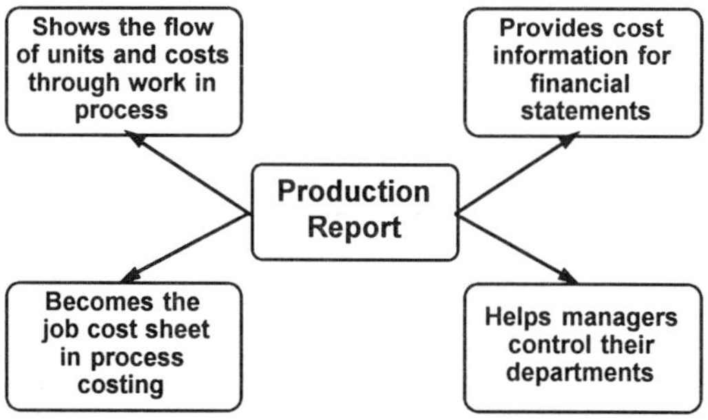




## Production Report

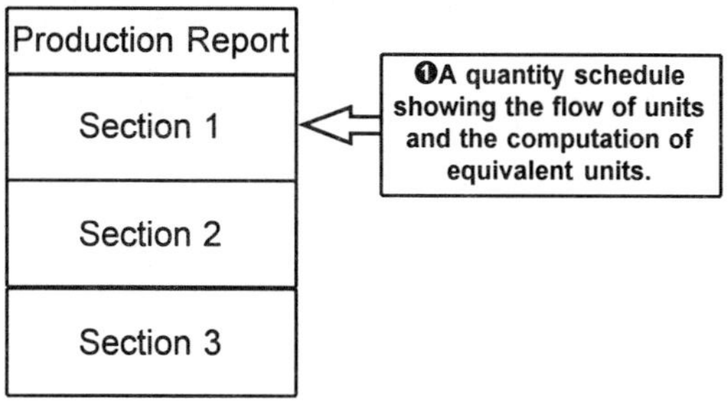

## 4 Production Report

Production Report

- Section 1
- Section 2
- Section 3

❷A computation of total and unit costs. (→ Section 2)



## 4 Production Report

Production Report

- Section 1
- Section 2
- Section 3

❸ A reconciliation of cost flows for the period, including: (→ Section 3)

- ❖Total cost for units completed and transferred from the processing department.
- ❖Total cost for partially completed units remaining in work in process.



## 4 Production Report Example

- ✦ Double Diamond Skis uses process costing to determine unit costs in its Shaping and Milling Department.
- ✦ Double Diamond uses the weighted average cost procedure.
- ✦ Using the following information for the month of May, let's prepare a production report for Shaping and Milling.

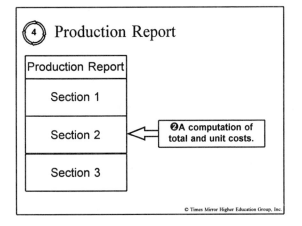

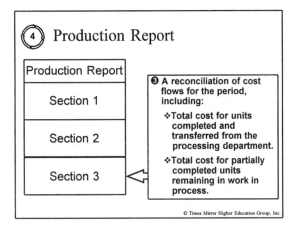

## Production Report Example

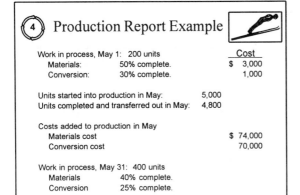

| | | | Cost |
|---|---|---|---|
| Work in process, May 1: 200 units | | | |
| Materials: | 50% complete. | | $ 3,000 |
| Conversion: | 30% complete. | | 1,000 |
| Units started into production in May: | | 5,000 | |
| Units completed and transferred out in May: | | 4,800 | |
| Costs added to production in May | | | |
| Materials cost | | | $ 74,000 |
| Conversion cost | | | 70,000 |
| Work in process, May 31: 400 units | | | |
| Materials | 40% complete. | | |
| Conversion | 25% complete. | | |



## Production Report Example

Section 1: Quantity Schedule with Equivalent Units

| | | Equivalent units | |
|---|---|---|---|
| | | Materials | Conversion |
| **Units to be accounted for:** | | | |
| Work in process, May 1 | 200 | | |
| Started into production | 5,000 | | |
| Total units | 5,200 | | |
| **Units accounted for as follows:** | | | |
| Completed and transferred | ? | ? | ? |
| Work in process, May 31 | ? | ? | ? |
| | 5,200 | ? | ? |



## Production Report Example

Section 2: Compute total and unit costs

| | Total Cost | Materials | Conversion |
|---|---|---|---|
| **Cost to be accounted for:** | | | |
| Work in process, May 1 | ? | ? | ? |
| Costs added in the Shipping and Milling Department | ? | ? | ? |
| Total cost | ? | ? | ? |
| Equivalent units | | 4,960 | 4,900 |
| Unit Costs | | ? | ? |
| Total unit cost | ? | | |

## Production Report Example

### Section 3: Cost Reconciliation

| | Total Cost | Equivalent Units Materials | Equivalent Units Conversion |
|---|---|---|---|
| Cost accounted for as follows: | | | |
| Transferred out during May | ? | 4,800 | 4,800 |
| Work in process, May 31: | | | |
| Materials | ? | 160 | |
| Conversion | ? | | 100 |
| Total work in process, May 31 | ? | | |
| Total cost accounted for | ? | | |

## Operation Costing

**Operation costing employs some aspects of both job-order and process costing.**

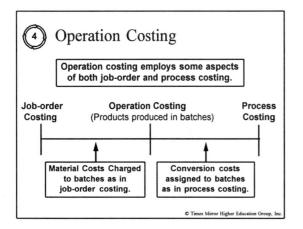

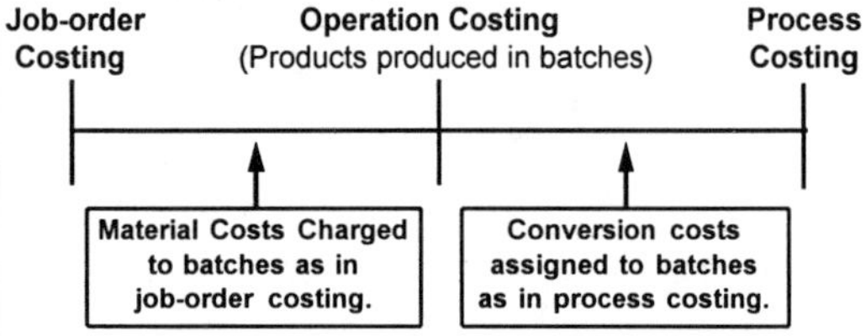
Job-order Costing
Operation Costing
(Products produced in batches)
Process Costing
Material Costs Charged to batches as in job-order costing.
Conversion costs assigned to batches as in process costing.

## Process Costing
### Typical Accounting Entries

GENERAL JOURNAL — Page 4

| Date | | Description | Post. Ref. | Debit | Credit |
|---|---|---|---|---|---|
| | | Raw Materials | | XXXXX | |
| | | Accounts Payable | | | XXXXX |
| | | *To record the purchase of material.* | | | |
| | | | | | |
| | | | | | |
| | | | | | |
| | | | | | |
| | | | | | |

## Process Costing
### Typical Accounting Entries

| GENERAL JOURNAL | | | | Page 4 |
|---|---|---|---|---|
| Date | Description | Post. Ref. | Debit | Credit |
| | Raw Materials | | XXXXX | |
| | Accounts Payable | | | XXXXX |
| | *To record the purchase of material.* | | | |
| | | | | |
| | Work in Process - Department A | | XXXXX | |
| | Work in Process - Department B | | XXXXX | |
| | Raw Materials | | | XXXXX |
| | *To record the use of direct material.* | | | |



## Process Costing
### Typical Accounting Entries

| GENERAL JOURNAL | | | | Page 4 |
|---|---|---|---|---|
| Date | Description | Post. Ref. | Debit | Credit |
| | Work in Process - Department A | | XXXXX | |
| | Work in Process - Department B | | XXXXX | |
| | Salaries and Wages Payable | | | XXXXX |
| | *To record direct labor costs.* | | | |
| | | | | |
| | | | | |
| | | | | |
| | | | | |



## Process Costing
### Typical Accounting Entries

| GENERAL JOURNAL | | | | Page 4 |
|---|---|---|---|---|
| Date | Description | Post. Ref. | Debit | Credit |
| | Work in Process - Department A | | XXXXX | |
| | Work in Process - Department B | | XXXXX | |
| | Manufacturing Overhead | | | XXXXX |
| | *To apply overhead to departments.* | | | |
| | | | | |
| | | | | |
| | | | | |
| | | | | |

## Process Costing
### Typical Accounting Entries

| GENERAL JOURNAL | | | | Page 4 |
|---|---|---|---|---|
| Date | Description | Post. Ref. | Debit | Credit |
| | Work in Process - Department B | | XXXXX | |
| | Work in Process - Department A | | | XXXXX |
| | *To record the transfer of goods from* | | | |
| | *Department A to Department B.* | | | |



## Process Costing
### Typical Accounting Entries

| GENERAL JOURNAL | | | | Page 4 |
|---|---|---|---|---|
| Date | Description | Post. Ref. | Debit | Credit |
| | Finished Goods | | XXXXX | |
| | Work in Process - Department B | | | XXXXX |
| | *To record the completion of goods* | | | |
| | *and their transfer from Department B* | | | |
| | *to finished goods inventory.* | | | |



## Process Costing
### Typical Accounting Entries

| GENERAL JOURNAL | | | | Page 4 |
|---|---|---|---|---|
| Date | Description | Post. Ref. | Debit | Credit |
| | Accounts Receivable | | XXXXX | |
| | Sales | | | XXXXX |
| | *To record sales on account.* | | | |
| | | | | |
| | Cost of Goods Sold | | XXXXX | |
| | Finished Goods | | | XXXXX |
| | *To record cost of goods sold.* | | | |

# End of Chapter 4

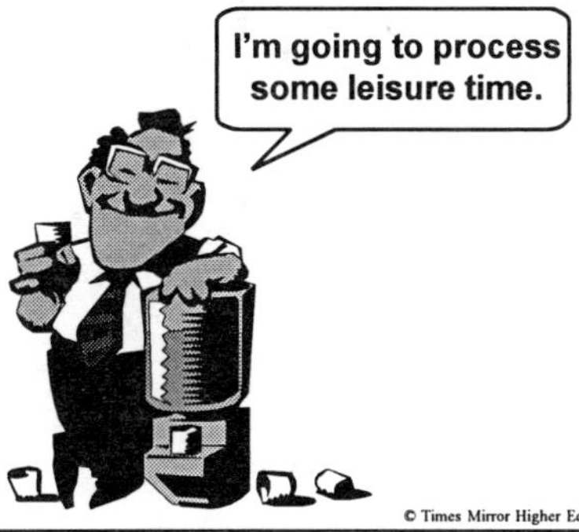
I'm going to process
some leisure time.

GARRISON

# MANAGERIAL

Eighth Edition

# ACCOUNTING

NOREEN

---

5

Chapter 5

## Systems Design:
## Activity-Based Costing and Quality Management



---

5

## The Concept of Activity Based Costing (ABC)

One of the most difficult tasks in computing accurate unit costs lies in determining the proper amount of overhead cost to assign to each job or to each unit of product.

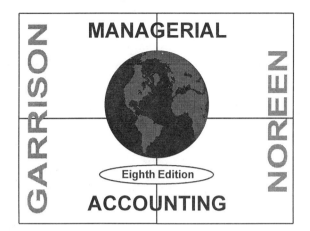

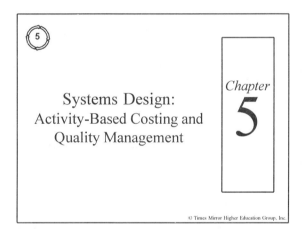

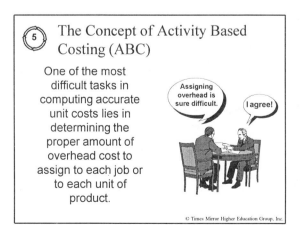

## The Concept of Activity Based Costing (ABC)

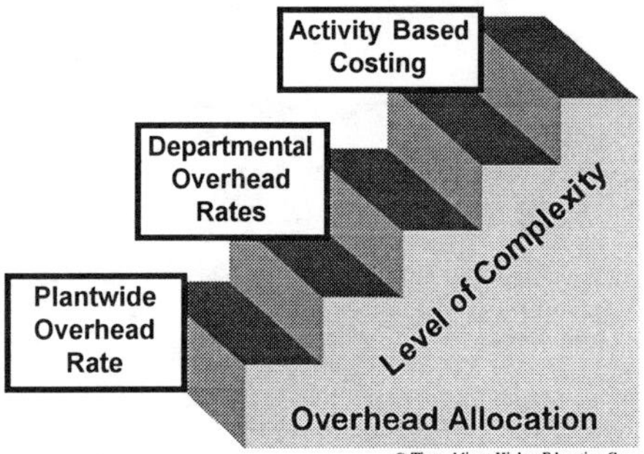




## Plantwide Overhead Rate

Companies tend to use direct labor as the overhead allocation base.



## Departmental Overhead Rates

**A two stage process is necessary because different departments may have different cost drivers.**

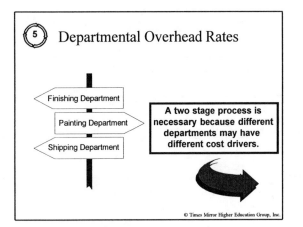

## Departmental Overhead Rates

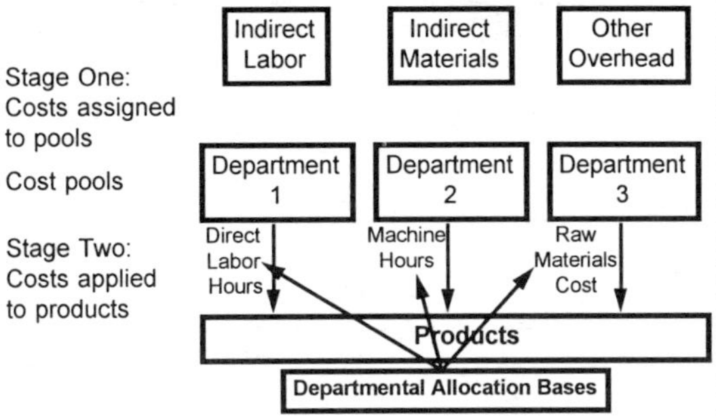




## Activity-Based Costing

**In the ABC method, we recognize that many activities within a department drive overhead costs.**



## Design of an ABC System

Activities Required

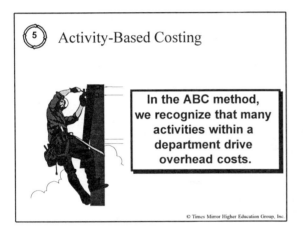

❶ Process Value Analysis (PVA)
❷ Identifying Activity Centers
❸ Assigning Costs to Activity Centers
❹ Selecting Cost Drivers

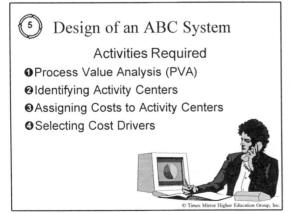

## Process Value Analysis (PVA)

1. Analyze activities required to make our product or perform our service.
2. Classify each activity as value-added or non-value-added
3. Identify ways to either reduce or eliminate the non-value-added activities.

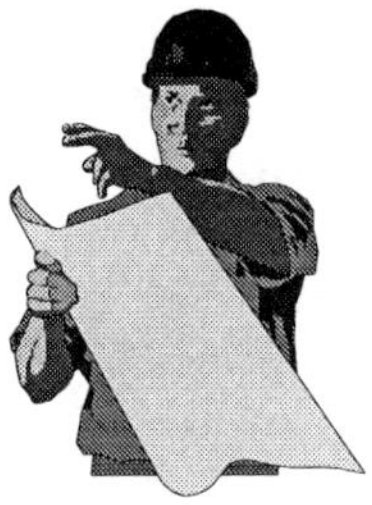



## Process Value Analysis (PVA)

Suppose our production process looks like this

| Receiving | Store Raw Materials | Operation 1 | Move and Wait | Operation 2 | Store Finished Goods | Pack & Ship |
|---|---|---|---|---|---|---|
| NVA | NVA | VA | NVA | VA | NVA | VA |

VA = Valued-added activity
NVA = Non-value-added activity



## Identifying Activity Centers

A part of the production process for which management wants a separate reporting of the costs of the activity involved.

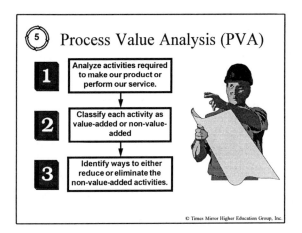

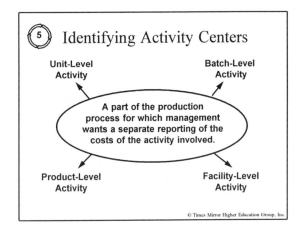

- Unit-Level Activity
- Batch-Level Activity
- Product-Level Activity
- Facility-Level Activity

## Assigning Costs to Activity Centers

Assign costs to the activity centers where they are accumulated while waiting to be applied to products.

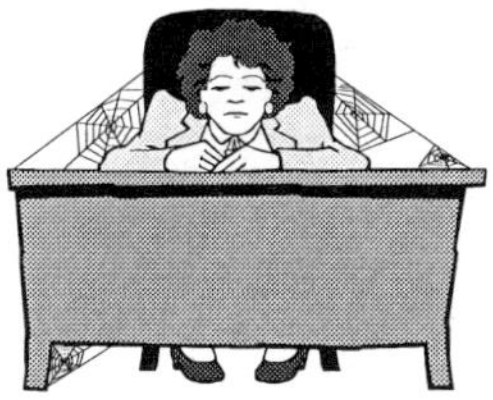



## Select Cost Drivers

Assign costs from the activity center to the product using appropriate cost drivers.

When selecting a cost driver consider:

❶ The ease of obtaining data.

❷ The degree to which the cost driver measures actual consumption by products.



## ABC Example

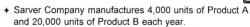

- Sarver Company manufactures 4,000 units of Product A and 20,000 units of Product B each year.
- The company currently uses direct labor hours to assign overhead cost to products.
- The predetermined overhead rate (POHR) is:

$$\frac{\text{Mfg. overhead cost}}{\text{Direct labor hours}} = \frac{\$900,000}{50,000} = \$18/\text{DLH}$$

- Product A requires 2.5 DLH and Product B requires 2.0 DLH to produce.

## 5 ABC Example

- Sarver uses a plantwide overhead allocation rate. Using this method, the unit product cost is:

| | Product A | Product B |
|---|---|---|
| Direct material | $ 36.00 | $ 30.00 |
| Direct labor | 17.50 | 14.00 |
| Manufacturing overhead | | |
| 2.5 DLH × $18/DLH | 45.00 | |
| 2.0 DLH × $18/DLH | | 36.00 |
| Total unit product cost | $ 98.50 | $ 80.00 |



## 5 ABC Example

- Management at Sarver believes that overhead costs are actually caused by the following five activities:

| Activity | Traceable Cost |
|---|---|
| Machine setups | $ 255,000 |
| Quality inspections | 160,000 |
| Production orders | 81,000 |
| Machine-hours worked | 314,000 |
| Material receipts | 90,000 |
| Total | $ 900,000 |



## 5 ABC Example

- The following transaction data has been complied by management of Sarver:

| Activity | Total | Product A | Product B |
|---|---|---|---|
| Machine setups | 5,000 | 3,000 | 2,000 |
| Quality inspections | 8,000 | 5,000 | 3,000 |
| Production orders | 600 | 200 | 400 |
| Machine-hours worked | 40,000 | 12,000 | 28,000 |
| Material receipts | 750 | 150 | 600 |

## ABC Example

- These data can be used to develop overhead rates for each of the five activities:

| Activity | Costs | Total Transactions | Rate per Transaction |
|---|---|---|---|
| Machine setups | | | |
| Quality inspections | | | |
| Production orders | | | |
| Machine-hours worked | | | |
| Material receipts | | | |



## ABC Example

- The activity based overhead rates we just calculated can be used to assign overhead costs to Sarver's two products.

| | Product A | | |
|---|---|---|---|
| Activity | ABC Rate | Transactions | Amount |
| Machine setups | $ 51.00 | | |
| Quality inspections | 20.00 | | |
| Production orders | 135.00 | | |
| Machine-hours worked | 7.85 | | |
| Material receipts | 120.00 | | |
| Total overhead assigned | | | |
| Number of units produced | | | |
| Overhead per unit | | | |



## ABC Example

- The activity based overhead rates we just calculated can be used to assign overhead costs to Sarver's two products.

| | Product B | | |
|---|---|---|---|
| Activity | ABC Rate | Transactions | Amount |
| Machine setups | $ 51.00 | | |
| Quality inspections | 20.00 | | |
| Production orders | 135.00 | | |
| Machine-hours worked | 7.85 | | |
| Material receipts | 120.00 | | |
| Total overhead assigned | | | |
| Number of units produced | | | |
| Overhead per unit | | | |

## 5 ABC Example

- Let's compute the product cost for A and B using our ABC overhead rates:

| Activity Based Costing | Product A | Product B |
|---|---|---|
| Direct materials | $ 36.00 | $ 30.00 |
| Direct labor | 17.50 | 14.00 |
| Manufacturing overhead | 98.05 | 25.39 |
| Total unit product cost | $ 151.55 | $ 69.39 |



## 5 ABC Example

- Now compare the unit product costs using the old costing system and our ABC system.

| *Costing Method* | Product A | Product B |
|---|---|---|
| Activity-based costing | $ 151.55 | $ 69.39 |
| Old costing system | 98.50 | 80.00 |



## 5 ABC and Service Industries

Implementation Problems

**Activities tend to be nonrepetitive human tasks.**

**High proportion of facility-level costs**

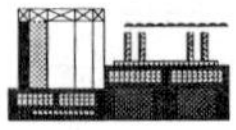

## International Use of ABC

The most extensive application of activity - based costing has been in the U.S., with some applications having been made in Northern Europe.

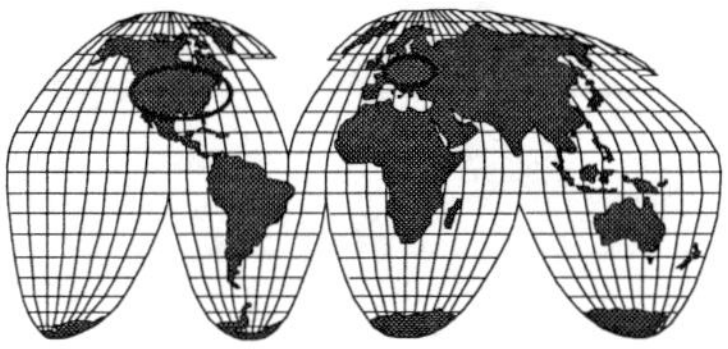



## Quality Management

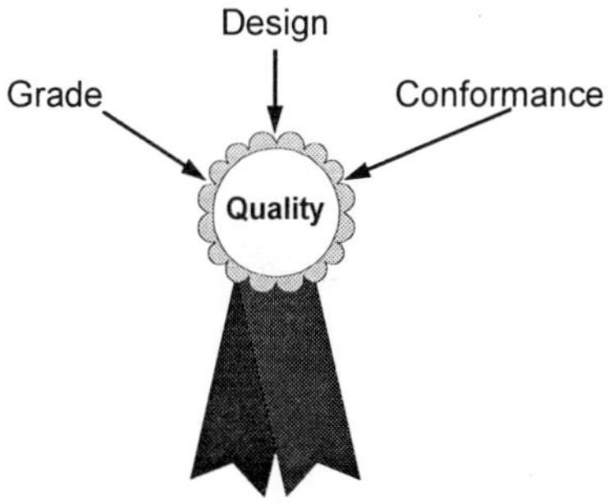




## Quality Management

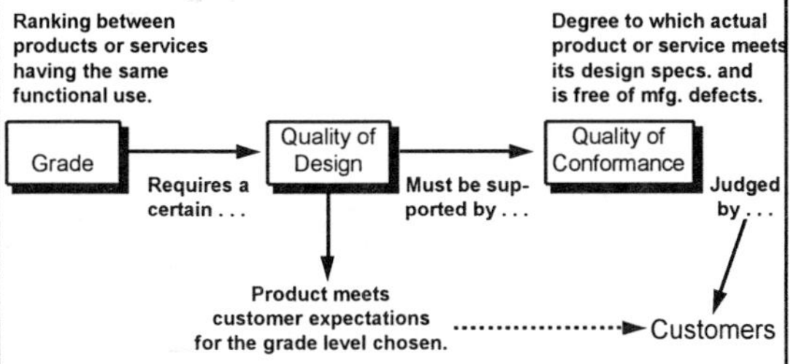

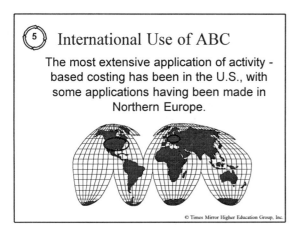

## Quality Conformance - A Closer Look

- The bulk of all quality costs usually are associated with the quality of conformance.
- These costs can be broken down as follows:
  - ❶Prevention costs,
  - ❷Appraisal costs,
  - ❸Internal failure costs, and
  - ❹External failure costs.

## Quality Cost Reports

- The report contains a break down of quality costs.
- Sarver's Quality Cost Report may look like this:

Sarver Company
Quality Cost Report
For the Year Ended December 31, 19X1

| | |
|---|---|
| Prevention Costs | $ 270,000 |
| Appraisal Costs | 40,000 |
| Internal Failure Costs | 210,000 |
| External Failure Costs | 47,000 |
| Total Quality Costs | $ 567,000 |



## International Aspects of Quality

- In the 1960's, both European and Japanese companies began to make large investment in quality training programs.
- By the 1980's the European and Japanese companies were setting the world standards for quality products.

## The ISO 9000 Standards

- Quality standards for products sold to companies in Europe.
- Set by the International Standards Organization.
- Companies must demonstrate that. . .
  - a quality control system is in use,
  - the system is fully operational, and
  - the level of quality is being achieved.

## End of Chapter 5

I call this quality time!

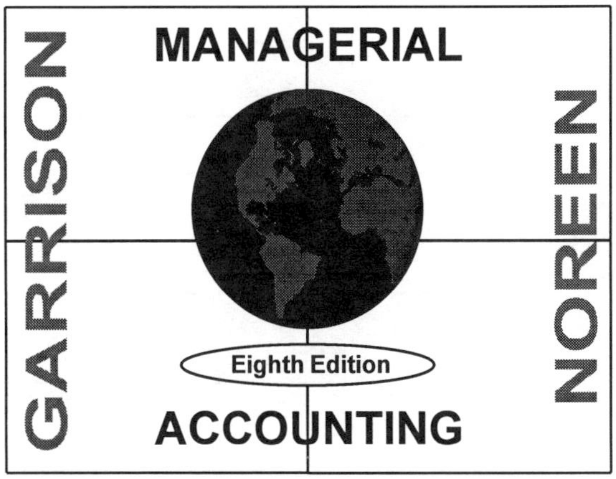


6

# Cost Behavior: Analysis and Use

*Chapter* 6



6

## Types of Cost Behavior Patterns

**Recall the summary of our cost behavior discussion from Chapter 2.**

| Summary of Variable and Fixed Cost Behavior | | |
|---|---|---|
| Cost | In Total | Per Unit |
| Variable | Total variable cost changes as activity level changes. | Variable cost per unit remains the same over wide ranges of activity. |
| Fixed | Total fixed cost remains the same even when the activity level changes within the relevant range. | Fixed cost per unit goes down as activity level goes up. |

## 6 Total Variable Cost Example

Your total long distance telephone bill is based on how many minutes you talk.

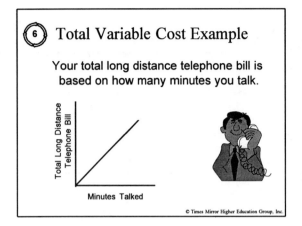

## 6 Variable Cost Per Unit Example

The cost per minute talked is constant. For example, 10 cents per minute.

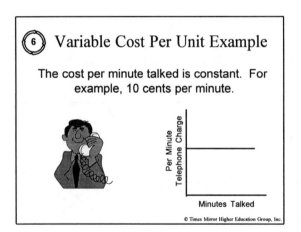

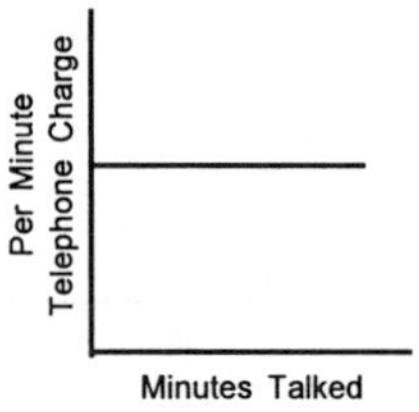




## 6 Total Fixed Cost Example

Your monthly basic telephone bill is probably fixed and does not change when you make more local calls.

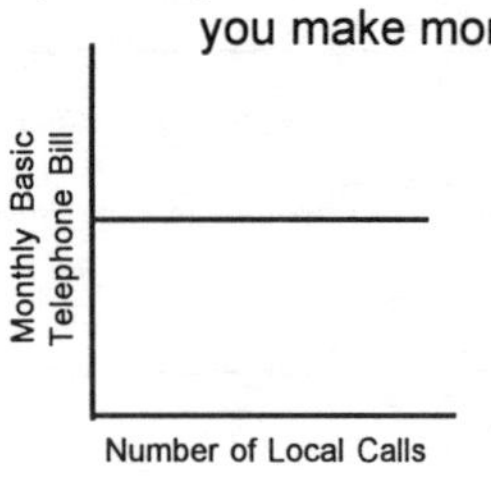

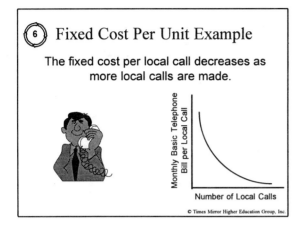

## 6 Fixed Cost Per Unit Example

The fixed cost per local call decreases as more local calls are made.

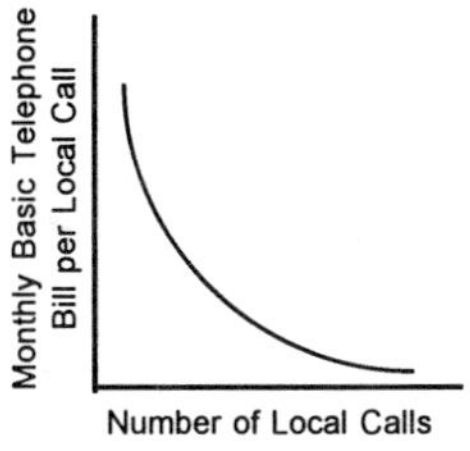




## 6 Cost Behavior

**Examples of variable costs**

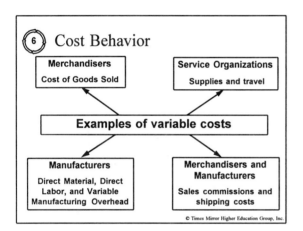

- **Merchandisers**: Cost of Goods Sold
- **Service Organizations**: Supplies and travel
- **Manufacturers**: Direct Material, Direct Labor, and Variable Manufacturing Overhead
- **Merchandisers and Manufacturers**: Sales commissions and shipping costs



## 6 Cost Behavior

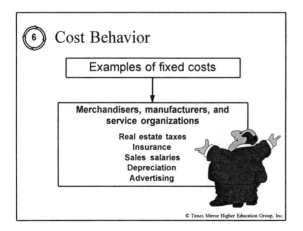

Examples of fixed costs

**Merchandisers, manufacturers, and service organizations**

Real estate taxes
Insurance
Sales salaries
Depreciation
Advertising

## 6 The Activity Base

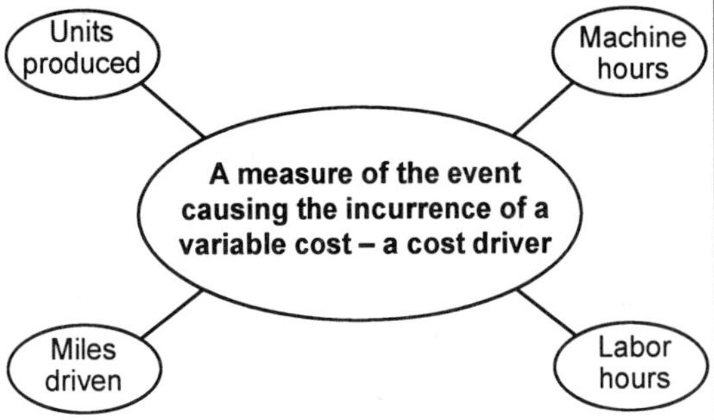




## 6 Step-Variable Costs

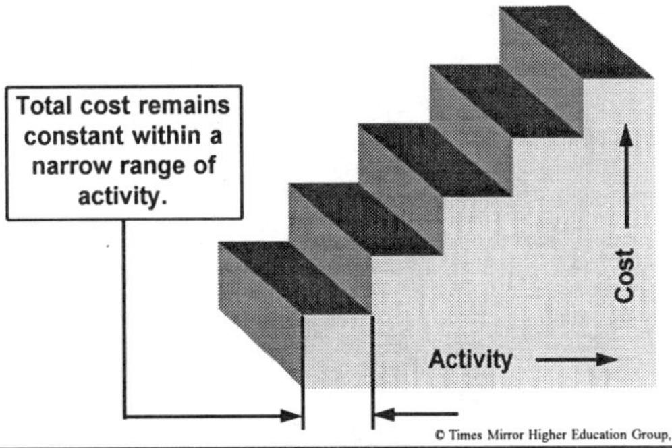




## 6 Step-Variable Costs

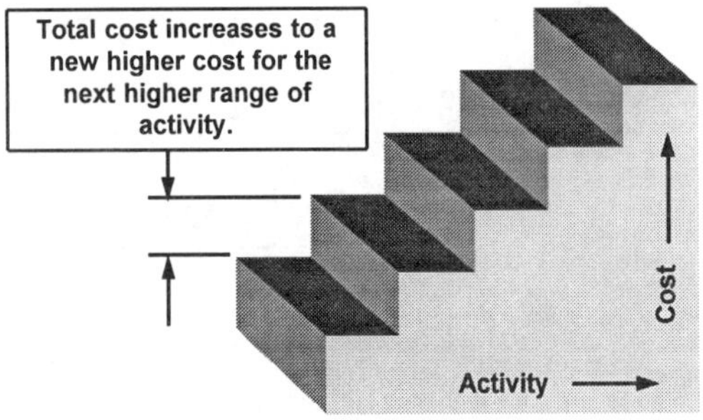

## 6 The Linearity Assumption and the Relevant Range

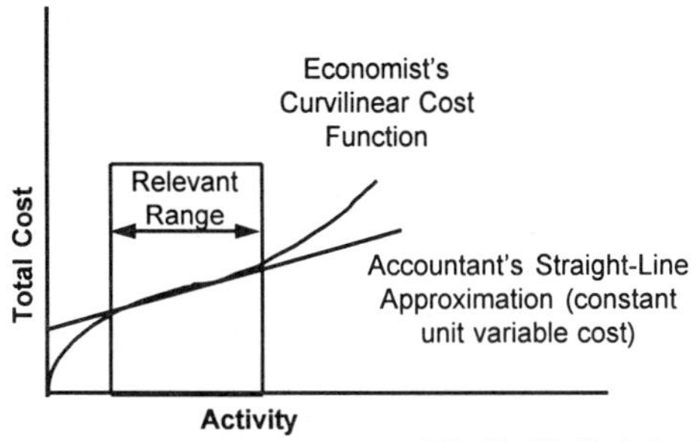




## 6 The Linearity Assumption and the Relevant Range

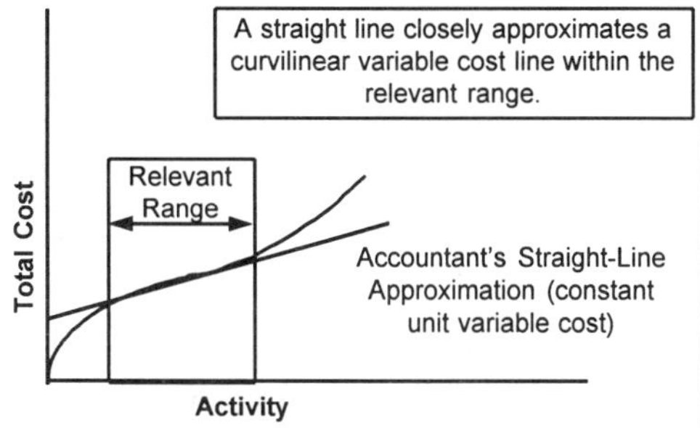




## 6 Types of Fixed Costs

**Fixed Costs**

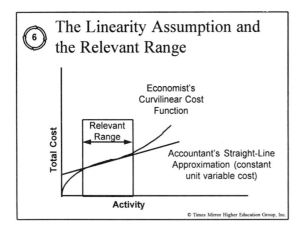

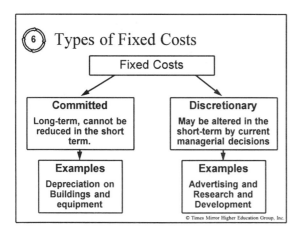

- **Committed**
  Long-term, cannot be reduced in the short term.
  - **Examples**
    Depreciation on Buildings and equipment
- **Discretionary**
  May be altered in the short-term by current managerial decisions
  - **Examples**
    Advertising and Research and Development

## 6 Trend Toward Fixed Costs

Increased automation.

Permanent work force on a short-term basis.

**Implications**

**Managers are more "locked-in" with fewer decision alternatives.**

**Planning becomes more crucial because fixed costs are difficult to change with current operating decisions.**



## 6 Fixed Costs and Relevant Range

Example: Office space is available at a rental rate of $30,000 per year in increments of 1,000 square feet. As the business grows more space is rented, increasing the total cost.

**Continue**



## 6 Fixed Costs and Relevant Range

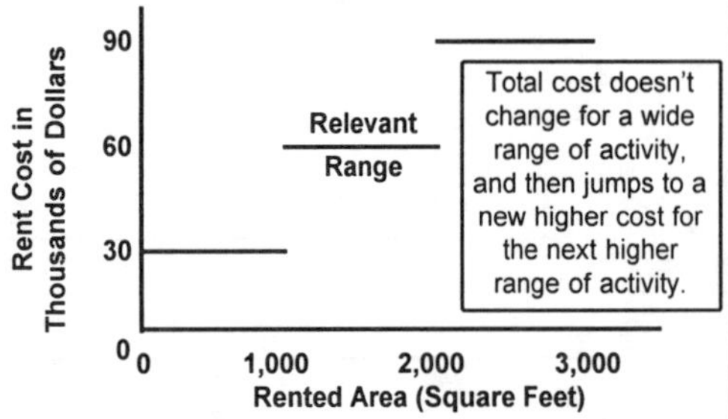

## 6 Fixed Costs and Relevant Range

How does this type of fixed cost differ from a step-variable cost?

Step-variable costs can be adjusted more quickly and . . .

The width of the activity steps is much wider for the fixed cost.



## 6 Mixed Costs

A mixed cost is partly fixed and partly variable.

Consider the following electric utility example.



## 6 Mixed Costs

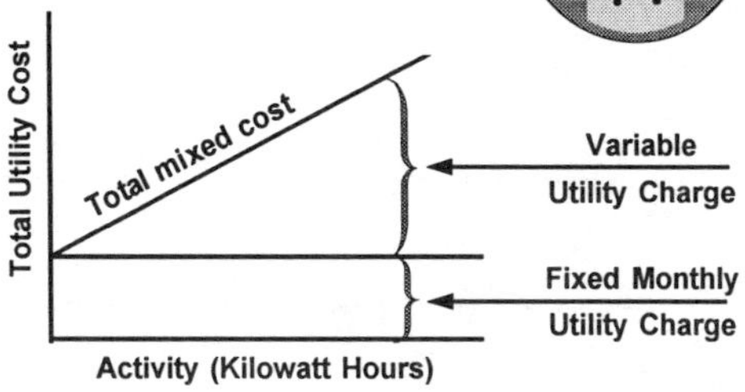

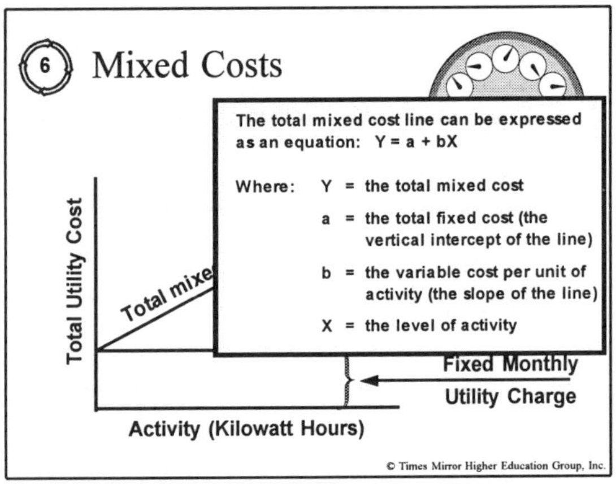
6
Mixed Costs
The total mixed cost line can be expressed as an equation: Y = a + bX
Where: Y = the total mixed cost
a = the total fixed cost (the vertical intercept of the line)
b = the variable cost per unit of activity (the slope of the line)
X = the level of activity
Total Utility Cost
Total mixe
Fixed Monthly Utility Charge
Activity (Kilowatt Hours)
© Times Mirror Higher Education Group, Inc.

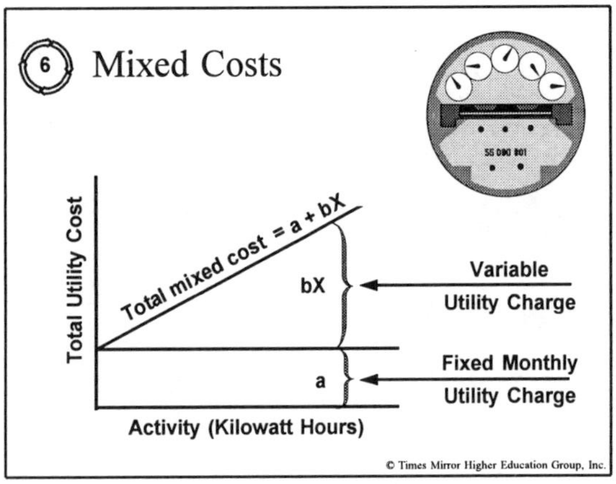
6
Mixed Costs
Total Utility Cost
Total mixed cost = a + bX
bX
Variable Utility Charge
a
Fixed Monthly Utility Charge
Activity (Kilowatt Hours)
© Times Mirror Higher Education Group, Inc.

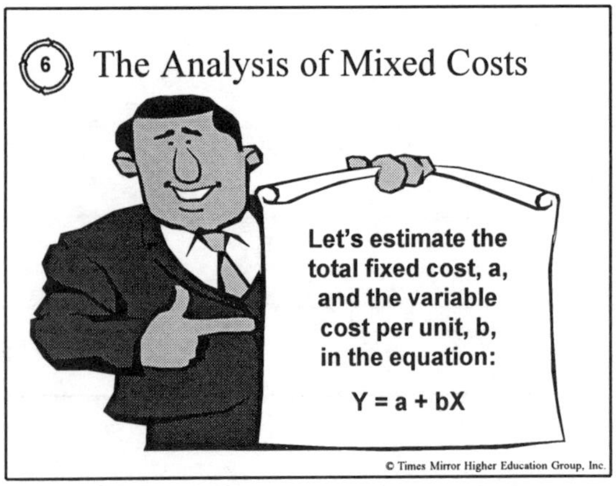
6
The Analysis of Mixed Costs
Let's estimate the total fixed cost, a, and the variable cost per unit, b, in the equation:
Y = a + bX
© Times Mirror Higher Education Group, Inc.

## ⑥ The Analysis of Mixed Costs

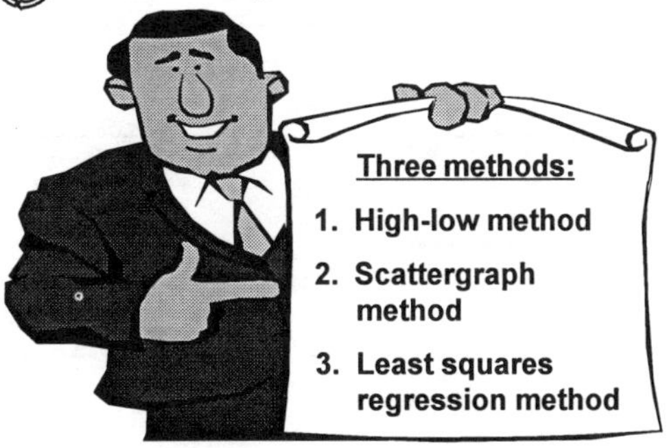
Three methods:
1. High-low method
2. Scattergraph method
3. Least squares regression method

## ⑥ The High-Low Method

WiseCo recorded the following production activity and maintenance costs for two months:

| | Units | Cost |
|---|---|---|
| High activity level | 9,000 | $ 9,700 |
| Low activity level | 5,000 | 6,100 |
| Change | 4,000 | $ 3,600 |

Using these two levels of activity, compute:

❶ the variable cost per unit;
❷ the fixed cost; and then
❸ express the costs in equation form Y = a + bX.

## ⑥ The High-Low Method

| | Units | Cost |
|---|---|---|
| High activity level | 9,000 | $ 9,700 |
| Low activity level | 5,000 | 6,100 |
| Change | 4,000 | $ 3,600 |

**❶ Unit variable cost = $3,600 ÷ 4,000 units = $.90 per unit**
**❷ Fixed cost = Total cost – Total variable cost**
**Fixed cost = $9,700 – ($.90 per unit × 9,000 units)**
**Fixed cost = $9,700 – $8,100 = $1,600**
**❸ Total cost = Fixed cost + Variable cost (Y = a + bX)**
**Y = $1,600 + $0.90X**

## 6 The High-Low Method Question 1

If sales commissions are $10,000 when 80,000 units are sold and $14,000 when 120,000 units are sold, what is the variable portion of sales commission per unit sold?

a. $.08 per unit
b. $.10 per unit
c. $.12 per unit
d. $.125 per unit



## 6 The High-Low Method Question 2

If sales commissions are $10,000 when 80,000 units are sold and $14,000 when 120,000 units are sold, what is the fixed portion of the sales commission?

a. $ 2,000
b. $ 4,000
c. $10,000
d. $12,000



## 6 The Scattergraph Method

A scattergraph of past cost behavior may be helpful in analyzing mixed costs.

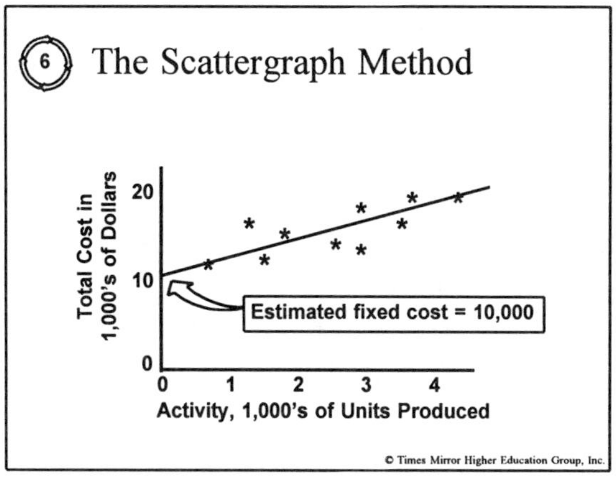
6
The Scattergraph Method
Total Cost in 1,000's of Dollars
20
10
0
0 1 2 3 4
Activity, 1,000's of Units Produced
Estimated fixed cost = 10,000
© Times Mirror Higher Education Group, Inc.

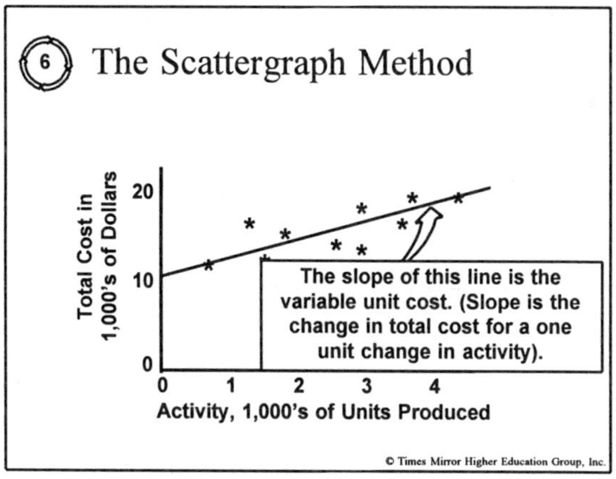
6
The Scattergraph Method
Total Cost in 1,000's of Dollars
20
10
0
0 1 2 3 4
Activity, 1,000's of Units Produced
The slope of this line is the variable unit cost. (Slope is the change in total cost for a one unit change in activity).
© Times Mirror Higher Education Group, Inc.

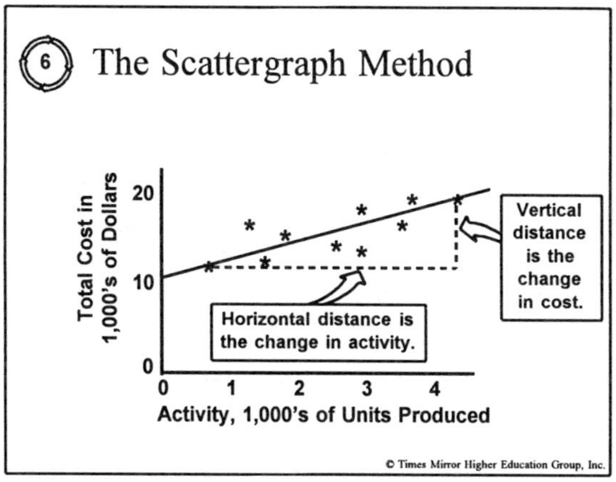
6
The Scattergraph Method
Total Cost in 1,000's of Dollars
20
10
0
0 1 2 3 4
Activity, 1,000's of Units Produced
Horizontal distance is the change in activity.
Vertical distance is the change in cost.
© Times Mirror Higher Education Group, Inc.

## The Scattergraph Method

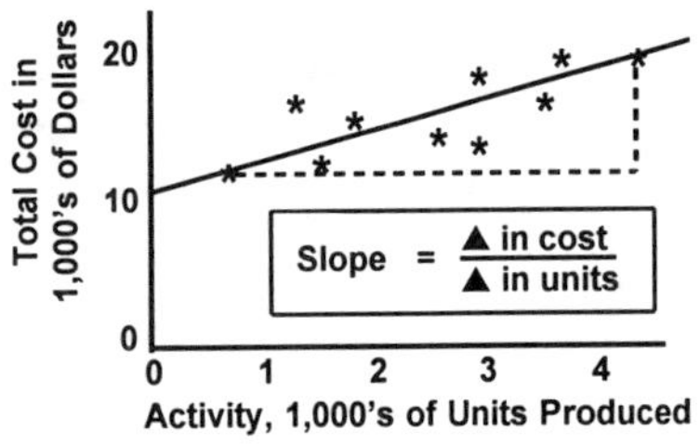




## Least-Squares Regression Method

Least-squares regression is usually covered in statistics courses. It is commonly used with computer software because of the large number of calculations required.

**The objective of the cost analysis remains the same:**

**Y = a + bX**



## The Contribution Format

| | Total | Unit |
|---|---|---|
| Sales Revenue | $ 100,000 | $ 50 |
| Less: Variable costs | 60,000 | 30 |
| Contribution margin | $ 40,000 | $ 20 |
| Less: Fixed costs | 30,000 | |
| Net income | $ 10,000 | |

**The contribution format income statement makes use of the cost analysis that has identified fixed and variable costs.**

## The Contribution Format

| | Total | Unit |
|---|---|---|
| Sales Revenue | $ 100,000 | $ 50 |
| Less: Variable costs | 60,000 | 30 |
| Contribution margin | $ 40,000 | $ 20 |
| Less: Fixed costs | 30,000 | |
| Net income | $ 10,000 | |

**Contribution margin is the amount by which revenue exceeds variable costs.**



## The Contribution Format

**Comparison of the Contribution Income Statement with the Traditional Income Statement**

| Traditional Approach (costs organized by function) | | Contribution Approach (costs organized by behavior) | |
|---|---|---|---|
| Sales | $ 100,000 | Sales | $ 100,000 |
| Less cost of goods sold | 70,000 | Less variable expenses | 60,000 |
| Gross Margin | $ 30,000 | Contribution margin | $ 40,000 |
| Less operating expenses | 20,000 | Less fixed expenses | 30,000 |
| Net income | $ 10,000 | Net income | $ 10,000 |



## End of Chapter 6

GARRISON

MANAGERIAL

Eighth Edition

ACCOUNTING

NOREEN

---

7

Cost-Volume-Profit Relationships

*Chapter*

7



---

7

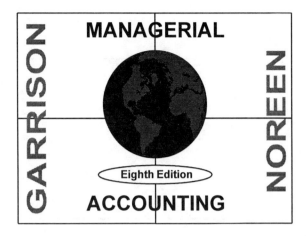

## The Basics of Cost-Volume-Profit (CVP) Analysis

| | |
|---|---|
| Sales (500 bikes) | $ 250,000 |
| Less: variable expenses | 150,000 |
| Contribution margin | 100,000 |
| Less: fixed expenses | 80,000 |
| Net income | $ 20,000 |

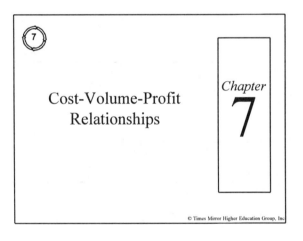

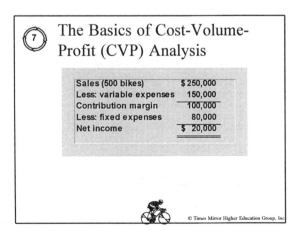

## 7 The Basics of Cost-Volume-Profit (CVP) Analysis

CVP analysis is concerned with the relationships among:

- *Product Prices*
- *Unit Sales Volume*
- *Unit Variable Costs*
- *Total Fixed Costs*
- *Mix of Products Sold*



## 7 The Contribution Approach

Consider the following information developed by the accountant at Nord Co.:

| | Total | Per Unit | Percent |
|---|---|---|---|
| Sales (500 bikes) | $250,000 | $ 500 | 100% |
| Less: variable expenses | 150,000 | 300 | 60% |
| Contribution margin | $100,000 | $ 200 | 40% |
| Less: fixed expenses | 80,000 | | |
| Net income | $ 20,000 | | |



## 7 The Contribution Approach

If Nord sells 400 units in a month, it will be operating at the break-even point.

| | Total | Per Unit | Percent |
|---|---|---|---|
| Sales (400 bikes) | $200,000 | $ 500 | 100% |
| Less: variable expenses | 120,000 | 300 | 60% |
| Contribution margin | $ 80,000 | $ 200 | 40% |
| Less: fixed expenses | 80,000 | | |
| Net income | $ - | | |

## 7 The Contribution Approach

If Nord sells one additional unit (401 bikes), net income will increase by $200.

| | Total | Per Unit | Percent |
|---|---|---|---|
| Sales (401 bikes) | $ 200,500 | $ 500 | 100% |
| Less: variable expenses | 120,300 | 300 | 60% |
| Contribution margin | $ 80,200 | $ 200 | 40% |
| Less: fixed expenses | 80,000 | | |
| Net income | $ 200 | | |



## 7 The Contribution Approach

✦ The break-even point can be defined either as:

❶ The point where total sales revenue equals total expenses (variable and fixed).

❷ The point where total contribution margin equals total fixed expenses.

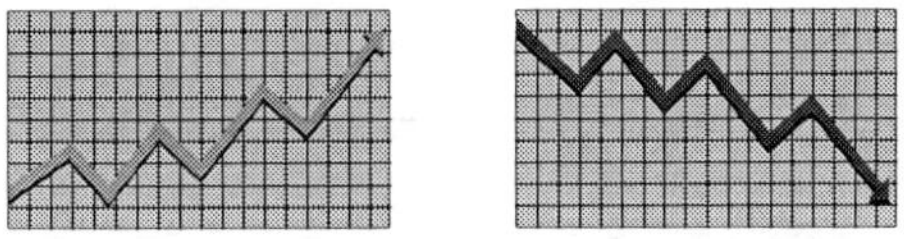



## 7 The Contribution Approach

Once the break-even point is reached, net income increases by the amount of the unit contribution margin for each additional unit sold.

| | Total | Per Unit | Percent |
|---|---|---|---|
| Sales (401 bikes) | $ 200,500 | $ 500 | 100% |
| Less: variable expenses | 120,300 | 300 | 60% |
| Contribution margin | $ 80,200 | $ 200 | 40% |
| Less: fixed expenses | 80,000 | | |
| Net income | $ 200 | | |

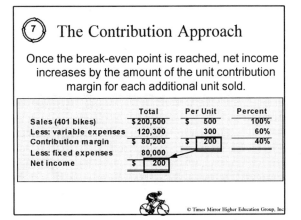

## Contribution Margin Ratio

- The contribution margin ratio is defined as follows:

$$\frac{\text{Contribution margin}}{\text{Sales}} = \text{CM Ratio}$$



## Contribution Margin Ratio

At Nord, each $1.00 increase in sales revenue results in a total contribution margin increase of 40¢.

If sales increase by $50,000, what will be the increase in total contribution margin?

## Contribution Margin Ratio

| | 400 Bikes | 500 Bikes |
|---|---|---|
| Sales | $ 200,000 | $ 250,000 |
| Less: variable expenses | 120,000 | 150,000 |
| Contribution margin | 80,000 | 100,000 |
| Less: fixed expenses | 80,000 | 80,000 |
| Net income | $ - | $ 20,000 |

A $50,000 increase in sales revenue

## 7 Contribution Margin Ratio

| | 400 Bikes | 500 Bikes |
|---|---|---|
| Sales | $ 200,000 | $ 250,000 |
| Less: variable expenses | 120,000 | 150,000 |
| Contribution margin | 80,000 | 100,000 |
| Less: fixed expenses | 80,000 | 80,000 |
| Net income | $ - | $ 20,000 |

A $50,000 increase in sales revenue results in a $20,000 increase in CM. ($50,000 × 40% = $20,000)



## 7 Changes in Fixed Costs and Sales Volume

- Nord is currently selling 500 bikes per month.
- The company's sales manager believes that an increase of $10,000 in the monthly advertising budget, would increase bike sales to 540 units.

Should we authorize the requested increase in the advertising budget?



## 7 Changes in Fixed Costs and Sales Volume

| | Current Sales (500 Bikes) | Proposed Sales (540 Bikes) |
|---|---|---|
| Sales | $ 250,000 | |
| Less: variable expenses | 150,000 | |
| Contribution margin | $ 100,000 | |
| Less: fixed expenses | 80,000 | |
| Net income | $ 20,000 | |

## Changes in Fixed Costs and Sales Volume

The Shortcut Solution

- Revenue increases by $20,000, so total CM increases by $8,000 ($20,000 × 40% = $8,000).
- The increase in CM ($8,000) is less than the increase in fixed costs ($10,000).
- So, net income will **decrease** by $2,000.

## Break-Even Analysis

- The break-even point is the point where
  - ❶Total sales revenue = total expenses or
  - ❷Total contribution margin = total fixed expenses.
- Break-even analysis can be approached in two ways:
  - ❶Equation method
  - ❷Contribution margin method.

## Equation Method

Sales – (Variable expenses + Fixed expenses) = Profits

**OR**

Sales = Variable expenses + Fixed expenses + Profits

## Equation Method

Here is the information from the Nord Co.:

| | Total | Per Unit | Percent |
|---|---|---|---|
| Sales (500 bikes) | $ 250,000 | $ 500 | 100% |
| Less: variable expenses | 150,000 | 300 | 60% |
| Contribution margin | $ 100,000 | $ 200 | 40% |
| Less: fixed expenses | 80,000 | | |
| Net income | $ 20,000 | | |



## Equation Method

We calculate the break-even point as follows:

Sales = Variable expenses + Fixed expenses + Profits



## Equation Method

We can also use the following equation to compute the break-even point in sales dollars.

Sales = Variable expenses + Fixed expenses + Profits

## 7 Contribution Margin Method

The contribution margin method is a variation of the equation method.

$$\frac{\text{Fixed expenses}}{\text{Unit contribution margin}} = \begin{array}{c}\text{Break-even point}\\ \text{in units sold}\end{array}$$



## 7 Contribution Margin Method

We can calculate the break-even point in total sales dollars as follows:

$$\frac{\text{Fixed expenses}}{\text{CM ratio}} = \begin{array}{c}\text{Break-even point in}\\ \text{total sales dollars}\end{array}$$



## 7 CVP Relationships in Graphic Form

- Viewing CVP relationships in a graph gives managers a perspective that can be obtained in no other way.
- Consider the following information for Nord Co.:

| | Income 300 units | Income 400 units | Income 500 units |
|---|---|---|---|
| Sales | $ 150,000 | $ 200,000 | $ 250,000 |
| Less: variable expenses | 90,000 | 120,000 | 150,000 |
| Contribution margin | $ 60,000 | $ 80,000 | $ 100,000 |
| Less: fixed expenses | 80,000 | 80,000 | 80,000 |
| Net income (loss) | $ (20,000) | $ - | $ 20,000 |

## 7 CVP Graph

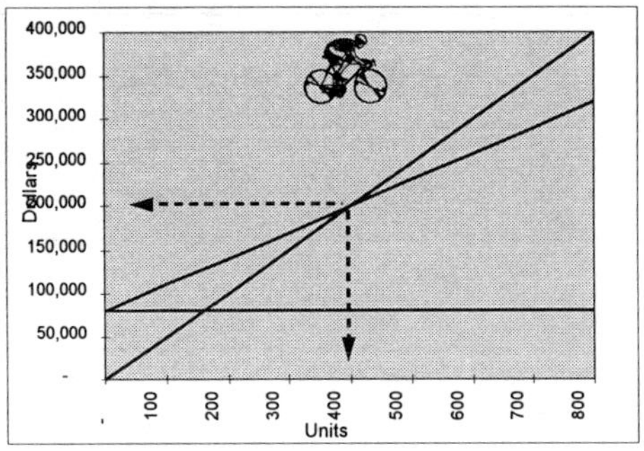




## 7 Profit Graph

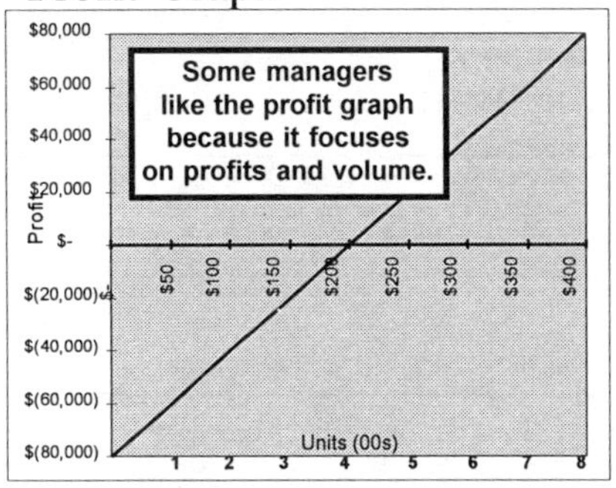




## 7 Profit Graph

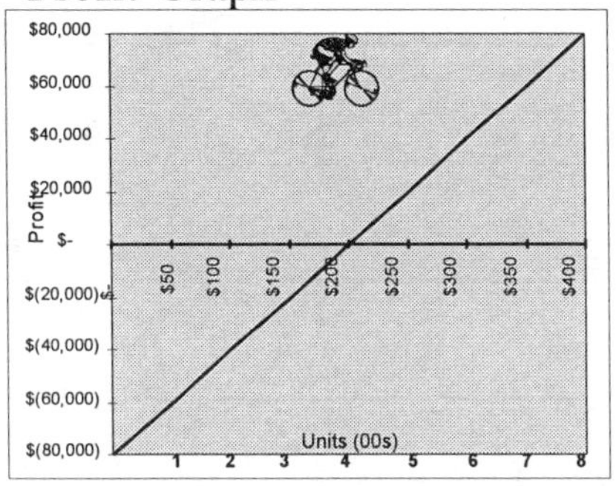

## 7 Target Net Profit Analysis

Suppose Nord Co. wants to know how many bikes must be sold to earn a profit of $100,000.

We can use our CVP formula to determine the sales volume needed to achieve a target net profit figure.



## 7 The CVP Equation

Sales = Variable expenses + Fixed expenses + Profits



## 7 The Contribution Margin Approach

We can determine the number of bikes that must be sold to earn a profit of $100,000 using the contribution margin approach.

$$\frac{\textbf{Fixed expenses + Target profit}}{\textbf{Unit contribution margin}} = \textbf{Units sold to attain the target profit}$$

## 7 The Margin of Safety

- Excess of budgeted (or actual) sales over the break-even volume of sales.
- Amount by which sales can drop before losses begin to be incurred.

**Total sales - Break-even sales = Margin of safety**

Let's calculate the margin of safety for Nord.



## 7 The Margin of Safety

Nord has a break-even point of $200,000. If actual sales are $250,000, the margin of safety is $50,000 or 100 bikes.

| | Break-even sales 400 units | Actual sales 500 units |
|---|---|---|
| Sales | $ 200,000 | $ 250,000 |
| Less: variable expenses | 120,000 | 150,000 |
| Contribution margin | 80,000 | 100,000 |
| Less: fixed expenses | 80,000 | 80,000 |
| Net income | $ - | $ 20,000 |

## 7 Operating Leverage

- A measure of the extent to which fixed costs are being used in an organization.
- Operating leverage is . . .
  - greatest in companies that have a high proportion of fixed costs in relation to variable costs.
  - lowest in companies that have a low proportion of fixed costs in relation to variable costs.

$$\frac{\textbf{Contribution margin}}{\textbf{Net income}} = \textbf{Degree of operating leverage}$$

## 7 Operating Leverage

| | Actual sales 500 Bikes |
|---|---|
| Sales | $ 250,000 |
| Less: variable expenses | 150,000 |
| Contribution margin | 100,000 |
| Less: fixed expenses | 80,000 |
| Net income | $ 20,000 |



## 7 Operating Leverage

A measure of how a percentage change in sales will affect profits.

If Nord increases its sales by 10%, what will be the percentage increase in net income?



## 7 The Concept of Sales Mix

- For a company with more than one product, sales mix is the relative combination in which a company's products are sold.
- Different products have different selling prices, cost structures, and contribution margins.

Let's assume Nord sells bikes and carts and see how we deal with break-even analysis.

## The Concept of Sales Mix

Nord provides us with the following information:

| | Bikes | | Carts | | Total | |
|---|---|---|---|---|---|---|
| Sales | $ 250,000 | 100% | $ 300,000 | 100% | $550,000 | 100% |
| Var. exp. | 150,000 | 60% | 135,000 | 45% | 285,000 | 52% |
| Contrib. margin | $ 100,000 | 40% | $ 165,000 | 55% | 265,000 | 48% |
| Fixed exp. | | | | | 170,000 | |
| Net income | | | | | $ 95,000 | |



## Assumptions of CVP Analysis

❶ Selling price is constant throughout the entire relevant range.

❷ Costs are linear throughout the entire relevant range.

❸ In multi-product companies, the sales mix is constant.

❹ In manufacturing companies, inventories do not change (units produced = units sold).

## End of Chapter 7

# MANAGERIAL ACCOUNTING

GARRISON

NOREEN

Eighth Edition

---

8

Chapter 8

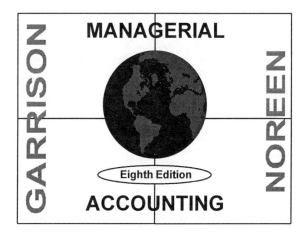

# Variable Costing: A Tool for Management



---

8

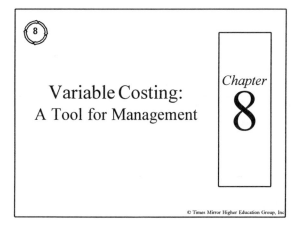

## Overview of Absorption and Variable Costing

| Absorption Costing | | Variable Costing |
|---|---|---|
| Product costs ← | Direct materials<br>Direct labor<br>Variable mfg. overhead | → Product costs |
| Period costs ← | Fixed mfg. overhead (absorption: product cost)<br>Selling & Admin. exp. | → Period costs |

## The Controversy over Fixed Overhead Cost

## The Controversy over Fixed Overhead Cost

## The Controversy over Fixed Overhead Cost

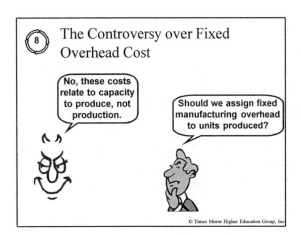

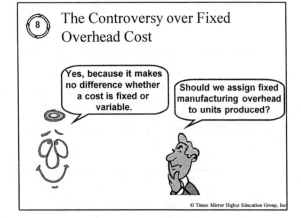

## 8 The Controversy over Fixed Overhead Cost

## 8 The Controversy over Fixed Overhead Cost

**Let's put some numbers to the controversy and see if it will sharpen our understanding.**

## 8 The Controversy over Fixed Overhead Cost

Harvey Co. produces a single product with the following information available:

| | |
|---|---|
| Number of units produced annually | 25,000 |
| Variable costs per unit: | |
| Direct materials, direct labor and variable mfg. overhead | $ 10 |
| Selling & administrative expenses | $ 3 |
| Fixed costs per year: | |
| Mfg. overhead | $ 150,000 |
| Selling & administrative expenses | $ 100,000 |

# The Controversy over Fixed Overhead Cost

Unit product cost is determined as follows:

| | Absorption Costing | Variable Costing |
|---|---|---|
| Direct materials, direct labor, and variable mfg. overhead | $ 10 | $ 10 |
| Fixed mfg. overhead ($150,000 ÷ 25,000 units) | 6 | - |
| Unit product cost | $ 16 | $ 10 |



# Income Comparison of Absorption and Variable Costing

Harvey Co. had no beginning inventory, produced 25,000 units and sold 20,000 units this year.

| | Absorption Costing | |
|---|---|---|
| Sales (20,000 × $30) | | $ 600,000 |
| Less cost of goods sold: | | |
| Beginning inventory | | |
| Add COGM | | |
| Goods available for sale | | |
| Ending inventory | | |
| Gross margin | | |
| Less selling & admin. exp. | | |
| Variable | | |
| Fixed | | |
| Net income | | |



# Income Comparison of Absorption and Variable Costing

Now let's look at variable costing by Harvey Co.

| | Variable Costing | |
|---|---|---|
| Sales (20,000 × $30) | | $ 600,000 |
| Less variable expenses: | | |
| Beginning inventory | | |
| Add COGM | | |
| Goods available for sale | | |
| Ending inventory | | |
| Variable cost of goods sold | | |
| Variable selling & administrative expenses | | |
| Contribution margin | | |
| Less fixed expenses: | | |
| Manufacturing overhead | | |
| Selling & administrative expenses | | |
| Net income | | |

## Income Comparison of Absorption and Variable Costing

Let's compare the methods.

| | Cost of Goods Sold | Ending Inventory | Period Expense | Total |
|---|---|---|---|---|
| Absorption costing | | | | |
| Variable mfg. costs | | | | |
| Fixed mfg. costs | | | | |
| | | | | |
| Variable costing | | | | |
| Variable mfg. costs | | | | |
| Fixed mfg. costs | | | | |
| | | | | |



## Reconciliation

We can reconcile the difference between absorption and variable net income as follows:

| | |
|---|---|
| Variable costing net income | $ 90,000 |
| Add: Fixed mfg. overhead costs deferred in inventory (5,000 units × $6 per unit) | 30,000 |
| Absorption costing net income | $ 120,000 |

$$\frac{\text{Fixed mfg. overhead}}{\text{Units produced}} \quad \frac{\$150,000}{25,000} = \$6.00 \text{ per unit}$$



## Extending the Example

Let's look at the second year of operations for Harvey Company.

## 8 Harvey Co. Year 2

In its second year of operations, Harvey Co. started with an inventory of 5,000 units, produced 25,000 units and sold 30,000 units.

| | | |
|---|---|---|
| Number of units produced annually | | 25,000 |
| Variable costs per unit: | | |
| Direct materials, direct labor and variable mfg. overhead | $ | 10 |
| Selling & administrative expenses | $ | 3 |
| Fixed costs per year: | | |
| Mfg. overhead | $ | 150,000 |
| Selling & administrative expenses | $ | 100,000 |



## 8 Harvey Co. Year 2

Unit product cost is determined as follows:

| | Absorption Costing | | Variable Costing | |
|---|---|---|---|---|
| Direct materials, direct labor, and variable mfg. overhead | $ | 10 | $ | 10 |
| Fixed mfg. overhead ($150,000 ÷ 25,000 units) | | 6 | | - |
| Unit product cost | $ | 16 | $ | 10 |

**There has been no change in Harvey's cost structure.**



## 8 Harvey Co. Year 2

**Now let's look at Harvey's income statement assuming absorption costing is used.**

## Harvey Co. Year 2

| | | Absorption Costing |
|---|---|---|
| Sales (30,000 × $30) | | $ 900,000 |
| Less cost of goods sold: | | |
| Beg. inventory (5,000 x $16) | $ 80,000 | |
| Add COGM (25,000 × $16) | 400,000 | |
| Goods available for sale | 480,000 | |
| Ending inventory | - | 480,000 |
| Gross margin | | 420,000 |
| Less selling & admin. exp. | | |
| Variable (20,000 × $3) | $ 60,000 | |
| Fixed | 100,000 | 160,000 |
| Net income | | $ 260,000 |



## Harvey Co. Year 2

**Next, we'll look at Harvey's income statement assuming variable costing is used.**

## Harvey Co. Year 2

| | | Variable Costing |
|---|---|---|
| Sales (30,000 × $30) | | $ 900,000 |
| Less variable expenses: | | |
| Beg. inventory (5,000 × $10) | $ 50,000 | |
| Add COGM (25,000 × $10) | 250,000 | |
| Goods available for sale | 300,000 | |
| Ending inventory | - | |
| Variable cost of goods sold | 300,000 | |
| Variable selling & administrative expenses (20,000 × $3) | 60,000 | 360,000 |
| Contribution margin | | 540,000 |
| Less fixed expenses: | | |
| Manufacturing overhead | $ 150,000 | |
| Selling & administrative expenses | 100,000 | 250,000 |
| Net income | | $ 290,000 |

## 8 Summary

**Income Comparison**

| Costing Method | 1st Period | 2nd Period | Total |
|---|---|---|---|
| Absorption | $ 120,000 | $ 260,000 | $ 380,000 |
| Variable | 90,000 | 290,000 | 380,000 |



## 8 Summary

Let's see if we can get an overview of what we have done.

## 8 Summary

| Relation between production and sales of the period | Effect on Inventories | Relation between absorption and variable net incomes |
|---|---|---|
| Production > Sales | Inventories Increase | Absorption > Variable |
| Production < Sales | Inventories decrease | Absorption < Variable |
| Production = Sales | No change | Absorption = Variable |

## Other Factors in Choosing a Costing Method

- CVP Analysis and Absorption Costing
  - CVP includes all fixed costs to compute breakeven.
  - Absorption costing defers fixed costs into inventory.
- Pricing Decisions
  - When absorption costing is used, there is a tendency to reject any price that is less than full cost.
- External Reporting and Income Taxes
  - External reporting and income tax law require that absorption costing be used.



## Advantages of the Contribution Approach

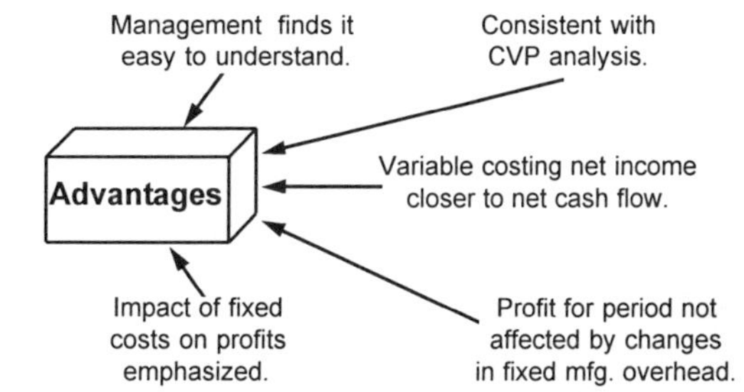

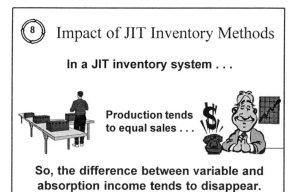

## Impact of JIT Inventory Methods

**In a JIT inventory system . . .**

**Production tends to equal sales . . .**

**So, the difference between variable and absorption income tends to disappear.**

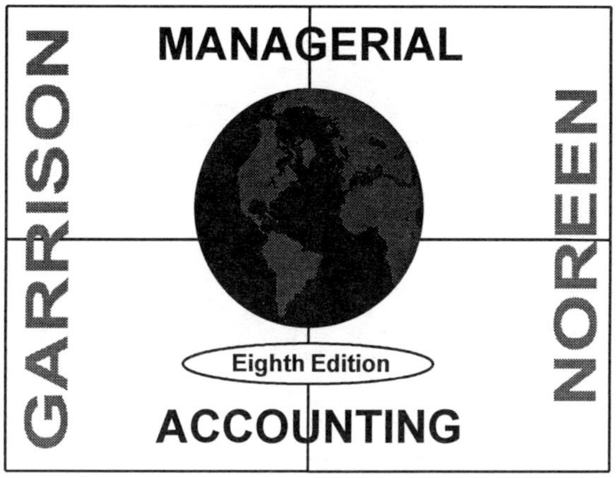


# Chapter 9

## Profit Planning



## The Basic Framework of Budgeting

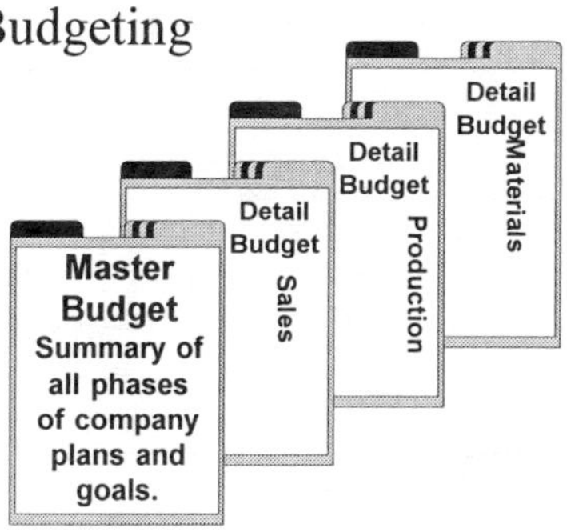

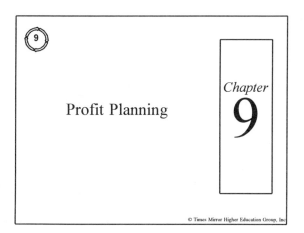

## 9 Planning and Control

- Planning -- involves developing objectives and preparing various budgets to achieve these objectives.
- Control -- involves the steps taken by management that attempt to ensure the objectives are attained.

## 9 Advantages of Budgeting

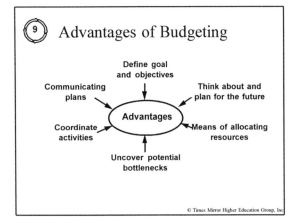

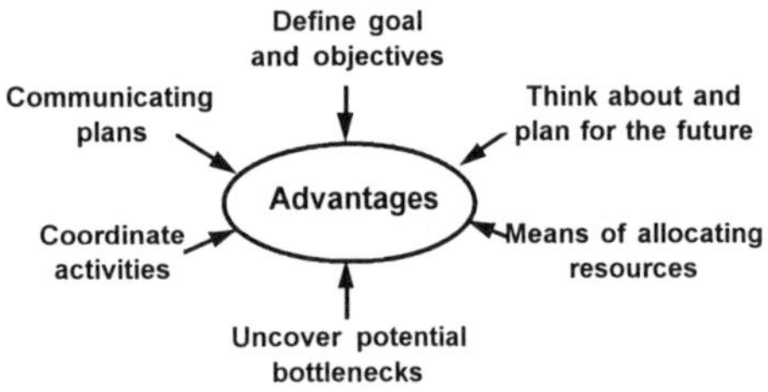




## 9 Responsibility Accounting

Managers should be evaluated by how well they manage those items — and only those items — under their control.

## 9 Choosing the Budget Period

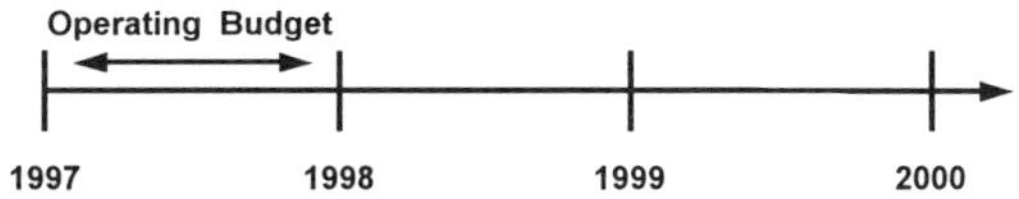


The annual operating budget may be divided into quarterly or monthly budgets.



## 9 Choosing the Budget Period

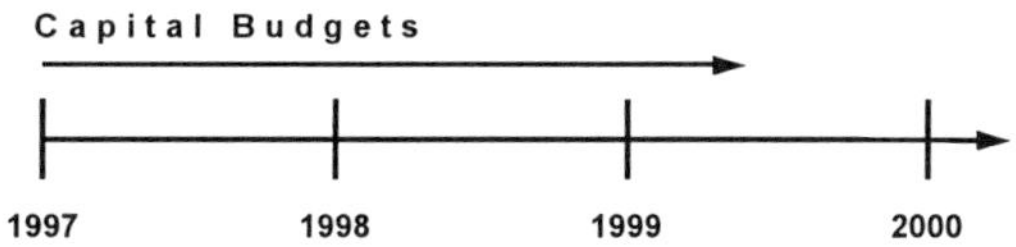




## 9 Choosing the Budget Period

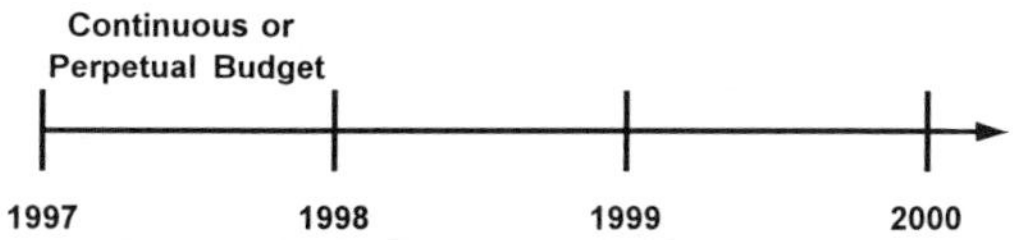


**This budget is usually a twelve-month budget that rolls forward one month as the current month is completed.**

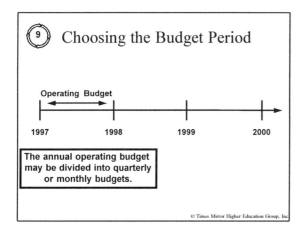

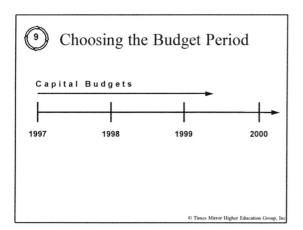

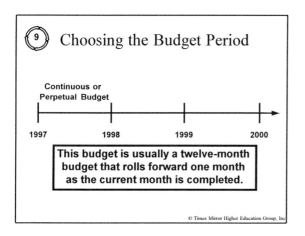

## Participative Budget System

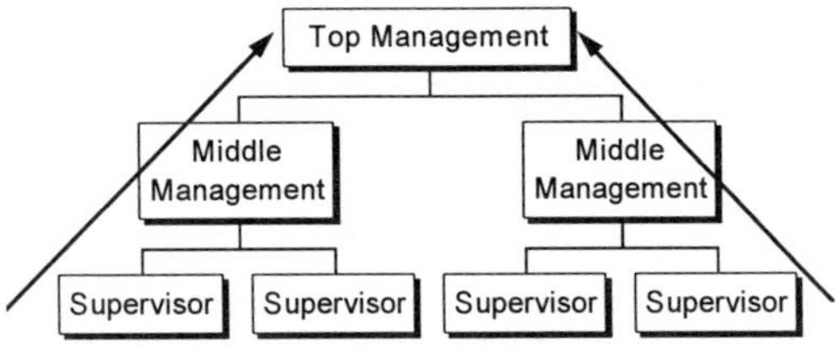


**Flow of Budget Data**



## The Budget Committee

- A standing committee responsible for
  - overall policy matters relating to the budget
  - coordinating the preparation of the budget

## The Master Budget

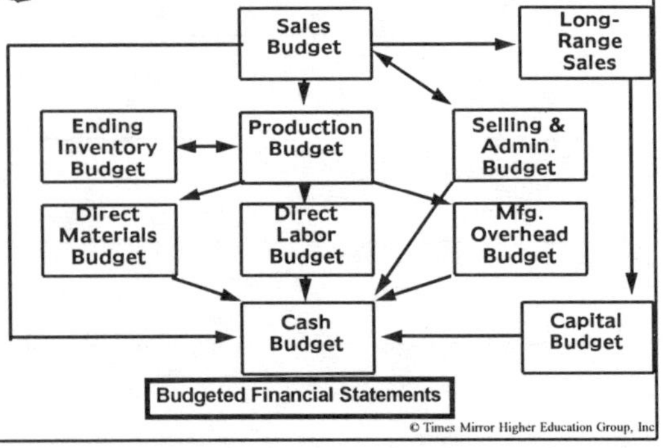

## 9 The Sales Budget

Detailed schedule showing expected sales for the coming periods expressed in units and dollars.

## 9 Budgeting Example

❶Royal Company is preparing budgets for the quarter ending June 30.

❷Budgeted sales for the next five months are:

| | |
|---|---|
| **April** | **20,000 units** |
| **May** | **50,000 units** |
| **June** | **30,000 units** |
| **July** | **25,000 units** |
| **August** | **15,000 units.** |

❸The selling price is $10 per unit.



## 9 The Sales Budget

| | April | May | June | Quarter |
|---|---|---|---|---|
| Budgeted sales (units) | 20,000 | 50,000 | 30,000 | 100,000 |
| Selling price per unit | | | | |
| Budgeted sales ($) | $ - | $ - | $ - | $ - |

## Expected Cash Collections

- All sales are on account.
- Royal's collection pattern is:
  - 70% collected in the month of sale,
  - 25% collected in the month following sale,
  - 5% is uncollected.
- The March 31 accounts receivable balance of $30,000 will be collected in full.



## Expected Cash Collections

| | April | May | June | Quarter |
|---|---|---|---|---|
| Accounts rec. - 3/31 | $ 30,000 | | | $ 30,000 |
| Total cash collections | | | | |



## The Production Budget

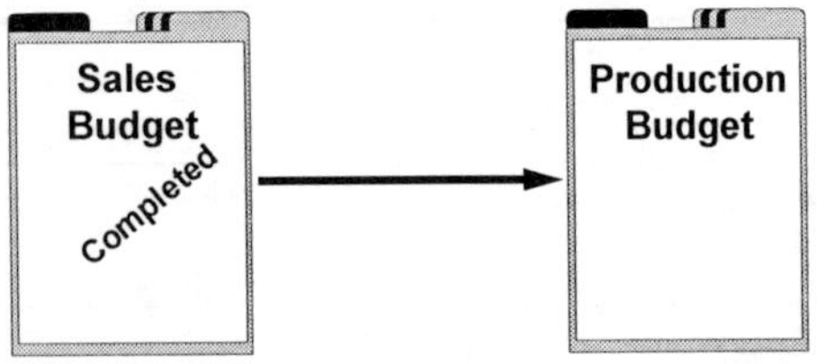


**Production must be adequate to meet budgeted sales and provide for sufficient ending inventory.**

## The Production Budget

- Royal Company wants ending inventory to be equal to 20% of the following month's budgeted sales in units.
- On March 31, 4,000 units were on hand.

Let's prepare the production budget.



## The Production Budget

| | April | May | June | Quarter |
|---|---|---|---|---|
| Sales in units | 20,000 | | | |
| **Add**: desired ending inventory | | | | |
| Total needed | | - | - | - |
| **Less**: beginning inventory | | | | |
| Production in units | - | - | - | - |



## The Direct Materials Budget

- At Royal Company, five pounds of material are required per unit of product.
- Management wants materials on hand at the end of each month equal to 10% of the following month's production.
- On March 31, 13,000 pounds of material are on hand. Material cost $.40 per pound.

Let's prepare the direct materials budget.

## The Direct Materials Budget

| | April | May | June | Quarter |
|---|---|---|---|---|
| Production in units | 26,000 | 46,000 | 29,000 | 101,000 |
| Materials per unit | | | | |
| Production needs | | | | |
| **Add:** desired **ending** inventory | | | | |
| Total needed | | | | |
| **Less:** beginning inventory | | | | |
| Materials to be purchased | - | - | - | - |



## Expected Cash Disbursement

- Royal pays $0.40 per pound for its materials.
- One-half of a month's purchases are paid for in the month of purchase; the other half is paid in the following month.
- No discounts are available.
- The March 31 accounts payable balance is $12,000.

Let's calculate expected cash disbursements.



## Expected Cash Disbursement

| | April | May | June | Quarter |
|---|---|---|---|---|
| Accounts pay. 3/31 | $ 12,000 | | | $ 12,000 |
| Total cash payments for materials | | | | |

## The Direct Labor Budget

- At Royal Company, each unit of product requires 0.05 hours of direct labor.
- The Company has a "no layoff" policy so all employees will be paid for 40 hours of work each week.
- In exchange for the "no layoff" policy, workers agreed to a wage rate of $10 per hour regardless of the hours worked (No overtime pay).
- For the next three months, the direct labor workforce will be paid for a minimum of 1,500 hours per month.

**Let's prepare the direct labor budget.**



## The Direct Labor Budget

| | April | May | June | Quarter |
|---|---|---|---|---|
| Production in units | 26,000 | 46,000 | 29,000 | 101,000 |
| Direct labor hours | | | | |
| Labor hours required | - | - | - | - |
| Guaranteed labor hours | | | | |
| Labor hours paid | | | | |
| Wage rate | | | | |
| Total direct labot cost | $ - | $ - | $ - | $ - |



## Manufacturing Overhead Budget

- Royal Company uses a variable manufacturing overhead of $1 per unit **produced**.
- Fixed manufacturing overhead is $50,000 per month and includes $20,000 of noncash costs (primarily depreciation of plant assets).

**Let's prepare the manufacturing overhead budget.**

## Manufacturing Overhead Budget

| | April | May | June | Quarter |
|---|---|---|---|---|
| Production in units | 26,000 | 46,000 | 29,000 | 101,000 |
| Variable mfg. OH rate | | | | |
| Variable mfg. OH costs | | | | |
| Fixed mfg. OH costs | | | | |
| Total mfg. OH costs | | | | |
| **Less**: noncash costs | | | | |
| Cash disbursements for manufacturing OH | | | | |



## Ending Finished Goods Inventory Budget

- Now, Royal can complete the ending finished goods inventory budget.
- At Royal, manufacturing overhead is applied to units of product on the basis of direct labor hours.

**Let's calculate ending finished goods inventory.**



## Ending Finished Goods Inventory Budget

| Production costs per unit | Quantity | Cost | Total |
|---|---|---|---|
| Direct materials | 5.00 lbs. | $ 0.40 | $ 2.00 |
| Direct labor | | | - |
| Manufacturing overhead | | | - |
| | | | |
| **Budgeted finished goods inventory** | | | |
| Ending inventory in units | | | |
| Unit product cost | | | |
| Ending finished goods inventory | | | |

## Selling and Administrative Expense Budget

- At Royal, variable selling and administrative expenses are $0.50 per unit sold.
- Fixed selling and administrative expenses are $70,000 per month.
- The fixed selling and administrative expenses include $10,000 in costs – primarily depreciation – that are not cash outflows of the current month.



## Selling and Administrative Expense Budget

| | April | May | June | Quarter |
|---|---|---|---|---|
| Sales in units | 20,000 | 50,000 | 30,000 | 100,000 |
| Variable selling and admin. rate | | | | |
| Variable expense | | | | |
| Fixed selling and admin. expense | | | | |
| Total expense | | | | |
| **Less**: noncash expenses | | | | |
| Cash disbursements for selling & admin. | | | | |



## The Cash Budget

- Royal:
  - Maintains a 16% open line of credit for $75,000.
  - Maintains a minimum cash balance of $30,000.
  - Borrows on the first day of the month and repays loans on the last day of the month.
  - Pays a cash dividend of $49,000 in April.
  - Purchases $143,700 of equipment in May and $48,300 in June paid in cash.
  - Has an April 1 cash balance of $40,000.

## 9 The Cash Budget

| | April | May | June | Quarter |
|---|---|---|---|---|
| Beginning cash balanc | $ 40,000 | | | |
| **Add**: cash collections | 170,000 | | | |
| Total cash available | 210,000 | | | |
| **Less**: disbursements | | | | |
| Materials | | | | |
| Direct labor | | | | |
| Mfg. overhead | | | | |
| Selling and admin. | | | | |
| Equipment purchase | | | | |
| Dividends | | | | |
| Total disbursements | | | | |
| Excess (deficiency) of Cash available over disbursements | | | | |



## 9 Financing and Repayment

| | April | May | June | Quarter |
|---|---|---|---|---|
| Excess (deficiency) of Cash available over disbursements | $(20,000) | | | |
| **Financing:** | | | | |
| Borrowing | 50,000 | | | |
| Repayments | - | | | |
| Interest | - | | | |
| Total financing | 50,000 | - | - | - |
| Ending cash balance | $ 30,000 | $ - | $ - | $ - |



## 9 Financing and Repayment

| | April | May | June | Quarter |
|---|---|---|---|---|
| Excess (deficiency) of Cash available over disbursements | $(20,000) | $ 30,000 | $ 95,000 | |
| **Financing:** | | | | |
| Borrowing | 50,000 | - | - | |
| Repayments | - | - | (50,000) | |
| Interest | - | - | (2,000) | |
| Total financing | 50,000 | - | (52,000) | - |
| Ending cash balance | $ 30,000 | $ 30,000 | $ 43,000 | $ - |

**$50,000 × 16% × 3/12 = $2,000**

## 9 The Cash Budget

| | April | May | June | Quarter |
|---|---|---|---|---|
| Beginning cash balanc | $ 40,000 | $ 30,000 | $ 30,000 | $ 40,000 |
| **Add**: cash collections | 170,000 | 400,000 | 335,000 | 905,000 |
| Total cash available | 210,000 | 430,000 | 365,000 | 945,000 |
| **Less**: disbursements | | | | |
| Materials | 40,000 | 72,300 | 72,700 | 185,000 |
| Direct labor | 15,000 | 23,000 | 15,000 | 53,000 |
| Mfg. overhead | 56,000 | 76,000 | 59,000 | 191,000 |
| Selling and admin. | 70,000 | 85,000 | 75,000 | 230,000 |
| Equipment purchase | - | 143,700 | 48,300 | 192,000 |
| Dividends | 49,000 | - | - | 49,000 |
| Total disbursements | 230,000 | 400,000 | 270,000 | 900,000 |
| Excess (deficiency) of Cash available over disbursements | $(20,000) | $ 30,000 | $ 95,000 | $ 45,000 |



## 9 Financing and Repayment

| | April | May | June | Quarter |
|---|---|---|---|---|
| Excess (deficiency) of Cash available over disbursements | $(20,000) | $ 30,000 | $ 95,000 | $ 45,000 |
| **Financing:** | | | | |
| Borrowing | 50,000 | - | - | 50,000 |
| Repayments | - | - | (50,000) | (50,000) |
| Interest | - | - | (2,000) | (2,000) |
| Total financing | 50,000 | - | (52,000) | (2,000) |
| Ending cash balance | $ 30,000 | $ 30,000 | $ 43,000 | $ 43,000 |



## 9 The Budgeted Income Statement

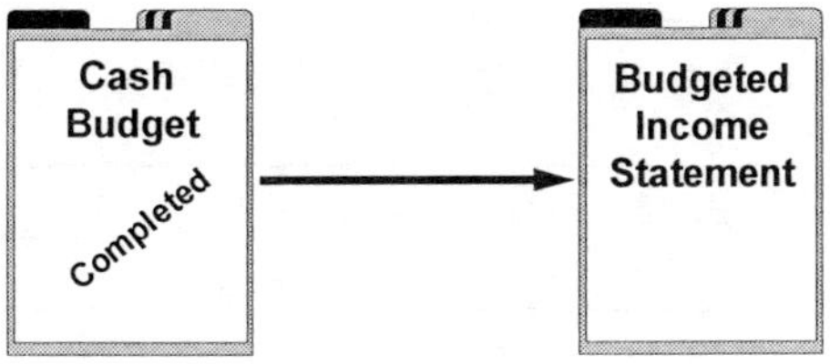

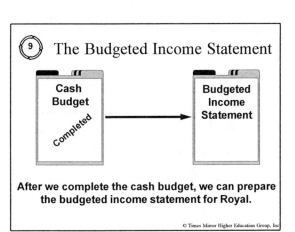

**After we complete the cash budget, we can prepare the budgeted income statement for Royal.**

# The Budgeted Income Statement

| Royal Company<br>Budgeted Income Statement<br>For the Three Months Ended June 30 | |
|---|---|
| Sales (100,000 units @ $10) | $ 1,000,000 |



# The Budgeted Balance Sheet

- Royal reports the following account balances on June 30 prior to preparing its budgeted financial statements:
  - Land - $50,000
  - Building (net) - $175,000
  - Common stock - $200,000
  - Retained earnings - $146,150



# The Budgeted Balance Sheet

Royal Company
Budgeted Balance Sheet
June 30

| | |
|---|---|
| Current assets | |
| Cash | $ 43,000 |
| Accounts receivable | 75,000 |
| Raw materials inventory | 4,600 |
| Finished goods inventory | 24,950 |
| Total current assets | 147,550 |
| Property and equipment | |
| Land | 50,000 |
| Building | 175,000 |
| Equipment | 192,000 |
| Total property and equipment | 417,000 |
| Total assets | $ 564,550 |
| | |
| Accounts payable | $ 28,400 |
| Common stock | 200,000 |
| Retained earnings | 336,150 |
| Total liabilities and equities | $ 564,550 |

## JIT Purchasing

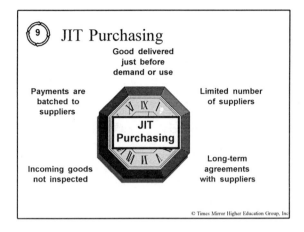

Good delivered just before demand or use

Payments are batched to suppliers

Limited number of suppliers

Incoming goods not inspected

Long-term agreements with suppliers



## International Aspects of Budgeting

- Multinational companies face special problems when preparing a budget.
  - Fluctuations in foreign currency exchange rates.
  - High inflation rates in some foreign countries.
  - Differences in local economic conditions.
  - Local governmental policies.

## End of Chapter 9

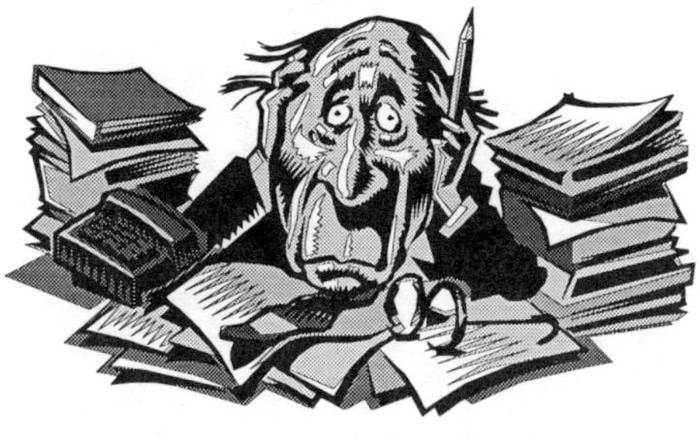

GARRISON

MANAGERIAL

Eighth Edition

ACCOUNTING

NOREEN

---

10

Standard Costs and Operating Performance Measures

*Chapter* 10



---

10 Standard Costs

- Based on carefully predetermined amounts.
- Used for planning labor, material and overhead requirements.
- The expected level of performance.
- Benchmarks for measuring performance.

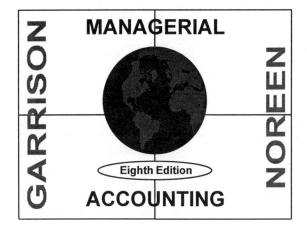

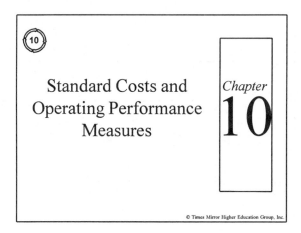

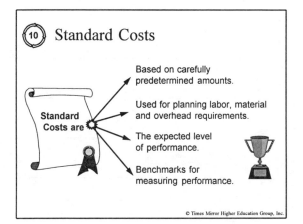

## (10) Standard Costs

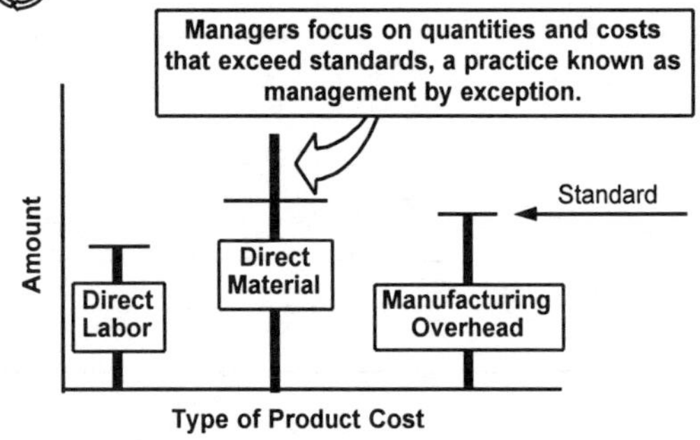




Managers focus on quantities and costs that exceed standards, a practice known as management by exception.

## (10) Setting Standard Costs

Accountants, engineers, personnel administrators, and production managers combine efforts to set standards based on experience and expectations.

## (10) Setting Standard Costs

Should we use practical standards or ideal standards?

## (10) Setting Standard Costs

Practical standards should be set at levels that are currently attainable with reasonable and efficient effort.

## (10) Setting Standard Costs

I agree. Ideal standards, that are based on perfection, are unattainable and therefore discouraging to most employees.

© Times Mirror Higher Education Group, Inc.

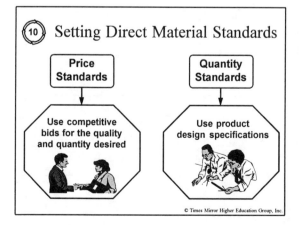

## (10) Setting Direct Material Standards

**Price Standards** → Use competitive bids for the quality and quantity desired

**Quantity Standards** → Use product design specifications

© Times Mirror Higher Education Group, Inc.

## (10) Setting Direct Material Standards

**The standard material cost for one unit of product is:**

standard price for one unit of material × standard quantity of material required for one unit of product

## (10) Setting Direct Labor Standards

**Rate Standards** → Use wage surveys and labor contracts

**Time Standards** → Use time and motion studies for each labor operation

## (10) Setting Direct Labor Standards

**The standard labor cost for one unit of product is:**

standard wage rate for one hour × standard number of labor hours for one unit of product

## Setting Variable Overhead Standards

**Rate Standards**

The rate is the variable portion of the predetermined overhead rate

**Activity Standards**

The activity is the cost driver used to calculate the predetermined overhead

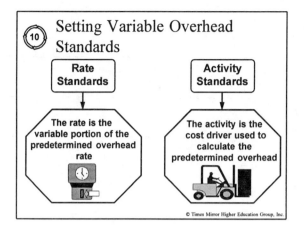

## Setting Variable Overhead Standards

The standard variable overhead cost for one unit of product is:

standard variable overhead rate for one unit of activity × standard number of activity units for one unit of product

## Standard Cost Card – Variable Production Cost

A standard cost card might look like this:

| Inputs | Standard Quantity or Hours | Standard Price or Rate | Standard Cost |
|---|---|---|---|
| Direct materials | 3.0 lbs. | $ 4.00 per lb. | $ 12.00 |
| Direct labor | 2.5 hours | 14.00 per hour | 35.00 |
| Variable mfg. overhead | 2.5 hours | 3.00 per hour | 7.50 |
| Total standard unit cost | | | $ 54.50 |

## 10 Standards vs. Budgets

**Are standards the same as budgets?**

**A standard is the expected cost for one unit.**

**A budget is the expected cost for all units.**



## 10 Advantages of Standard Costs

Possible reductions in production costs

Management by exception

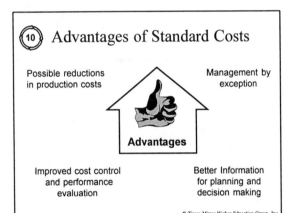

Improved cost control and performance evaluation

Better Information for planning and decision making



## 10 Disadvantages of Standard Costs

Emphasis on negative exceptions may impact morale.

Emphasis on negative exceptions may lead to cover ups.

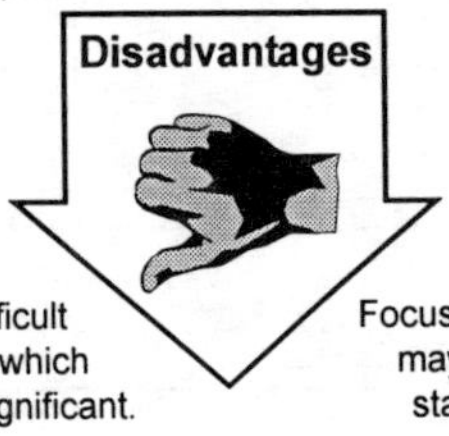


It may be difficult to determine which variances are significant.

Focus on big variances may obscure early stages of trends.

## (10) Standard Cost Variances

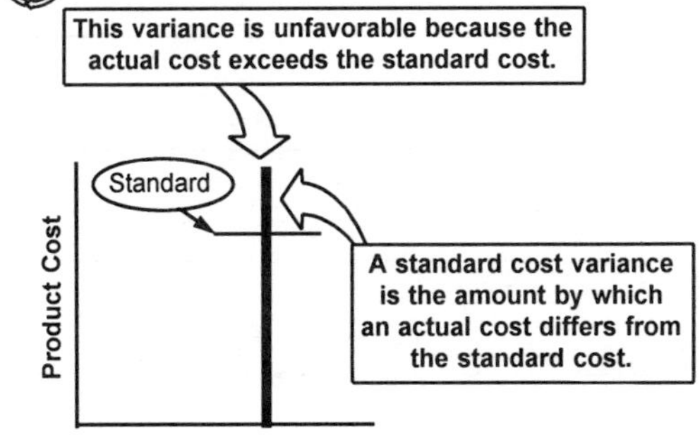




## (10) Standard Cost Variances

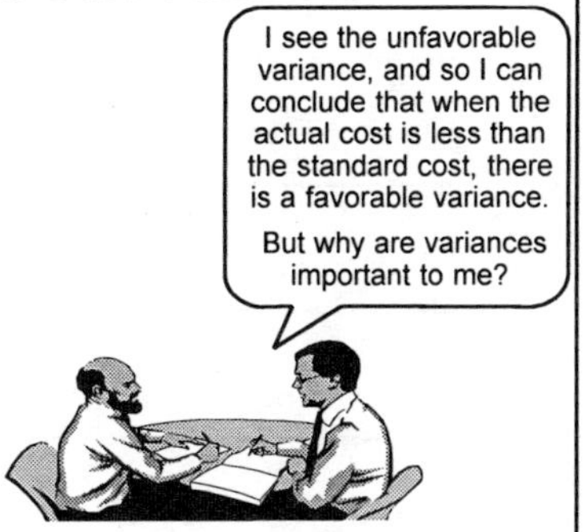




## (10) Standard Cost Variances

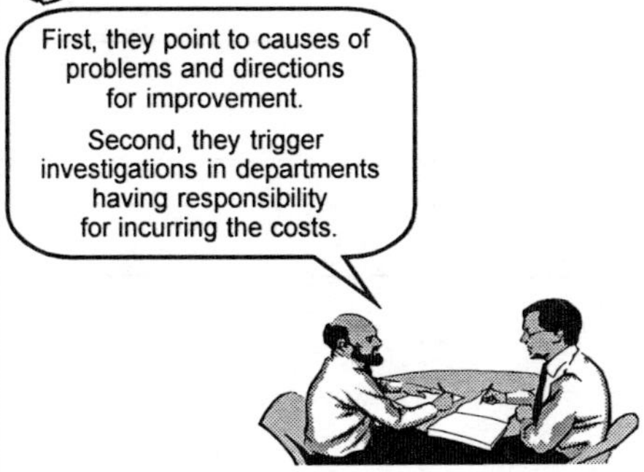

## (10) Variance Analysis Cycle

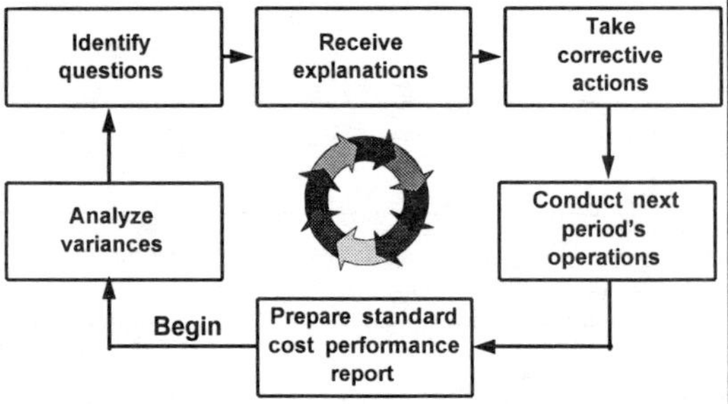




## (10) Standard Cost Variances

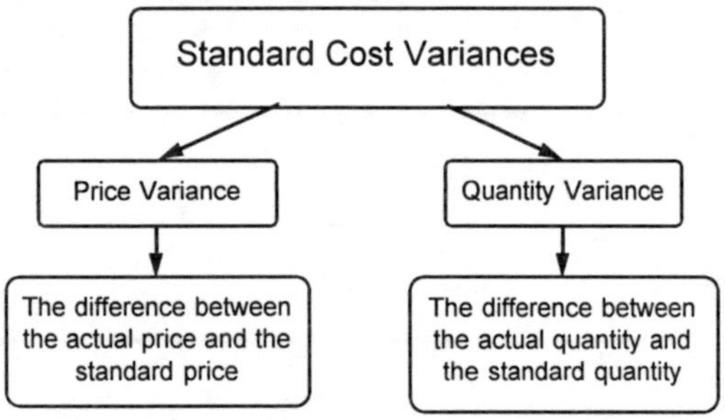




## (10) A General Model for Variance Analysis

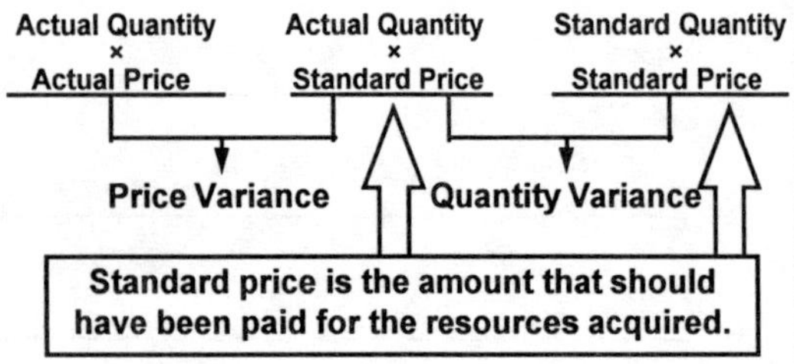

## A General Model for Variance Analysis

| Actual Quantity × Actual Price | Actual Quantity × Standard Price | Standard Quantity × Standard Price |
|---|---|---|

Price Variance (Actual Quantity × Actual Price vs. Actual Quantity × Standard Price)

Quantity Variance (Actual Quantity × Standard Price vs. Standard Quantity × Standard Price)

**Standard quantity is the quantity allowed for the actual good output.**



## A General Model for Variance Analysis

| Actual Quantity × Actual Price | Actual Quantity × Standard Price | Standard Quantity × Standard Price |
|---|---|---|

Price Variance (Actual Quantity × Actual Price vs. Actual Quantity × Standard Price)

Quantity Variance (Actual Quantity × Standard Price vs. Standard Quantity × Standard Price)

| AQ(AP - SP) | SP(AQ - SQ) |
|---|---|
| AQ = Actual Quantity | SP = Standard Price |
| AP = Actual Price | SQ = Standard Quantity |



## Material Variances Example

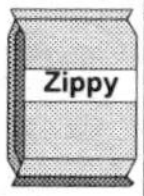


Hanson Inc. has the following direct material standard to manufacture one Zippy:

1.5 pounds per Zippy at $4.00 per pound

Last week 1,700 pounds of material were purchased and used to make 1,000 Zippies. The material cost a total of $6,630.

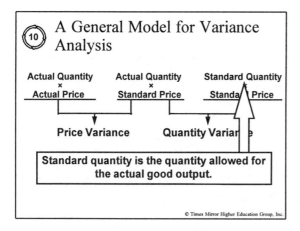

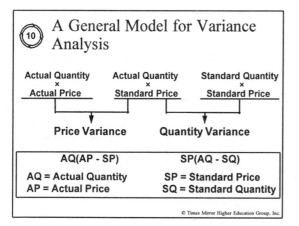

## Material Variances Question 1

What is the actual price per pound paid for the material?

a. $4.00 per pound.
b. $4.10 per pound.
c. $3.90 per pound.
d. $6.63 per pound.



## Material Variances Question 2

Hanson's material price variance (MPV) for the week was:

a. $170 unfavorable.
b. $170 favorable.
c. $800 unfavorable.
d. $800 favorable.



## Material Variances Question 3

The standard quantity of material that should have been used to produce 1,000 Zippies is:

a. 1,700 pounds.
b. 1,500 pounds.
c. 2,550 pounds.
d. 2,000 pounds.

## Material Variances Question 4

Hanson's material quantity variance (MQV) for the week was:

a. $170 unfavorable.
b. $170 favorable.
c. $800 unfavorable.
d. $800 favorable.



## Material Variances Summary

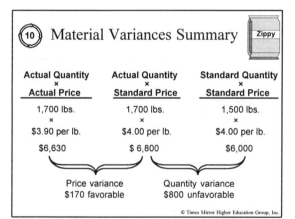

| Actual Quantity × Actual Price | Actual Quantity × Standard Price | Standard Quantity × Standard Price |
|---|---|---|
| 1,700 lbs. × $3.90 per lb. | 1,700 lbs. × $4.00 per lb. | 1,500 lbs. × $4.00 per lb. |
| $6,630 | $ 6,800 | $6,000 |

Price variance $170 favorable

Quantity variance $800 unfavorable



## Material Variances

**Hanson purchased and used 1,700 pounds. How are the variances computed if the amount purchased differs from the amount used?**

**The price variance is computed on the entire quantity purchased.**

**The quantity variance is computed only on the quantity used.**

## 10 Material Variances Continued

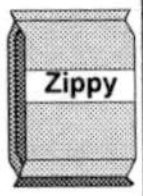


Hanson Inc. has the following material standard to manufacture one Zippy:

1.5 pounds per Zippy at $4.00 per pound

Last week 2,800 pounds of material were purchased at a total cost of $10,920, and 1,700 pounds were used to make 1,000 Zippies.



## 10 Material Variances Continued

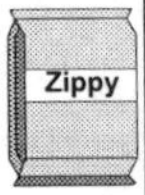


| Actual Quantity Purchased × Actual Price | Actual Quantity Purchased × Standard Price |
|---|---|
| 2,800 lbs. × $3.90 per lb. | 2,800 lbs. × $4.00 per lb. |
| $10,920 | $11,200 |

Price variance $280 favorable

Price variance increases because quantity purchased increases.



## 10 Material Variances Continued

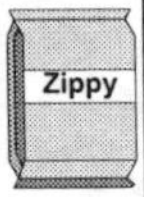


| Actual Quantity Used × Standard Price | Standard Quantity × Standard Price |
|---|---|
| 1,700 lbs. × $4.00 per lb. | 1,500 lbs. × $4.00 per lb. |
| $6,800 | $6,000 |

Quantity variance is unchanged because actual and standard quantities are unchanged.

Quantity variance $800 unfavorable

## 10 Isolation of Material Variances

I need the variances as soon as possible so that I can better identify problems and control costs.
You accountants just don't understand the problems we production managers have.
Okay. I'll start computing the price variance when material is purchased and the quantity variance as soon as material is used.



## 10 Responsibility for Material Variances

I am not responsible for this unfavorable material quantity variance.
You purchased cheap material, so my people had to use more of it.
You used too much material because of poorly trained workers and poorly maintained equipment.
Also, your poor scheduling sometimes requires me to rush order material at a higher price, causing unfavorable price variances.



## 10 Labor Variances Example

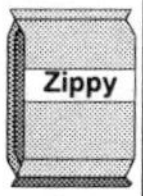


**Hanson Inc. has the following direct labor standard to manufacture one Zippy:**

**1.5 standard hours per Zippy at $6.00 per direct labor hour**

**Last week 1,550 direct labor hours were worked at a total labor cost of $9,610 to make 1,000 Zippies.**

## 10 Labor Variances Question 1

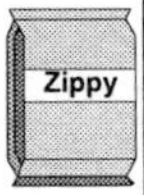


**What was Hanson's actual rate (AR) for labor for the week?**

a. **$6.20 per hour.**
b. **$6.00 per hour.**
c. **$5.80 per hour.**
d. **$5.60 per hour.**



## 10 Labor Variances Question 2

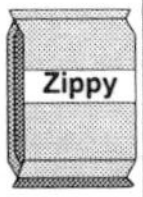


**Hanson's labor rate variance (LRV) for the week was:**

a. **$310 unfavorable.**
b. **$310 favorable.**
c. **$300 unfavorable.**
d. **$300 favorable.**



## 10 Labor Variances Question 3

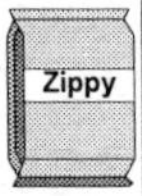


**The standard hours (SH) of labor that should have been worked to produce 1,000 Zippies is:**

a. **1,550 hours.**
b. **1,500 hours.**
c. **1,700 hours.**
d. **1,800 hours.**

## (10) Labor Variances Question 4

**Hanson's labor efficiency variance (LEV) for the week was:**

a. **$290 unfavorable.**
b. **$290 favorable.**
c. **$300 unfavorable.**
d. **$300 favorable.**



## (10) Labor Variances Summary

| Actual Hours × Actual Rate | Actual Hours × Standard Rate | Standard Hours × Standard Rate |
|---|---|---|
| 1,550 hours × $6.20 per hour | 1,550 hours × $6.00 per hour | 1,500 hours × $6.00 per hour |
| $9,610 | $9,300 | $9,000 |

Rate variance
$310 unfavorable

Efficiency variance
$300 unfavorable



## (10) Labor Rate Variance – A Closer Look

Using highly paid skilled workers to perform unskilled tasks results in an unfavorable rate variance.

High skill, high rate

Low skill, low rate

Production managers who make work assignments are generally responsible for rate variances.

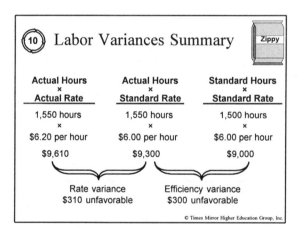

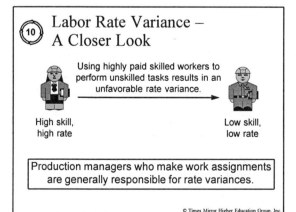

## Labor Efficiency Variance – A Closer Look

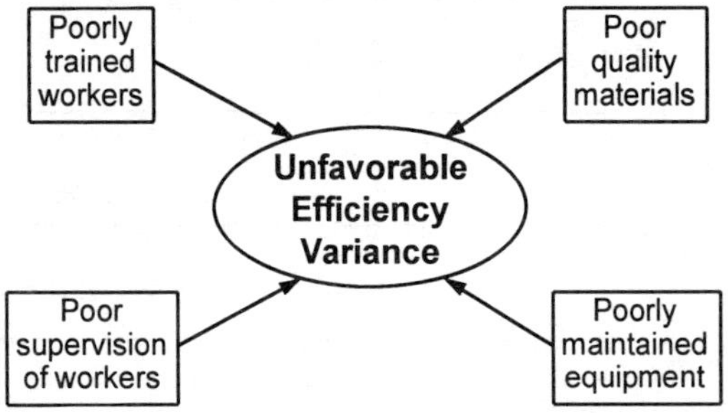




## Responsibility for Labor Variances

## Responsibility for Labor Variances

## Variable Manufacturing Overhead Variances Example

10

**Hanson Inc. has the following variable manufacturing overhead standard to manufacture one Zippy:**

**1.5 standard hours per Zippy at $3.00 per direct labor hour**

**Last week 1,550 hours were worked to make 1,000 Zippies, and $5,115 was spent for variable manufacturing overhead.**



## Variable Manufacturing Overhead Variances Question 1

10

**What was Hanson's actual rate (AR) for variable manufacturing overhead rate for the week?**

a. **$3.00 per hour.**
b. **$3.19 per hour.**
c. **$3.30 per hour.**
d. **$4.50 per hour.**



## Variable Manufacturing Overhead Variances Question 2

10

**Hanson's spending variance (SV) for variable manufacturing overhead for the week was:**

a. **$465 unfavorable.**
b. **$400 favorable.**
c. **$335 unfavorable.**
d. **$300 favorable.**

## Variable Manufacturing Overhead Variances Question 3

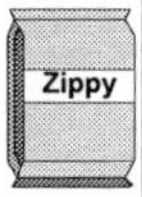


**Hanson's efficiency variance (EV) for variable manufacturing overhead for the week was:**

a. **$435 unfavorable.**
b. **$435 favorable.**
c. **$150 unfavorable.**
d. **$150 favorable.**



## Variable Manufacturing Overhead Variances

| Actual Hours × Actual Rate | Actual Hours × Standard Rate | Standard Hours × Standard Rate |
|---|---|---|
| 1,550 hours × $3.30 per hour | 1,550 hours × $3.00 per hour | 1,500 hours × $3.00 per hour |
| $5,115 | $4,650 | $4,500 |

Spending variance $465 unfavorable (between $5,115 and $4,650)

Efficiency variance $150 unfavorable (between $4,650 and $4,500)



## Variable Manufacturing Overhead Variances – A Closer Look

**Spending Variance**

Results from paying more or less than expected for overhead items such as supplies and utilities.

**Efficiency Variance**

A function of the selected cost driver.

It does not reflect overhead control.

## Variance analysis and Management by Exception

How do I know which variances to investigate?

Larger variances, in dollar amount or as a percentage of the standard, are investigated first.



## Standard Costs and the New Competitive Environment

Standard costing may be inappropriate in some modern manufacturing environments.

Undue concern for variances and cost minimization may lead to lower quality.

Automation reduces labor costs and the significance of labor variances.

The desire to "keep everyone busy" – even at non-bottleneck workstations – can lead to excessive work in process inventories.



## Operating Performance Measures

1. Quality control
2. Material control
3. Inventory control
4. Machine performance
5. Delivery performance

The focus is on continuous improvement rather than meeting a particular standard.

## (10) Operating Performance Measures

**Quality Control**
1. Warranty claims
2. Customer complaints
3. Defective products
4. Cost of rework

**Material Control**
1. Quality
2. Lead time
3. Cost of scrap

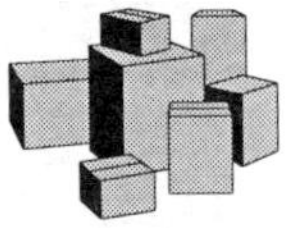



## (10) Operating Performance Measures

**Inventory Control**
1. Turnover ratio
2. Number of inventoried items

**Machine Performance**
1. Availability
2. Downtime
3. Usage
4. Setup time

## (10) Delivery Performance Measures

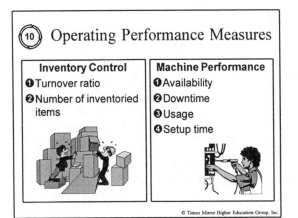

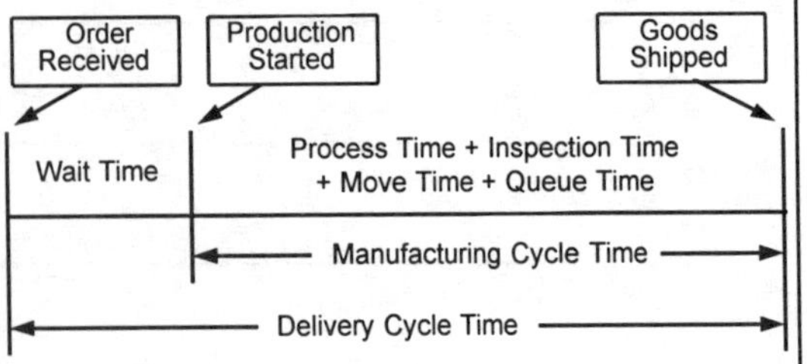

End of Chapter 10

GARRISON

# MANAGERIAL

Eighth Edition

# ACCOUNTING

NOREEN

---

11

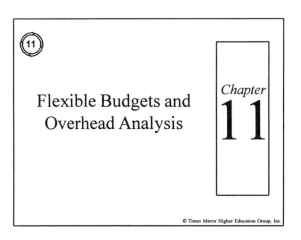

Flexible Budgets and Overhead Analysis

*Chapter* 11



---

11

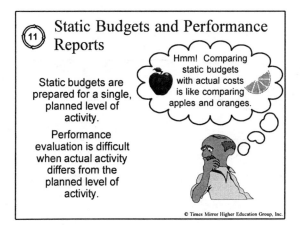

## Static Budgets and Performance Reports

Static budgets are prepared for a single, planned level of activity.

Performance evaluation is difficult when actual activity differs from the planned level of activity.

Hmm! Comparing static budgets with actual costs is like comparing apples and oranges.

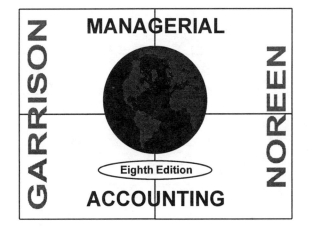

## 11 Static Budgets and Performance Reports

| | Static Budget | Actual Results | Variances |
|---|---|---|---|
| Machine hours | 10,000 | 8,000 | 2,000 U |
| Variable costs | | | |
| Indirect labor | $ 40,000 | $ 34,000 | $6,000 F |
| Indirect materials | 30,000 | 25,500 | 4,500 F |
| Power | 5,000 | 3,800 | 1,200 F |
| Fixed costs | | | |
| Depreciation | 12,000 | 12,000 | 0 |
| Insurance | 2,000 | 2,000 | 0 |
| Total overhead costs | $ 89,000 | $ 77,300 | $11,700 F |



## 11 Static Budgets and Performance Reports

| | Static Budget | Actual Results | Variances |
|---|---|---|---|
| Machine hours | 10,000 | 8,000 | 2,000 U |
| Variable costs | | | |
| Indirect labor | $ 40,000 | $ 34,000 | $6,000 F |
| Indirect materials | 30,000 | 25,500 | 4,500 F |
| Power | 5,000 | 3,800 | 1,200 F |
| | | | 0 |
| Insurance | 2,000 | 2,000 | 0 |
| Total overhead costs | $ 89,000 | $ 77,300 | $11,700 F |

**Since cost variances are favorable, have we done a good job controlling costs?**



## 11 Static Budgets and Performance Reports

I don't think I can answer this question using a static budget.
I do know that actual activity is below budgeted activity which is unfavorable.
But shouldn't variable costs be lower if actual activity is below budgeted activity?

## Static Budgets and Performance Reports

- The relevant question is . . .

  "How much of the favorable cost variance is due to lower activity, and how much is due to good cost control?"

- To answer the question, we must **flex** the budget to the actual level of activity.

## Flexible Budgets

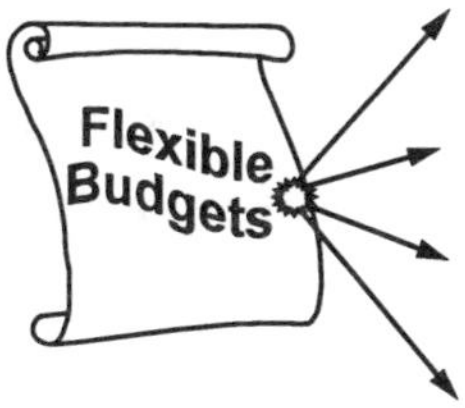


- Show revenues and expenses that should have occurred at the actual level of activity.
- May be prepared for any activity level in the relevant range.
- Reveal variances due to good cost control or lack of cost control.
- Improve performance evaluation.



## Flexible Budgets

Central Concept

If you can tell me what your activity was for the period, I will tell you what your costs and revenue should have been.

## 11 Preparing a Flexible Budget

- To flex a budget for different activity levels, we must know how costs behave with changes in activity levels.
  - Total variable costs change in direct proportion to changes in activity.
  - Total fixed costs remain unchanged within the relevant range.

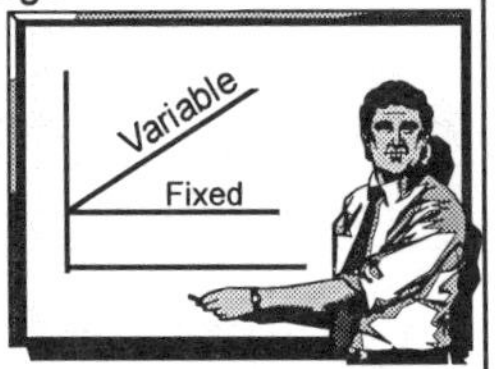




## 11 Preparing a Flexible Budget

Let's prepare flexible budgets for the Cheese Company.



## 11 Preparing a Flexible Budget

| | Cost Formula Per Hour | Total Fixed Cost | Flexible Budgets 8,000 Hours | 10,000 Hours | 12,000 Hours |
|---|---|---|---|---|---|
| Machine hours | | | 8,000 | 10,000 | 12,000 |
| Variable costs | | | | | |
| Indirect labor | 4.00 | | | | |
| Indirect material | 3.00 | | | | |
| Power | 0.50 | | | | |
| Total variable cost | $ 7.50 | | | | |
| Fixed costs | | | | | |
| Depreciation | | $12,000 | | | |
| Insurance | | 2,000 | | | |
| Total fixed cost | | | | | |
| Total overhead costs | | | | | |

## (11) Preparing a Flexible Budget

| | Cost Formula Per Hour | Total Fixed Cost | Flexible Budgets: 8,000 Hours | 10,000 Hours | 12,000 Hours |
|---|---|---|---|---|---|
| Machine hours | | | 8,000 | 10,000 | 12,000 |
| Variable costs | | | | | |
| Indirect labor | 4.00 | | $ 32,000 | $ 40,000 | $ 48,000 |
| Indirect material | 3.00 | | 24,000 | 30,000 | 36,000 |
| Power | 0.50 | | 4,000 | 5,000 | 6,000 |
| Total variable cost | $ 7.50 | | $ 60,000 | $ 75,000 | $ 90,000 |
| Fixed costs | | | | | |
| Depreciation | | $12,000 | $ 12,000 | $ 12,000 | $ 12,000 |
| Insurance | | 2,000 | 2,000 | 2,000 | 2,000 |
| Total fixed cost | | | $ 14,000 | $ 14,000 | $ 14,000 |
| Total overhead costs | | | $ 74,000 | $ 89,000 | $ 104,000 |



## (11) Flexible Budget Performance Report

Now let's prepare a flexible budget performance report at 8,000 actual machine hours for the Cheese Co.




## (11) Flexible Budget Performance Report

| | Cost Formula Per Hour | Total Fixed Costs | Flexible Budget | Actual Results | Variances |
|---|---|---|---|---|---|
| Machine hours | | | 8,000 | 8,000 | 0 |
| Variable costs | | | | | |
| Indirect labor | $ 4.00 | | $ 32,000 | $ 34,000 | $ 2,000 U |
| Indirect material | 3.00 | | 24,000 | 25,500 | 1,500 U |
| Power | 0.50 | | 4,000 | 3,800 | 200 F |
| Total variable costs | $ 7.50 | | $ 60,000 | $ 63,300 | $ 3,300 U |
| Fixed Expenses | | | | | |
| Depreciation | | $12,000 | $ 12,000 | $ 12,000 | 0 |
| Insurance | | 2,000 | 2,000 | 2,000 | 0 |
| Total fixed costs | | | $ 14,000 | $ 14,000 | 0 |
| Total overhead costs | | | $ 74,000 | $ 77,300 | $ 3,300 U |

# Flexible Budget Performance Report

# Static Budgets and Performance Reports

| | Static Budget | Actual Results | Variances |
|---|---|---|---|
| Machine hours | 10,000 | 8,000 | 2,000 U |
| Variable costs | | | |
| Indirect labor | $ 40,000 | $ 34,000 | $6,000 F |
| | | | 4,500 F |
| | | | 1,200 F |
| | | | 0 |
| Insurance | 2,000 | 2,000 | 0 |
| Total overhead costs | $ 89,000 | $ 77,300 | $11,700 F |

Recall our original variance of $11,700. We will use the flexible budget to answer the activity vs. cost control question.



# Flexible Budget Performance Report

**Overhead Variance Analysis**

| Static Overhead Budget at 10,000 Hours | Actual Overhead at 8,000 Hours |
|---|---|
| $ 89,000 | $ 77,300 |

Difference between original static budget and actual overhead = $11,700 F.

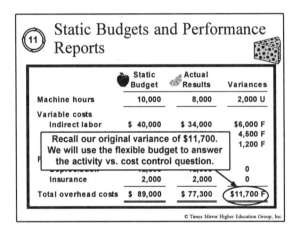

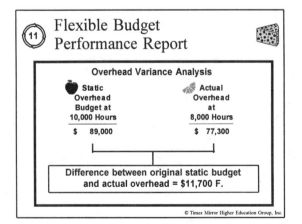

## Flexible Budget Performance Report

## Flexible Budget Performance Report

**Overhead Variance Analysis**

| Static Overhead Budget at 10,000 Hours | Flexible Overhead Budget at 8,000 Hours | Actual Overhead at 8,000 Hours |
|---|---|---|
| $ 89,000 | $ 74,000 | $ 77,300 |

Difference between original static budget and actual overhead = $11,700 F.



## Flexible Budget Performance Report

**Overhead Variance Analysis**

| Static Overhead Budget at 10,000 Hours | Flexible Overhead Budget at 8,000 Hours | Actual Overhead at 8,000 Hours |
|---|---|---|
| $ 89,000 | $ 74,000 | $ 77,300 |

Activity

This $15,000 variance is due to lower activity.

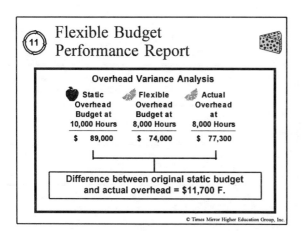

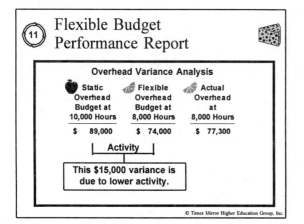

## Flexible Budget Performance Report

**Overhead Variance Analysis**

| Static Overhead Budget at 10,000 Hours | Flexible Overhead Budget at 8,000 Hours | Actual Overhead at 8,000 Hours |
|---|---|---|
| $ 89,000 | $ 74,000 | $ 77,300 |

**Cost control**

**This $3,300 flexible budget variance is due to poor cost control.**



## Flexible Budget Performance Report

There are two primary reasons for unfavorable variable overhead variances:

1. Spending too much for resources
2. Using the resources inefficiently

I see that flexible budgets reveal variable overhead variances that result from cost control, but what factors cause the variances?

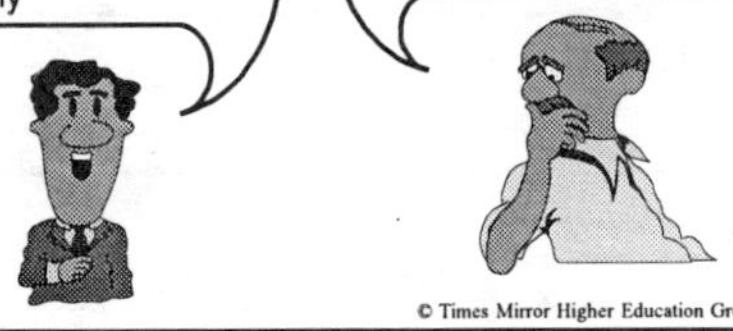

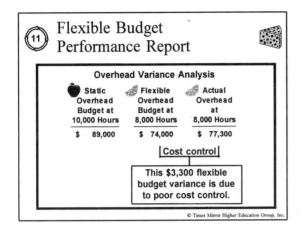

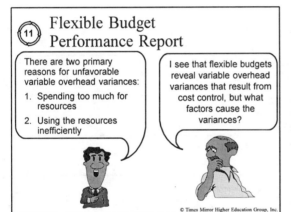

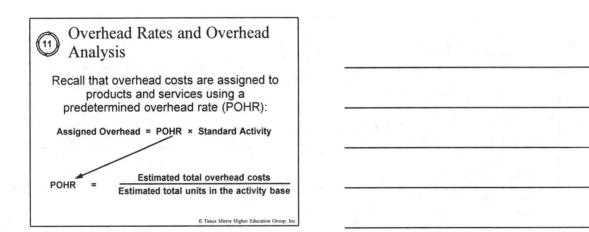

## Overhead Rates and Overhead Analysis

Recall that overhead costs are assigned to products and services using a predetermined overhead rate (POHR):

**Assigned Overhead = POHR × Standard Activity**

$$\text{POHR} = \frac{\text{Estimated total overhead costs}}{\text{Estimated total units in the activity base}}$$

## (11) Overhead Rates and Overhead Analysis – Example

Let's look at overhead
rates in a flexible
budget for ColaCo.




## (11) Overhead Rates and Overhead Analysis – Example

**ColaCo prepared this flexible budget for overhead:**

| Machine Hours | Total Variable Overhead | Variable Overhead Rate | Total Fixed Overhead | Fixed Overhead Rate |
|---|---|---|---|---|
| 2,000 | $ 4,000 | ? | $ 9,000 | ? |
| 4,000 | 8,000 | ? | 9,000 | ? |

**ColaCo applies overhead based on machine hour activity.**



## (11) Overhead Variances

Now that we can

let's use them to

## (11) Variable Overhead Variances

| Actual Variable Overhead Incurred | Flexible Budget for Variable Overhead at Actual Hours | Flexible Budget for Variable Overhead at Standard Hours |
|---|---|---|
| AH × AR | AH × SR | SH × SR |

Spending Variance (AH × AR vs. AH × SR)

Efficiency Variance (AH × SR vs. SH × SR)

AH = Actual Hours of Activity
AR = Actual Variable Overhead Rate
SR = Standard Variable Overhead Rate
SH = Standard Hours Allowed



## (11) Variable Overhead Variances

| Actual Variable Overhead Incurred | Flexible Budget for Variable Overhead at Actual Hours | Flexible Budget for Variable Overhead at Standard Hours |
|---|---|---|
| AH × AR | AH × SR | SH × SR |

Spending Variance (AH × AR vs. AH × SR)

Efficiency Variance (AH × SR vs. SH × SR)

Spending variance = AH(AR - SR)
Efficiency variance = SR(AH - SH)

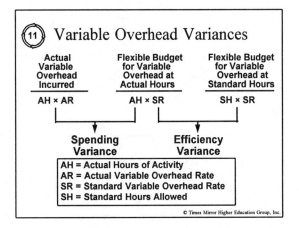

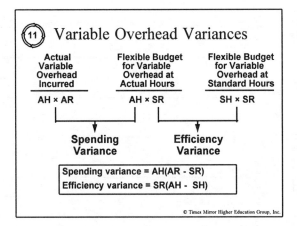

## (11) Variable Overhead Variances – Example

ColaCo's actual production for the period required 3,200 standard machine hours. Actual variable overhead incurred for the period was $6,740. Actual machine hours worked were 3,300.

Compute the variable overhead spending and efficiency variances.

## Variable Overhead Variances – Example

| Actual Variable Overhead Incurred | Flexible Budget for Variable Overhead at Actual Hours | Flexible Budget for Variable Overhead at Standard Hours |
|---|---|---|
| | 3,300 hours × $2.00 per hour | 3,200 hours × $2.00 per hour |
| $6,740 | $6,600 | $6,400 |

Spending variance $140 unfavorable

Efficiency variance $200 unfavorable



## Variable Overhead Variances – A Closer Look

**Spending Variance**

Results from paying more or less than expected for overhead items and from excessive usage of overhead items.

**Efficiency Variance**

A function of the selected cost driver.

It does not reflect overhead control.

## Overhead Variances

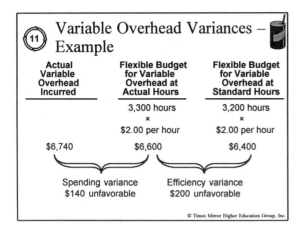

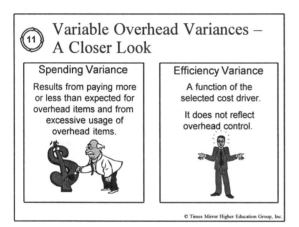

## (11) Fixed Overhead Variances

| Actual Fixed Overhead Incurred | Fixed Overhead Budget | Fixed Overhead Applied |
|---|---|---|
| | | SH × FR |

Actual Fixed Overhead Incurred vs. Fixed Overhead Budget → **Budget Variance**

Fixed Overhead Budget vs. Fixed Overhead Applied → **Volume Variance**

FR = Standard Fixed Overhead Rate
SH = Standard Hours Allowed



## (11) Overhead Rates and Overhead Analysis – Example

**ColaCo prepared this flexible budget for overhead:**

| Machine Hours | Total Variable Overhead | Variable Overhead Rate | Total Fixed Overhead | Fixed Overhead Rate |
|---|---|---|---|---|
| 2,000 | $ 4,000 | $ 2.00 | $ 9,000 | $ 4.50 |
| 4,000 | 8,000 | 2.00 | 9,000 | 2.25 |

What is ColaCo's fixed overhead rate for an estimated activity of 3,000 machine hours?



## (11) Fixed Overhead Variances – Example

ColaCo's actual production required 3,200 standard machine hours. Actual fixed overhead was $8,450.

Compute the fixed overhead budget and volume variances.

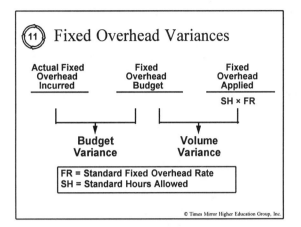

## 11 Fixed Overhead Variances – Example

| Actual Fixed Overhead Incurred | Fixed Overhead Budget | Fixed Overhead Applied |
|---|---|---|
| | | 3,200 hours × $3.00 per hour |
| $8,450 | $9,000 | $9,600 |

Budget variance $550 favorable (Actual Fixed Overhead Incurred vs. Fixed Overhead Budget)

Volume variance $600 favorable (Fixed Overhead Budget vs. Fixed Overhead Applied)



## 11 Fixed Overhead Variances – A Closer Look

**Budget Variance**

Results from paying more or less than expected for overhead items.

**Volume Variance**

Results from the inability to operate at the activity planned for the period.

## 11 Overhead Variances

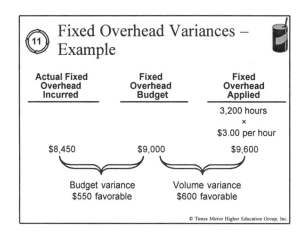

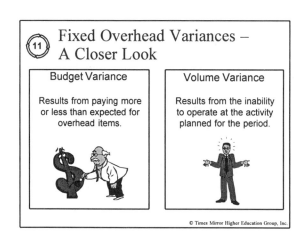

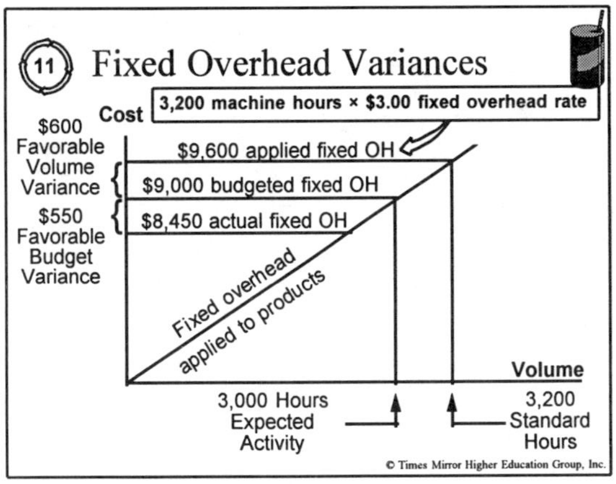
11
Fixed Overhead Variances
Cost
3,200 machine hours × $3.00 fixed overhead rate
$600 Favorable Volume Variance
$550 Favorable Budget Variance
$9,600 applied fixed OH
$9,000 budgeted fixed OH
$8,450 actual fixed OH
Fixed overhead applied to products
Volume
3,000 Hours Expected Activity
3,200 Standard Hours
© Times Mirror Higher Education Group, Inc.

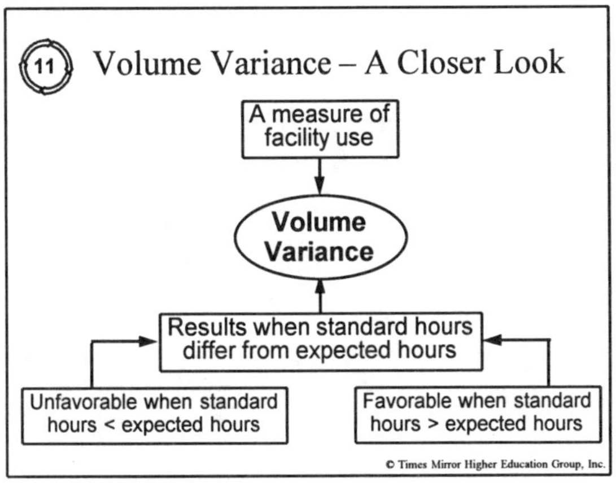
11
Volume Variance – A Closer Look
A measure of facility use
Volume Variance
Results when standard hours differ from expected hours
Unfavorable when standard hours < expected hours
Favorable when standard hours > expected hours
© Times Mirror Higher Education Group, Inc.

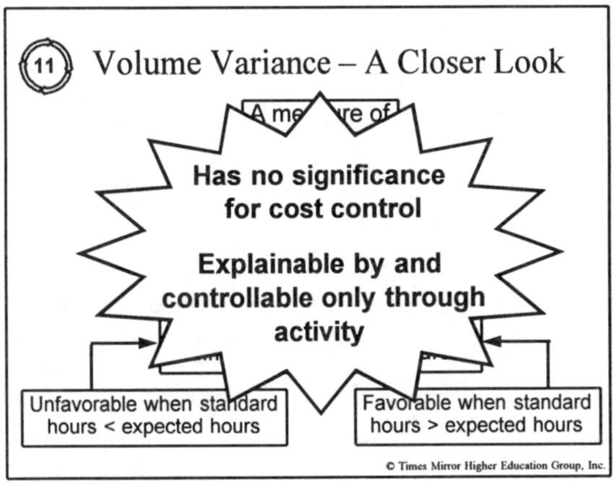
11
Volume Variance – A Closer Look
Has no significance for cost control
Explainable by and controllable only through activity
Unfavorable when standard hours < expected hours
Favorable when standard hours > expected hours
© Times Mirror Higher Education Group, Inc.

## Presentation of Overhead Variances on the Income Statement

**Summary of ColaCo's Overhead Variances**

| | | |
|---|---|---|
| **Variable Overhead** | | |
| Spending Variance | $ 140 | U |
| Efficiency Variance | 200 | U |
| Total | $ 340 | U |
| **Fixed Overhead** | | |
| Budget Variance | 550 | F |
| Volume Variance | 600 | F |
| Total | $ 1,150 | F |

**The $810 net result is shown on income statements prepared for management's own internal use.**



## Presentation of Overhead Variances on the Income Statement

ColaCo
Income Statement
For the Year Ended December 31, 19X8

| | Actual Results | Flexible Budget | Variance |
|---|---|---|---|
| Sales ($30 per unit) | $ 48,000 | $ 48,000 | $ – |
| Less cost of goods sold | | | |
| (standard cost, $20 per unit) | 31,190 | 32,000 | 810 F |
| Gross margin | 16,810 | 16,000 | 810 F |
| Less operating expenses: | | | |
| Selling expense | 3,500 | 3,500 | – |
| Administrative expense | 5,500 | 5,500 | – |
| Total operating expenses | 9,000 | 9,000 | – |
| Net income | $ 7,810 | $ 7,000 | $ 810 F |



## End of Chapter 11

I'm here to flex your budget. Are you ready to ante up?

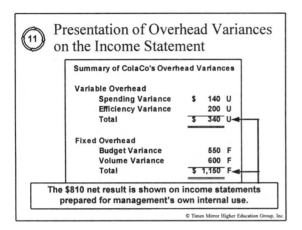

GARRISON

**MANAGERIAL**

Eighth Edition

**ACCOUNTING**

NOREEN

---

12

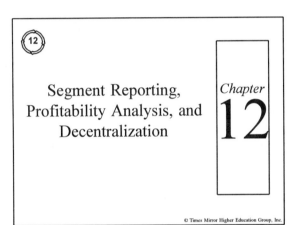

Segment Reporting, Profitability Analysis, and Decentralization

*Chapter* 12



---

12

## Segment Reporting

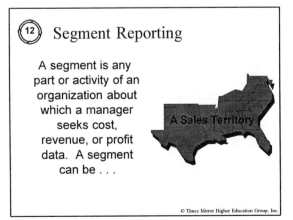

A segment is any part or activity of an organization about which a manager seeks cost, revenue, or profit data. A segment can be . . .

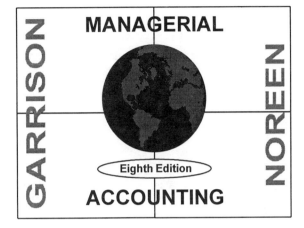

## 12 Segment Reporting

A segment is any part or activity of an organization about which a manager seeks cost, revenue, or profit data. A segment can be . . .

**An Individual Store**

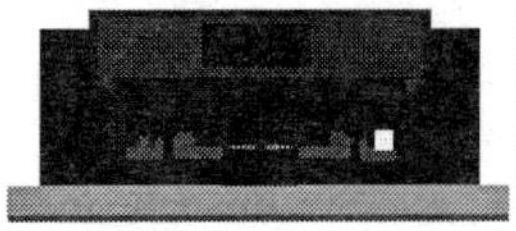



## 12 Segment Reporting

A segment is any part or activity of an organization about which a manager seeks cost, revenue, or profit data. A segment can be . . .

**A Service Center**



## 12 Traceable and Common Costs

**Fixed Costs**

**Traceable** — Costs arise because of the existence of a particular segment

**Common** — Costs arise because of overall operating activities.

## Cost Allocation Guidelines

✦ Two guidelines should be followed in allocating costs to the various segments of a company . . .

❶ According to cost behavior patterns.

❷ According to whether the costs are directly traceable to the segments involved.

## Hindrances to Proper Cost Assignment

**The Problems**

- **Omission of some costs in the assignment process.**
- **Assignment of costs to segments that are really common costs of the entire organization.**
- **The use of inappropriate methods for allocating costs among segments.**



## Omission of Costs

✦ Costs assigned to a segment should include all costs attributable to that segment from the company's entire value chain.

**Business Functions Making Up The Value Chain**

| | | | | | |
|---|---|---|---|---|---|
| R&D | Product Design | Manufacturing | Marketing | Distribution | Customer Service |

## Inappropriate Methods of Allocating Costs Among Segments

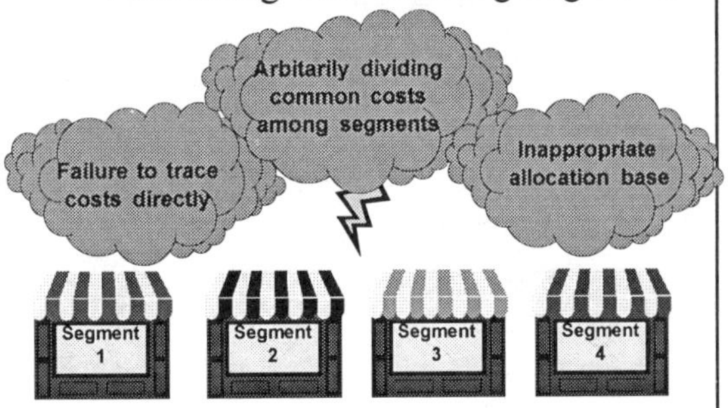




## Segment Reporting and Profitability Analysis

**Webber, Inc.**

**Computer Division** | **Television Division**

**Webber, Inc. has two divisions.**



## Segment Reporting and Profitability Analysis

Our approach to segment reporting uses the contribution format.

| Income Statement<br>Contribution Margin Format<br>Television Division | |
|---|---|
| Sales | $300,000 |
| Variable COGS | 120,000 |
| Other variable costs | 30,000 |
| Total variable costs | 150,000 |
| Contribution margin | 150,000 |
| Traceable fixed costs | 90,000 |
| Segment margin | $ 60,000 |

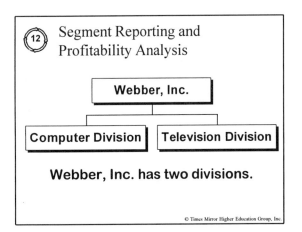

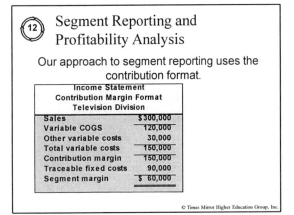

## Segment Reporting and Profitability Analysis

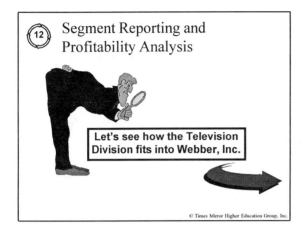

**Let's see how the Television Division fits into Webber, Inc.**

## Segment Reporting and Profitability Analysis

| Income Statement | Company | Television | Computer |
|---|---|---|---|
| Sales | | $ 300,000 | |
| Variable costs | | (150,000) | |
| CM | | 150,000 | |
| Traceable FC | | (90,000) | |
| Division margin | | 60,000 | |
| Common costs | | | |
| Net income | | | |

**Let's add the Computer Division's numbers.**



## Identifying Traceable Fixed Costs

Traceable costs would disappear over time if the segment itself disappeared.

**No computer division means . . .**

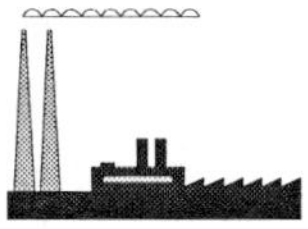

**No computer division manager.**

## (12) Identifying Common Fixed Costs

Common costs arise because of overall operation of the company and are not due to the existence of a particular segment.

**No computer division but . . .**

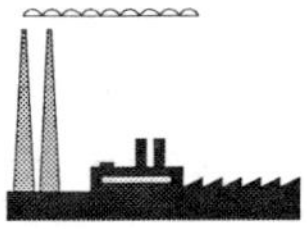

**We still have a company president.**

## (12) Traceable Costs Can Become Common Costs

Fixed costs that are traceable on one segmented statement can become common if the company is divided into smaller segments.

**Let's see how this works!**

## (12) Traceable Costs Can Become Common Costs

**Webber, Inc.**

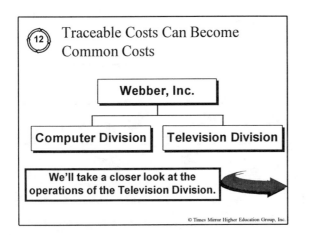

**Computer Division** | **Television Division**

**We'll take a closer look at the operations of the Television Division.**

## Traceable Costs Can Become Common Costs

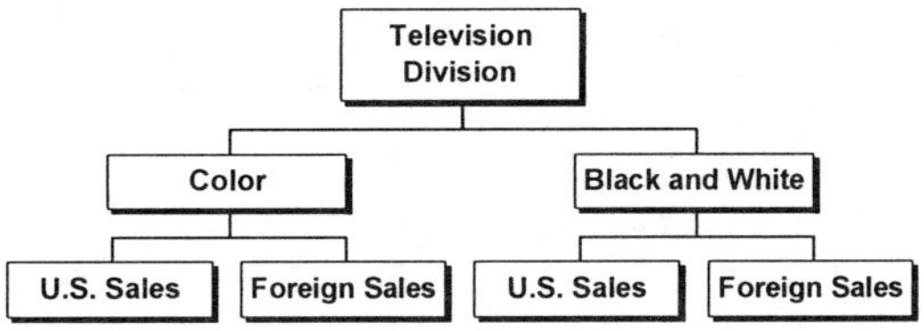




## Traceable Costs Can Become Common Costs

**Income Statement**

| | Television Division | Color | Black and White |
|---|---|---|---|
| Sales | | | |
| Variable costs | | | |
| CM | | | |
| Traceable FC | | | |
| Segment margin | | | |
| Common costs | | | |
| Net income | | | |

**We obtained the following information from the Color and Black and White segments.**



## Traceable Costs Can Become Common Costs

**Income Statement**

| | Television Division | Color | Black and White |
|---|---|---|---|
| Sales | $ 300,000 | $ 200,000 | $ 100,000 |
| Variable costs | (150,000) | (95,000) | (55,000) |
| CM | 150,000 | 105,000 | 45,000 |
| Traceable FC | (80,000) | (45,000) | (35,000) |
| Segment margin | 70,000 | 60,000 | 10,000 |
| Common costs | 10,000 | | |
| Net income | $ 60,000 | | |

## 12 Segment Margin

The segment margin is the best gauge of the long-run profitability of a segment.

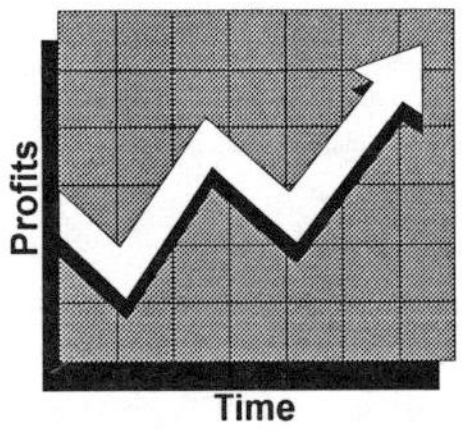




## 12 Customer Profitability Analysis

## 12 Customer Profitability Analysis

## 12 Decentralization and Segment Reporting

Segment reporting is of greatest value in organizations that are decentralized.

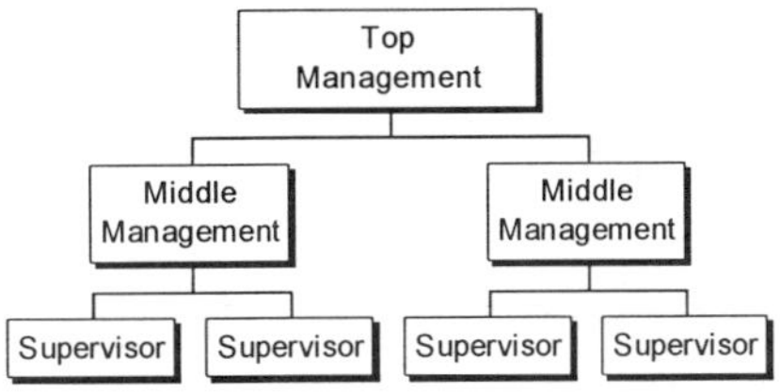




## 12 Benefits of Decentralization

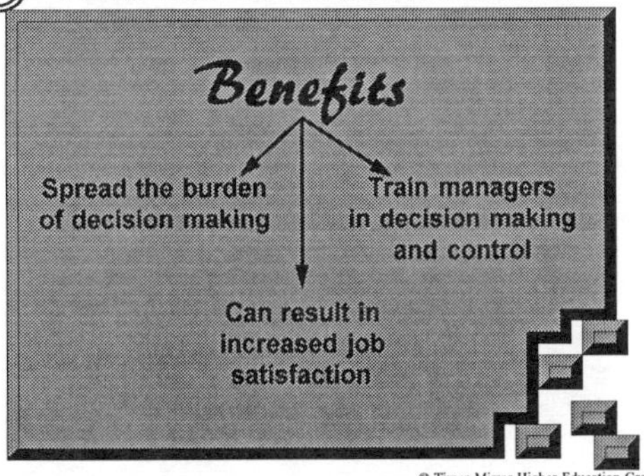

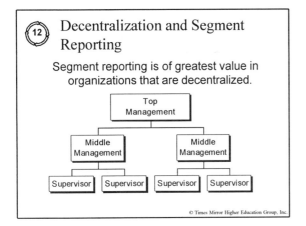

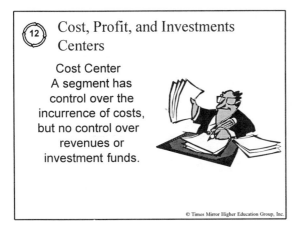

## 12 Cost, Profit, and Investments Centers

Cost Center
A segment has control over the incurrence of costs, but no control over revenues or investment funds.

## Cost, Profit, and Investments Centers

Profit Center
A segment has control over both costs and revenues, but no control over investment funds.

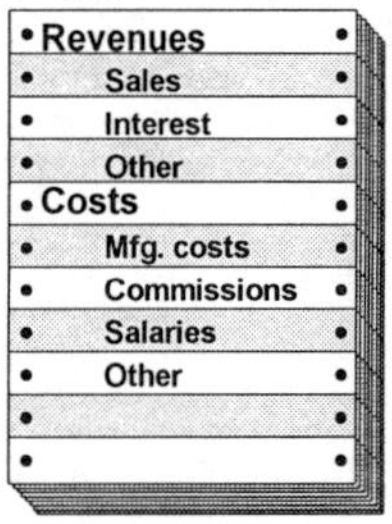




## Cost, Profit, and Investments Centers

Investment Center
A segment has control over costs, revenues, and investment funds.

Corporate Headquarters



## Measuring Management Performance

| | Evaluation Tool |
|---|---|
| Cost Center → | Cost standards |
| Profit Center → | Contribution income statement |
| Investment Center → | Rate of return on invested funds or residual income |

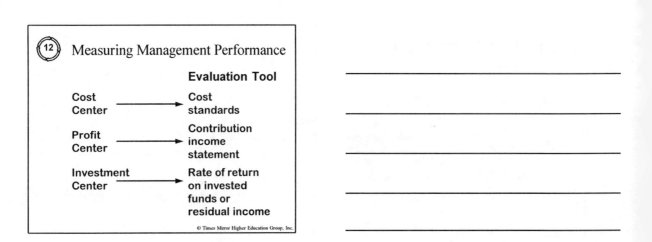

## Return on Investment (ROI) Formula

**Margin × Turnover = ROI**

$$\frac{\text{Net operating income}}{\text{Sales}} \times \frac{\text{Sales}}{\text{Average operating assets}} = \text{ROI}$$

## Return on Investment (ROI) Formula

Regal Company reports the following:

| | |
|---|---|
| Net operating income | $ 30,000 |
| Sales | $ 500,000 |
| Average operating assets | $ 200,000 |

**Let's calculate ROI.**



## Return on Investment (ROI) Formula

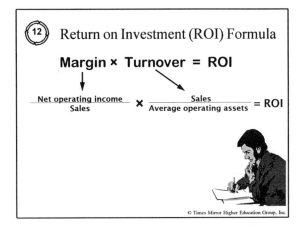

$$\frac{\text{Net operating income}}{\text{Sales}} \times \frac{\text{Sales}}{\text{Average operating assets}} = \text{ROI}$$

## Controlling the Rate of Return

Three ways to improve ROI . . .

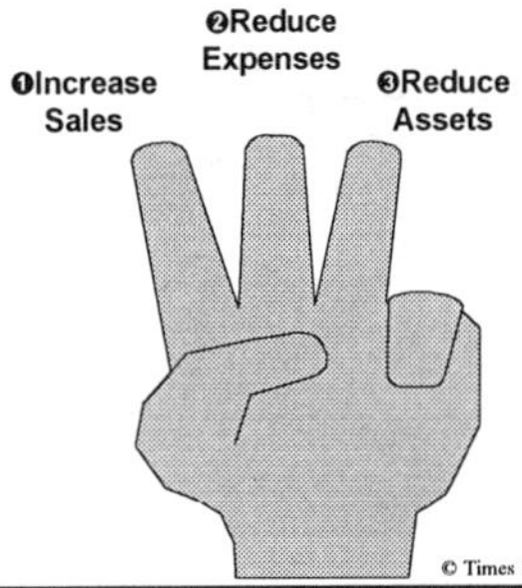




## Controlling the Rate of Return

- Regal's segment manager was able to increase sales to \$600,000 which increased net operating income to \$42,000.
- There was no change in the average operating assets of the segment.

**Let's calculate the new ROI.**



## Return on Investment (ROI) Formula

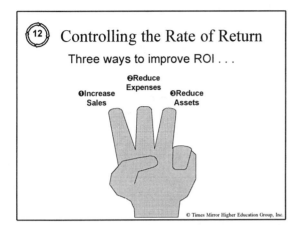

$$\frac{\text{Net operating income}}{\text{Sales}} \times \frac{\text{Sales}}{\text{Average operating assets}} = \text{ROI}$$

## Criticisms of ROI

- Tends to emphasize short-term performance
- Not consistent with cash flow models used for capital expenditures
- Not fully controllable by the segment manager

## Criticisms of ROI - Example

- As division manager at Winston, Inc., your compensation package includes a salary plus bonus based on your division's ROI -- the higher your ROI, the bigger your bonus.
- The company requires an ROI of 15% on all new investments -- your division has been producing an ROI of 30%.
- You have an opportunity to invest in a new project that will produce an ROI of 25%.

**As division manager would you invest in this project?**



## Criticisms of ROI - Example

As division manager, I wouldn't invest in that project because it would lower my pay!

## Criticisms of ROI - Example

Gee . . .
I thought we were
supposed to do what
was best for the
company!



## Residual Income - Another Measure of Performance

above some minimum
return on operating

## Residual Income

- A division of Zepher, Inc. has average operating assets of $100,000 and is required to earn a return of 20% on these assets.
- In the current period the division earns $30,000.

**Let's calculate residual income.**

## 12 Residual Income

| | | |
|---|---|---|
| Operating assets | | $100,000 |
| Required rate of return | × | 20% |
| Required return | | $ 20,000 |

| | |
|---|---|
| Actual return | $ 30,000 |
| Required return | (20,000) |
| Residual income | $ 50,000 |



## 12 Motivation and Residual Income

Residual income encourages managers to make profitable investments that would be rejected by managers using ROI.

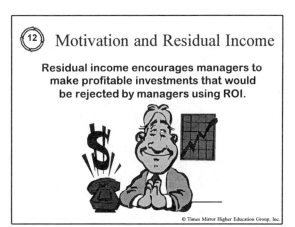

## 12 End of Chapter 12

*Let's work on my rate of return . . .*

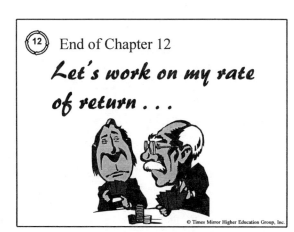

GARRISON

MANAGERIAL

Eighth Edition

ACCOUNTING

NOREEN

13

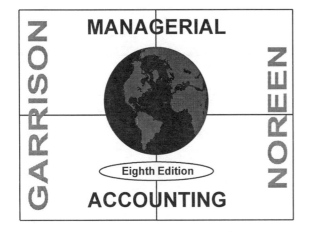

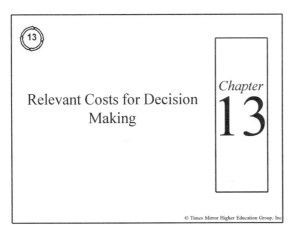

Relevant Costs for Decision Making

Chapter 13

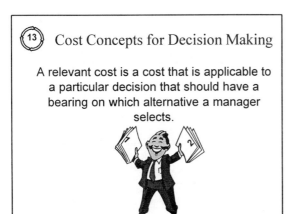

13 Cost Concepts for Decision Making

A relevant cost is a cost that is applicable to a particular decision that should have a bearing on which alternative a manager selects.

## 13 Identifying Relevant Costs

- Avoidable costs are relevant costs that can be eliminated (in whole or in part) as a result of choosing one alternative over another.
- All costs are avoidable, except:
  1. Sunk costs.
  2. Future costs that do not differ between the alternatives at hand.

## 13 Identifying Relevant Costs

Sunk cost -- a cost that has already been incurred and that cannot be avoided regardless of which course of action a manager may decide to take.

## 13 Identifying Relevant Costs

Well, I've assembled all the costs associated with the alternatives we are considering.

## 13 Identifying Relevant Costs

## 13 Identifying Relevant Costs

## 13 Identifying Relevant Costs

## 13 Sunk Costs are not Relevant Costs

Let's look at the White Company example.

## 13 Sunk Costs are not Relevant Costs

A manager at White Co. wants to replace an old machine with a new, more efficient machine.

| | |
|---|---|
| **New machine:** | |
| List price | $ 90,000 |
| Annual variable expenses | 80,000 |
| Expected life in years | 5 |
| **Old machine:** | |
| Original cost | $ 72,000 |
| Remaining book value | 60,000 |
| Disposal value now | 15,000 |
| Annual variable expenses | 100,000 |
| Remaining life in years | 5 |

## 13 Sunk Costs are not Relevant Costs

A manager at White Co. wants to replace an old machine with a new, more efficient machine.

- White's sales are $200,000 per year.
- Fixed expenses, other than depreciation, are $70,000 per year.

Should the manager purchase the new machine?

## Incorrect Analysis

The manger recommends that the company not purchase the new machine since disposal of the old machine would result in a loss:

| | |
|---|---|
| Remaining book value | $ 60,000 |
| Disposal value | (15,000) |
| Loss from disposal | $ 45,000 |



## Correct Analysis

Look at the comparative cost and revenue for the next five years.

| For Five Years | Keep Old Machine | Purchase New Machine | Difference |
|---|---|---|---|
| Sales | | | |
| Variable expenses | | | |
| Other fixed expenses | | | |
| Depreciation - new | | | |
| Depreciation - old | | | |
| Disposal of old machine | | | |
| Total net income | | | |



## Correct Analysis

Look at the comparative cost and revenue for the next five years.

| For Five Years | Keep Old Machine | Purchase New Machine | Difference |
|---|---|---|---|
| Sales | $ 1,000,000 | $ 1,000,000 | $ - |
| Variable expenses | (500,000) | (400,000) | 100,000 |
| Other fixed expenses | (350,000) | (350,000) | - |
| Depreciation - new | | (90,000) | (90,000) |
| Depreciation - old | (60,000) | (60,000) | - |
| Disposal of old machine | | 15,000 | 15,000 |
| Total net income | $ 90,000 | $ 115,000 | $ 25,000 |

**Would you recommend purchasing the new machine even though we will show a $45,000 loss on the old machine?**

## 13 Correct Analysis

## 13 Correct Analysis

We could prepare the analysis using only relevant costs:

| Relevant Cost Analysis | |
|---|---|
| Savings in variable expenses provided by the new machine ($20,000 × 5 yrs.) | $ 100,000 |
| Cost of the new machine | (90,000) |
| Disposal value of old machine | 15,000 |
| Net effect | $ 25,000 |



## 13 Future Costs

Any future cost that does not differ between the alternatives in a decision situation is not a relevant cost so far as the decision is concerned.

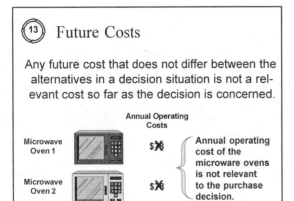

Annual Operating Costs

Microwave Oven 1  $X8

Microwave Oven 2  $X8

Annual operating cost of the microware ovens is not relevant to the purchase decision.

## Adding/Dropping Segments

One of the most important decisions managers make is whether to add or drop a business segment such as a product or a store.

Let's look at the concept of relevant costs should be used in such a decision.

## Adding/Dropping Segments

Due to the declining popularity of digital watches, Lovell Company's digital watch line has not reported a profit for several years. An income statement for last year is shown on the next screen.

## Adding/Dropping Segments

| Segment Income Statement<br>Digital Watches | | |
|---|---|---|
| Sales | | $ 500,000 |
| Less: variable expenses | | |
| Variable mfg. costs | $ 120,000 | |
| Variable shipping costs | 5,000 | |
| Commissions | 75,000 | 200,000 |
| Contribution margin | | $ 300,000 |
| Less: fixed expenses | | |
| General factory overhead | $ 60,000 | |
| Salary of line manager | 90,000 | |
| Depreciation of equipment | 50,000 | |
| Advertising - direct | 100,000 | |
| Rent - factory space | 70,000 | |
| General admin. expenses | 30,000 | 400,000 |
| Net loss | | $ (100,000) |

## (13) Adding/Dropping Segments

Segment Income Statement
Digital Watches

**If the digital watch line is dropped, the fixed general factory overhead and general administrative expenses will be allocated to other product lines because they are not avoidable.**

| | | |
|---|---|---|
| General factory overhead | $ 60,000 | |
| Salary of line manager | 90,000 | |
| Depreciation of equipment | 50,000 | |
| Advertising - direct | 100,000 | |
| Rent - factory space | 70,000 | |
| General admin. expenses | 30,000 | 400,000 |
| Net loss | | $ (100,000) |



## (13) Adding/Dropping Segments

Segment Income Statement
Digital Watches

**The equipment used to manufacture digital watches has no resale value or alternative use.**

| | | |
|---|---|---|
| | | $ 500,000 |
| | | 200,000 |
| Contribution margin | | $ 300,000 |
| Less: fixed expenses | | |
| General factory overhead | $ 60,000 | |
| Salary of line manager | 90,000 | |
| Depreciation of equipment | 50,000 | |
| Advertising - direct | 100,000 | |
| Rent - factory space | 70,000 | |
| General admin. expenses | 30,000 | 400,000 |
| Net loss | | $ (100,000) |



## (13) Adding/Dropping Segments

Segment Income Statement
Digital Watches

| | | |
|---|---|---|
| Sales | | $ 500,000 |
| Less: variable expenses | | |
| Variable mfg. costs | $ 120,000 | |
| Variable shipping costs | | |
| Commissions | | |
| Contribution margin | | |
| Less: fixed expenses | | |
| General factory overhead | $ 60,000 | |
| Salary of line manager | 90,000 | |
| Depreciation of equipment | 50,000 | |
| Advertising - direct | 100,000 | |
| Rent - factory space | 70,000 | |
| General admin. expenses | 30,000 | 400,000 |
| Net loss | | $ (100,000) |

**Should Lovell retain or drop the digital watch segment?**

## A Contribution Margin Approach

DECISION RULE

Lovell should drop the digital watch segment only if its fixed cost savings exceed lost contribution margin.

Let's look at this solution.



## A Contribution Margin Approach

| Contribution Margin Solution | | |
|---|---|---|
| Contribution margin lost if digital watches are dropped | | $ (300,000) |
| | | $ - |



## A Contribution Margin Approach

| Contribution Margin Solution | | |
|---|---|---|
| Contribution margin lost if digital watches are dropped | | $ (300,000) |
| Less fixed costs that can be avoided | | |
| Salary of the line manager | $ 90,000 | |
| Advertising - direct | 100,000 | |
| Rent - factory space | 70,000 | 260,000 |
| Net disadvantage | | $ (40,000) |

**Remember, depreciation on equipment with no resale value is not relevant to the decision since it is a sunk cost and therefore is not avoidable.**

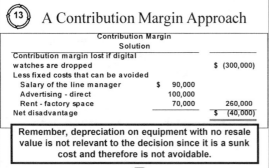

## 13 Comparative Income Approach

The Lovell solution can also be obtained by preparing comparative income statements showing results with and without the digital watch segment.

Let's look at this second approach.

## 13 Comparative Income Approach

Comparative Income Solution

| | Keep Digital Watches | Drop Digital Watches | Difference |
|---|---|---|---|
| Sales | $ 500,000 | | |
| Less variable expenses: | | | |
| Mfg. expenses | | | |
| Freight out | | | |
| Commissions | | | |
| Total variable expenses | | | |
| Contribution margin | | | |
| Less fixed expenses: | | | |
| General factory overhead | | | |
| Salary of line manager | | | |
| Depreciation | | | |
| Advertising - direct | | | |
| Rent - factory space | | | |
| General admin. expenses | | | |
| Total fixed expenses | | | |
| Net loss | | | |



## 13 Comparative Income Approach

Comparative Income Solution

| | Keep Digital Watches | Drop Digital Watches | Difference |
|---|---|---|---|
| Sales | $ 500,000 | $ - | $ (500,000) |
| Less variable expenses: | | - | |
| Mfg. expenses | 120,000 | - | 120,000 |
| Freight out | 5,000 | - | 5,000 |
| Commissions | 75,000 | - | 75,000 |
| Total variable expenses | 200,000 | - | 200,000 |
| Contribution margin | 300,000 | - | (300,000) |
| Less fixed expenses: | | | |
| General factory overhead | 60,000 | 60,000 | - |
| Salary of line manager | 90,000 | - | 90,000 |
| Depreciation | 50,000 | 50,000 | - |
| Advertising - direct | 100,000 | - | 100,000 |
| Rent - factory space | 70,000 | - | 70,000 |
| General admin. expenses | 30,000 | 30,000 | - |
| Total fixed expenses | 400,000 | 140,000 | 260,000 |
| Net loss | $ (100,000) | $ (140,000) | $ (40,000) |

## (13) Beware of Allocated Fixed Costs

## (13) Beware of Allocated Fixed Costs

## (13) Beware of Allocated Fixed Costs

## The Make or Buy Decision

A decision concerning whether an item should be produced internally or purchased from an outside supplier is called a "make or buy" decision.

Let's look at the Essex Company example.



## The Make or Buy Decision

- Essex manufactures part 457A that is currently used in one of its products.
- The unit cost to make this part is:

| | |
|---|---|
| Direct materials | $ 9 |
| Direct labor | 5 |
| Variable overhead | 1 |
| Depreciation of special equip. | 3 |
| Supervisor's salary | 2 |
| General factory overhead | 10 |
| Total cost per unit | $ 30 |



## The Make or Buy Decision

- The special equipment used to manufacture part 457A has no resale value.
- General factory overhead is allocated on the basis of direct labor hours.
- The $30 total unit cost is based on 20,000 parts produced each year.
- An outside supplier has offered to provide the 20,000 parts at a cost of $25 per part.

Should we accept the supplier's offer?

## 13 The Make or Buy Decision

| | Cost Per Unit | Cost of 20,000 Units Make | Buy |
|---|---|---|---|
| Outside purchase price | | | $ 500,000 |

**20,000 × $25 purchase price = $500,000**



## 13 The Make or Buy Decision

| | Cost Per Unit | Cost of 20,000 Units Make | Buy |
|---|---|---|---|
| Outside purchase price | | | $ 500,000 |
| Direct materials | $ 9 | 180,000 | |
| Direct labor | 5 | 100,000 | |
| Variable overhead | 1 | 20,000 | |
| Depreciation of equip. | 3 | - | |
| Supervisor's salary | 2 | 40,000 | |
| General factory overhead | 10 | - | |
| Total cost | $ 30 | $ 340,000 | $ 500,000 |

**Should we make or buy part 457A?**



## 13 The Make or Buy Decision

DECISION RULE

- In deciding whether to accept the outside supplier's offer, Essex isolated the relevant costs of making the part by eliminating:
  - The sunk costs.
  - The future costs that will not differ between making or buying the parts.

## The Matter of Opportunity Cost

- The economic benefits that are foregone as a result of pursuing some course of action
- Do not represent actual dollar outlays and are not recorded in the accounts of an organization

## Special Orders

- **Jet, Inc. receives a one-time order that is not considered part of its normal ongoing business.**
- **Jet, Inc. makes a single product with a unit variable cost of $8. Normal selling price is $20 per unit.**
- **A foreign distributor offers to purchase 3,000 units for $10 per unit.**
- **Annual capacity is 10,000 units, and annual fixed costs total $48,000, but Jet, Inc. is currently producing and selling only 5,000 units.**

**Should Jet accept the offer?**



## Special Orders

**Jet, Inc.**
**Contribution Income Statement**

| | | |
|---|---|---|
| Revenue (5,000 × $20) | | $ 100,000 |
| Variable costs: | | |
| Direct materials | $ 20,000 | |
| Direct labor | 5,000 | |
| Manufacturing overhead | 10,000 | |
| Marketing costs | 5,000 | |
| Total variable costs | | 40,000 |
| Contribution margin | | 60,000 |
| Fixed costs: | | |
| Manufacturing overhead | $ 28,000 | |
| Marketing costs | 20,000 | |
| Total fixed costs | | 48,000 |
| Net income | | $ 12,000 |

## Special Orders

If Jet accepts the offer, net income will increase by $6,000.

| | |
|---|---|
| Increase in revenue (3,000 × $10) | $30,000 |
| Increase in costs (3,000 × $8 variable cost) | 24,000 |
| Increase in net income | $ 6,000 |



## Special Orders

If Jet accepts the offer, net income will increase by $6,000.

| | |
|---|---|
| Increase in revenue (3,000 × $10) | $30,000 |
| Increase in costs (3,000 × $8 variable cost) | 24,000 |
| Increase in net income | $ 6,000 |

**Should Jet accept the special order?**



## Utilization of Scarce Resources

- Firms often face the problem of deciding how scarce resources are going to be utilized.
- Usually, fixed costs are not affected by this particular decision, so management can focus on maximizing total contribution margin.

Let's look at the Ensign Company example.

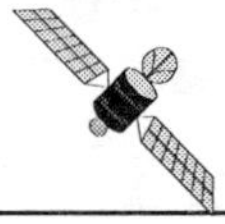

## Utilization of Scarce Resources

Ensign Company produces two products and selected data is shown below:

| | Products 1 | Products 2 |
|---|---|---|
| Selling price per unit | $ 60 | $ 50 |
| Less: variable expenses per unit | 36 | 35 |
| Contribution margin per unit | $ 24 | $ 15 |
| Current demand per week (units) | 2,000 | 2,200 |
| Contribution margin ratio | 40% | 30% |
| Processing time required on machine A1 per unit | 1.00 min. | 0.50 min. |



## Utilization of Scarce Resources

- Machine A1 is the scarce resource because there is excess capacity on other machines. Machine A1 is being used at 100% of its capacity.
- Machine A1 capacity is 2,400 minutes per week.

Should Ensign focus its efforts on Product 1 or 2?



## Utilization of Scarce Resources

Let's calculate the contribution margin per unit of the scarce resource, machine A1.

| | | Products 1 | | Products 2 |
|---|---|---|---|---|
| Contribution margin per unit | | $ 24 | | ? |
| Time required to produce one unit | ÷ | 1.00 min. | ÷ | ? min. |
| Contribution margin per minute | | $ 24 min. | | ? min. |

## Utilization of Scarce Resources

Let's calculate the contribution margin per unit of the scarce resource, machine A1.

| | Products 1 | | Products 2 | |
|---|---|---|---|---|
| Contribution margin per unit | $ 24 | | $ 15 | |
| Time required to produce one unit | ÷ 1.00 | min. | ÷ 0.50 | min. |
| Contribution margin per minute | $ 24 | min. | $ 30 | min. |

**If there are no other considerations, the best plan would be to produce to meet current demand for Product 2 and then use any capacity that remains to make Product 1.**



## Utilization of Scarce Resources

Let's see how this plan would work.

**Alloting Our Scarce Recource (Machine A1)**

| | | |
|---|---|---|
| Weekly demand for Product 2 | 2,200 | units |
| Time required per unit | × 0.50 | min. |
| Total time required to make Product 2 | 1,100 | min. |



## Utilization of Scarce Resources

According to the plan, we will produce 2,200 units of Product 2 and 1,300 of Product 1. Our contribution margin looks like this.

| | Product 1 | Product 2 |
|---|---|---|
| Production and sales (units) | 1,300 | 2,200 |
| Contribution margin per unit | $ 24 | $ 15.00 |
| Total contribution margin | $ 31,200 | $ 33,000 |

## Utilization of Scarce Resources

According to the plan, we will produce 2,200 units of Product 2 and 1,300 of Product 1. Our contribution margin looks like this.

| | Product 1 | Product 2 |
|---|---|---|
| Production and sales (units) | 1,300 | 2,200 |
| Contribution margin per unit | $ 24 | $ 15.00 |
| Total contribution margin | $ 31,200 | $ 33,000 |

**The total contribution margin for Ensign is $64,200.**

## Managing Constraints

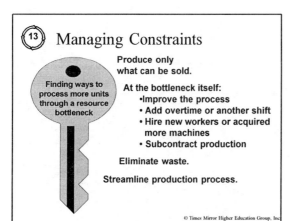

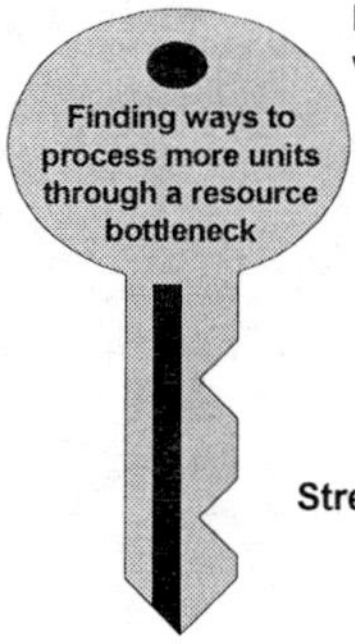
Finding ways to process more units through a resource bottleneck

**Produce only what can be sold.**

**At the bottleneck itself:**
- **Improve the process**
- **Add overtime or another shift**
- **Hire new workers or acquired more machines**
- **Subcontract production**

**Eliminate waste.**

**Streamline production process.**

## Joint Product Costs

- In some industries, a number of end products are produced from a single raw material input.
- Two or more products produced from a common input are called joint products.
- The point in the manufacturing process where each joint product can be recognized as a separate product is called the split-off point.

## Joint Products

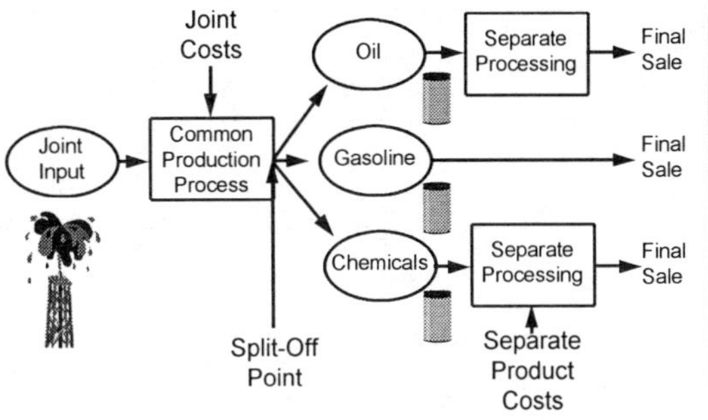




## The Pitfalls of Allocation

Joint costs are really common costs incurred to simultaneously produce a variety of end products.

Joint costs are commonly allocated to end products on the basis of the relative sales value of each product or on some other basis.

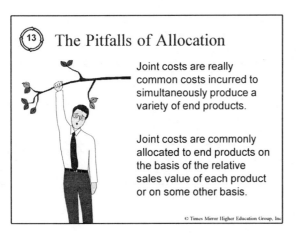

## Sell or Process Further

- Joint product costs are not relevant in decisions regarding what to do with a product after the split-off point forward. At the split-off point joint product costs have already been incurred and cannot be avoided.
- As a general rule . . .

It is always profitable to continue processing a joint product after the split-off point so long as the incremental revenue exceeds the incremental processing costs.

Let's look at the Sawmill, Inc. example.

## 13 Sell or Process Further

- Sawmill, Inc. cuts logs from which unfinished lumber and sawdust are the immediate joint products.
- Unfinished lumber is sold "as is" or processed further into finished lumber.
- Sawdust can also be sold "as is" to gardening wholesalers or processed further into "presto-logs."

## 13 Sell or Process Further

Data about Sawmill's joint products includes:

| | Per Log | |
|---|---|---|
| | Lumber | Sawdust |
| Sales value at the split-off point | $ 140 | $ 40 |
| Sales value after further processing | 270 | 50 |
| Allocated joint product costs | 176 | 24 |
| Cost of further processing | 50 | 20 |



## 13 Sell or Process Further

**Analysis of Sell or Process Further**

| | Per Log | |
|---|---|---|
| | Lumber | Sawdust |
| Sales value after further processing | $ 270 | $ 50 |
| | | |
| | | |
| | | |

## 13 Sell or Process Further

**Analysis of Sell or Process Further**

| | Per Log | |
|---|---|---|
| | Lumber | Sawdust |
| Sales value after further processing | $ 270 | $ 50 |
| Sales value at the split-off point | 140 | 40 |
| Incremental revenue | 130 | 10 |
| Cost of further processing | 50 | 20 |
| Profit (loss) from further processing | $ 80 | $ (10) |

**Should we process the lumber further and sell the sawdust "as is?"**



## 13 End of Chapter 13

**GARRISON**

# MANAGERIAL

Eighth Edition

# ACCOUNTING

**NOREEN**

---

14

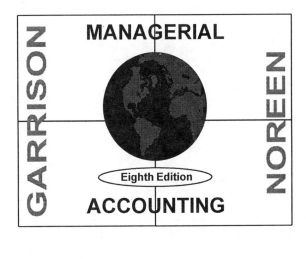

# Capital Budgeting Decisions

*Chapter* 14



---

14

## Capital Budgeting - An Investment Concept

Actions relating to the planning and financing of capital outlays, like the purchase of new equipment, introduction of new product lines, and modernization of plant facilities

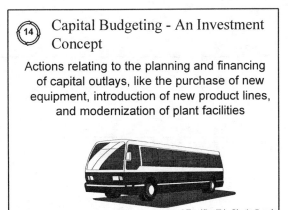

## Typical Capital Budgeting Decisions

Plant expansion

Equipment selection

Equipment replacement

Cost reduction

Lease or buy

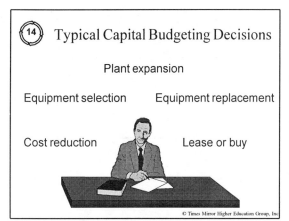

## Characteristics of Business Investments

- Business investments have two key characteristics . . .
  - ❶They involve depreciable assets, and
  - ❷The returns extend over long periods of time.

## Depreciable Assets

- Generally have little or no resale value at the end of their useful lives.
- Any returns from such assets must be sufficient to do two things . . .
  - ❶Provide a return on the original investment, and
  - ❷Return the total amount of the original investment.

## 14 Time Value of Money

- Business investments extend over long periods of time, so we must recognize the time value of money.
- Investments that promise returns earlier in time are preferable to those that promise returns later in time.

## 14 Time Value of Money

$$F_n = P(1 + r)^n$$

You would have $F_n$ dollars.

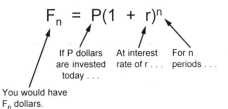

If P dollars are invested today . . .

At interest rate of r . . .

For n periods . . .



## 14 Time Value of Money

If $100 is invested today at 8% interest, how much will the investment be worth in two years?

## 14 Time Value of Money

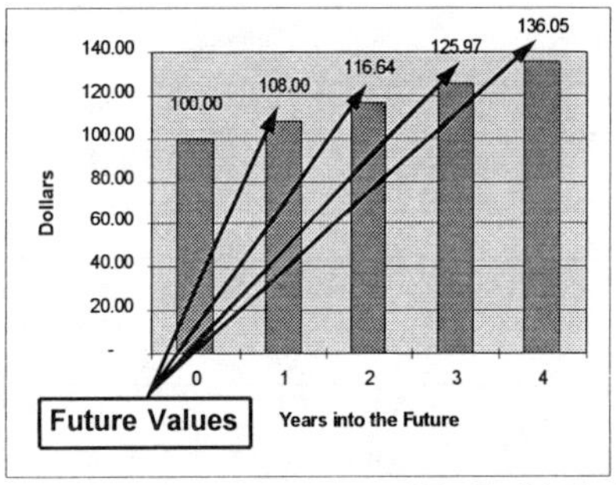




## 14 Time Value of Money

The present value of any sum to be received in the future can be computed by using the interest formula and solving for P . . .

$$P = \frac{F_n}{(1 + r)^n}$$

or

$$P = F_n \times \frac{1}{(1 + r)^n}$$



## 14 Time Value of Money

A bond will pay $100 in two years. What is the present value of the $100 if an investor can earn a return of 12% on the investment?

## (14) Time Value of Money

A bond will pay $100 in two years. What is the present value of the $100 if an investor can earn a return of 12% on the investment?

$$P = \$100 \times \frac{1}{(1 + .12)^2}$$

$$P = \$100 \times .797 = \$79.70$$



## (14) Time Value of Money

Excerpt from Present Value of $1 Table in the Appendix to Chapter 14

| | Discount rate | | |
|---|---|---|---|
| Periods | 10% | 12% | 14% |
| 1 | 0.909 | 0.893 | 0.877 |
| 2 | 0.826 | 0.797 | 0.769 |
| 3 | 0.751 | 0.712 | 0.675 |
| 4 | 0.683 | 0.636 | 0.592 |
| 5 | 0.621 | 0.567 | 0.519 |



## (14) Time Value of Money

An investment that involves a series of identical cash flows at the end of each year is called an annuity.

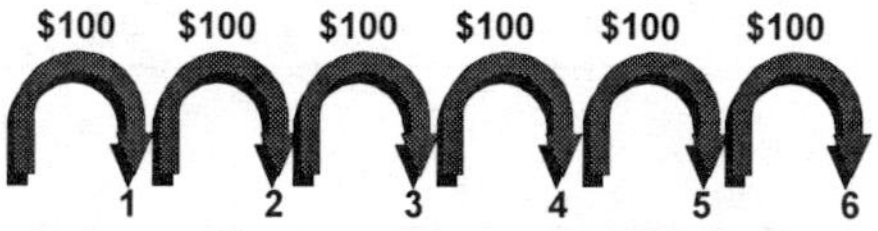

## Time Value of Money

An investment that involves a series of identical cash flows at the end of each year is called an annuity.

**Lacey Company purchased a tract of land on which a $60,000 payment will be due each year for the next five years. What is the present value of this stream of cash payments when the discount rate is 12%?**



## Time Value of Money

| Year | Cash Payment | 12% Factor | Present Value |
|---|---|---|---|
| 1 | $ 60,000 | 0.893 | $ 53,580 |

**Present value factor of $1 for 1 period at 12%.**



## Time Value of Money

| Year | Cash Payment | 12% Factor | Present Value |
|---|---|---|---|
| 1 | $ 60,000 | 0.893 | $ 53,580 |

**$60,000 × 0.893 = $53,580**

## Time Value of Money

| Year | Cash Payment | 12% Factor | Present Value |
|---|---|---|---|
| 1 | $ 60,000 | 0.893 | $ 53,580 |
| 2 | 60,000 | 0.797 | 47,820 |



## Time Value of Money

| Year | Cash Payment | 12% Factor | Present Value |
|---|---|---|---|
| 1 | $ 60,000 | 0.893 | $ 53,580 |
| 2 | 60,000 | 0.797 | 47,820 |

**This is the present value of $1 factor for 2 periods at 12% we used in the bond example.**



## Time Value of Money

| Year | Cash Payment | 12% Factor | Present Value |
|---|---|---|---|
| 1 | $ 60,000 | 0.893 | $ 53,580 |
| 2 | 60,000 | 0.797 | 47,820 |
| 3 | 60,000 | 0.712 | 42,720 |
| 4 | 60,000 | 0.636 | 38,160 |
| 5 | 60,000 | 0.567 | 34,020 |
| | | 3.605 | $216,300 |

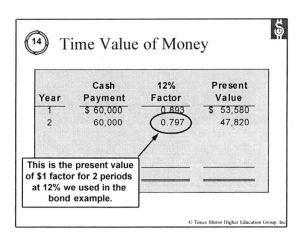

## Time Value of Money

| Year | Cash Payment | 12% Factor | Present Value |
|---|---|---|---|
| 1 | $ 60,000 | 0.893 | $ 53,580 |
| 2 | 60,000 | 0.797 | 47,820 |
| 3 | 60,000 | 0.712 | 42,720 |
| 4 | 60,000 | 0.636 | 38,160 |
| 5 | 60,000 | 0.567 | 34,020 |
| | | 3.605 | $216,300 |

**The present value of our 5 $60,000 payments is $216,300.**



## Time Value of Money

We could solve the problem like this . . .

$60,000 × 3.605 = $216,300



## Time Value of Money

We could solve the problem like this . . .

$60,000 × 3.605 = $216,300

| Year | Cash Payment | 12% Factor | Present Value |
|---|---|---|---|
| 1 | $ 60,000 | 0.893 | $ 53,580 |
| 2 | 60,000 | 0.797 | 47,820 |
| 3 | 60,000 | 0.712 | 42,720 |
| 4 | 60,000 | 0.636 | 38,160 |
| 5 | 60,000 | 0.567 | 34,020 |
| | | 3.605 | $216,300 |

## Time Value of Money

We could solve the problem like this . . .

$60,000 × 3.605 = $216,300

Look in Appendix C of this Chapter for the Present Value of an Annuity of $1 Table

| Periods | 10% | 12% | 14% |
|---|---|---|---|
| 1 | 0.909 | 0.893 | 0.877 |
| 2 | 1.736 | 1.690 | 1.647 |
| 3 | 2.487 | 2.402 | 2.322 |
| 4 | 3.170 | 3.037 | 2.914 |
| 5 | 3.791 | 3.605 | 3.433 |



## Net Present Value

- To determine net present value we . . .
  1. Calculate the present value of cash inflows,
  2. Calculate the present value of cash outflows,
  3. Subtract the present value of the outflows from the present value of the inflows.

## Time Value of Money

Let's look at how we use present value to make business decisions.

## Discounted Cash Flows - The Net Present Value Method

Lester Company has been offered a five year contract to provide component parts for a large manufacturer.

| Cost and revenue information | |
|---|---|
| Cost of special equipment | $160,000 |
| Working capital required | 100,000 |
| Relining equipment in 3 years | 30,000 |
| Salvage value of equipment in 5 years | 5,000 |
| Annual cash revenue and costs: | |
| Sales revenue from parts | 750,000 |
| Cost of parts sold | 400,000 |
| Salaries, shipping, etc. | 270,000 |



## Discounted Cash Flows - The Net Present Value Method

- At the end of five years the working capital will be released and may be used elsewhere by Lester.
- Lester Company uses a discount rate of 10%.

Should the contract be accepted?



## Discounted Cash Flows - The Net Present Value Method

Annual net cash inflows from operations

| | |
|---|---|
| Sales revenue | $ 750,000 |
| Cost of parts sold | 400,000 |
| Gross margin | 350,000 |
| Less out-of-pocket costs | 270,000 |
| Annual net cash inflows | $ 80,000 |

## Discounted Cash Flows - The Net Present Value Method

| | Years | Cash Flows | 10% Factor | Present Value |
|---|---|---|---|---|
| Investment in equipment | Now | $(160,000) | 1.0000 | $(160,000) |
| Net present value | | | | |



## Discounted Cash Flows - The Net Present Value Method

| | Years | Cash Flows | 10% Factor | Present Value |
|---|---|---|---|---|
| Investment in equipment | Now | $(160,000) | 1.0000 | $(160,000) |
| Working capital needed | Now | (100,000) | 1.0000 | (100,000) |
| Annual net cash inflows | 1-5 | 80,000 | 3.7910 | 303,280 |
| Relining of equipment | 3 | (30,000) | 0.7510 | (22,530) |
| Salvage value of equipment | 5 | 5,000 | 0.6210 | 3,105 |
| Net present value | | | | |



## Discounted Cash Flows - The Net Present Value Method

| | Years | Cash Flows | 10% Factor | Present Value |
|---|---|---|---|---|
| Investment in equipment | Now | $(160,000) | 1.0000 | $(160,000) |
| Working capital needed | Now | (100,000) | 1.0000 | (100,000) |
| Annual net cash inflows | 1-5 | 80,000 | 3.7910 | 303,280 |
| Relining of equipment | 3 | (30,000) | 0.7510 | (22,530) |
| Salvage value of equipment | 5 | 5,000 | 0.6210 | 3,105 |
| Working capital released | 5 | 100,000 | 0.6210 | 62,100 |
| Net present value | | | | $ 85,955 |

## Discounted Cash Flows - The Net Present Value Method

General decision rule . . .

| If the Net Present Value is . . . | Then the Project is . . . |
|---|---|
| Positive . . . | Acceptable, since it promises a return greater than the required rate of return. |
| Zero . . . | Acceptable, since it promises a return equal to the required rate of return. |
| Negative . . . | Not acceptable, since it promises a return less than the required rate of return. |



## Typical Cash Outflows

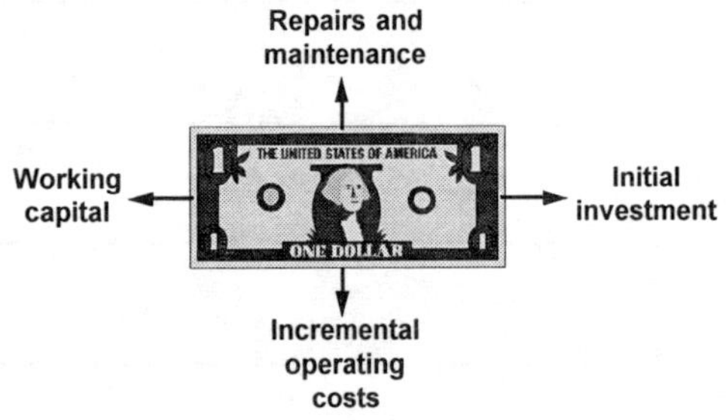




## Typical Cash Inflows

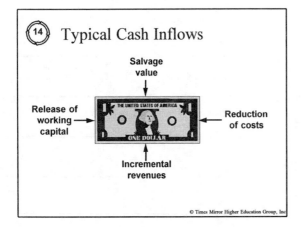

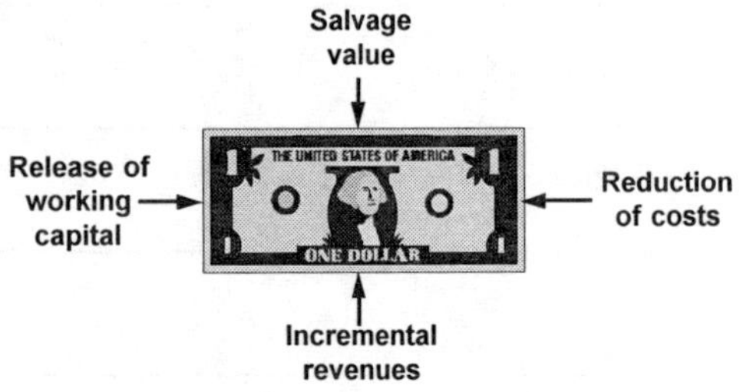

## 14 Recovery of the Original Investment

- Depreciation is not deducted in computing the present value of a project because . . .
  - ❶It does not involve a current cash outflow.
  - ❷Discounted cash flow methods automatically provide for return of the original investment.

## 14 Choosing a Discount Rate

- The discount rate generally is associated with the company's cost of capital.
- The cost of capital involves a blending of the costs of all sources of investment funds, both debt and equity.

## 14 Discounted Cash Flows - The Internal Rate of Return Method

- The internal rate of return is the interest yield promised by an investment project over its useful life.
- The internal rate of return is computed by finding the discount rate that will cause the net present value of a project to be zero.

## Discounted Cash Flows - The Internal Rate of Return Method

**Let's see how we calculate the internal rate of return!**

## Discounted Cash Flows - The Internal Rate of Return Method

- Decker Company can purchase a new machine at a cost of $104,320 that will save $20,000 per year in cash operating costs.
- The machine has a 10-year life.

## Discounted Cash Flows - The Internal Rate of Return Method

Future cash flows are the same every year in this example, so we can calculate the internal rate of return as follows:

$$\frac{\text{Investment required}}{\text{Net annual cash flows}} = \text{Present value factor}$$

14

## Discounted Cash Flows - The Internal Rate of Return Method

Here's the proof . . .

| | Year | Amount | 14% Factor | Present Value |
|---|---|---|---|---|
| Investment required | Now | $ (104,320) | 1.000 | (104,320) |
| Annual cost savings | 1-10 | 20,000 | 5.216 | 104,320 |
| Net present value | | | | $ - |



14

## Net Present Value vs. Internal Rate of Return

Net Present Value

- The cost of capital is used as the actual discount rate.
- Any project with a negative net present value is rejected.

14

## Net Present Value vs. Internal Rate of Return

Net Present Value

- The cost of capital is used as the actual discount rate.
- Any project with a negative net present value is rejected.

Internal Rate of Return

- The cost of capital is compared to the internal rate of return on a project.
- To be acceptable, a project's rate of return cannot be less than the cost of capital.

## Net Present Value vs. Internal Rate of Return

- The net present value method has the following advantages over the internal rate of return method . . .
  - ✓ Easier to use.
  - ✓ Easier to adjust for risk.
  - ✓ Provides more usable information.

## Expanding the Net Present Value Method

- To compare competing investment projects we can use the following net present value approaches:
  - Total-Cost Approach
  - Incremental-Cost Approach

## Total-Cost Approach

- White Co. is trying to decide whether to remodel an old car wash or remove it entirely and install a new one.
- The company uses a discount rate of 10%.

| | New Car Wash | Old Car Wash |
|---|---|---|
| Annual revenues | $ 90,000 | $ 70,000 |
| Annual cash operating costs | 30,000 | 25,000 |
| Net annual cash inflows | $ 60,000 | $ 45,000 |

## Total-Cost Approach

- The new washer costs $300,000 and will produce revenues for 10 years.
- The brushes have to be replaced at the end of 6 years at a cost of $50,000.
- The old washer has a current salvage value of $40,000.
- The estimated salvage value of the new washer will be $7,000 at the end of 10 years.
- Remodeling the old washer costs $175,000 and the brushes must be replaced at the end of 6 years at a cost of $80,000 .

Should White replace the washer?



## Total-Cost Approach

Install the New Washer

| | Year | Cash Flows | 10% Factor | Present Value |
|---|---|---|---|---|
| Initial investment | Now | $ (300,000) | 1.000 | $(300,000) |
| Replace brushes | 6 | (50,000) | 0.564 | (28,200) |
| Net annual cash inflows | 1-10 | 60,000 | 6.145 | 368,700 |
| Salvage of old equipment | Now | 40,000 | 1.000 | 40,000 |
| Salvage of new equipment | 10 | 7,000 | 0.386 | 2,702 |
| Net present value | | | | $ 83,202 |



## Total-Cost Approach

Install the New Washer

| | Year | Cash Flows | 10% Factor | Present Value |
|---|---|---|---|---|
| Initial investment | Now | $ (300,000) | 1.000 | $(300,000) |
| Replace brushes | 6 | (50,000) | 0.564 | (28,200) |
| Net annual cash inflows | 1-10 | 60,000 | 6.145 | 368,700 |
| Salvage of old equipment | Now | 40,000 | 1.000 | 40,000 |
| Salvage of new equipment | 10 | 7,000 | 0.386 | 2,702 |
| Net present value | | | | $ 83,202 |

**If we install the new washer, the investment will yield a positive net present value of $83,202.**

## 14 Total-Cost Approach

Now let's see what happens if we remodel the existing washer.

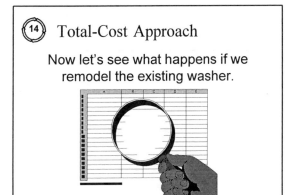

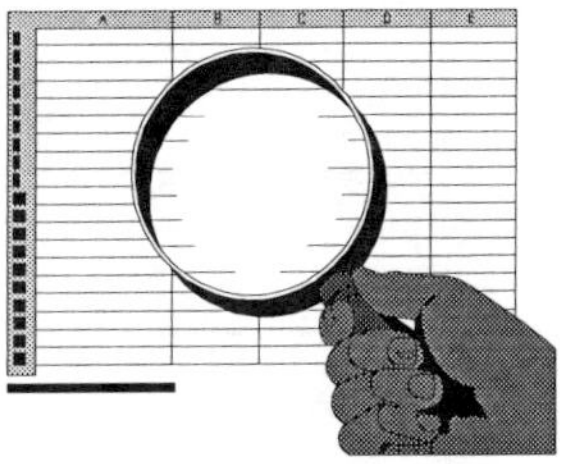



## 14 Total-Cost Approach

Remodel the Old Washer

| | Year | Cash Flows | 10% Factor | Present Value |
|---|---|---|---|---|
| Initial investment | Now | $ (175,000) | 1.000 | $(175,000) |
| Replace brushes | 6 | (80,000) | 0.564 | (45,120) |
| Net annual cash inflows | 1-10 | 45,000 | 6.145 | 276,525 |
| Net present value | | | | $ 56,405 |



## 14 Total-Cost Approach

**Both projects yield a positive net present value.**

| | Net Present Value |
|---|---|
| Invest in new washer | $ 83,202 |
| Remodel existing washer | 56,405 |
| In favor of new washer | $ 26,797 |

## Incremental-Cost Approach

Under the incremental-cost approach, only those cash flows that differ between the two alternatives are considered.

Let's look at an analysis of the White Co. decision using the incremental-cost approach.



## Incremental-Cost Approach

| | Year | Cash Flows | 10% Factor | Present Value |
|---|---|---|---|---|
| Incremental investment | Now | $(125,000) | 1.000 | $(125,000) |

**$300,000 new - $175,000 remodel = $125,000**



## Incremental-Cost Approach

| | Year | Cash Flows | 10% Factor | Present Value |
|---|---|---|---|---|
| Incremental investment | Now | $(125,000) | 1.000 | $(125,000) |
| Incremental cost of brushes | 6 | $ 30,000 | 0.564 | 16,920 |

**$80,000 remodel - $50,000 new = $30,000**

## Incremental-Cost Approach

| | Year | Cash Flows | 10% Factor | Present Value |
|---|---|---|---|---|
| Incremental investment | Now | $(125,000) | 1.000 | $(125,000) |
| Incremental cost of brushes | 6 | $ 30,000 | 0.564 | 16,920 |
| Increased net cash inflows | 1-10 | 15,000 | 6.145 | 92,175 |

**$60,000 new - $45,000 remodel = $15,000**



## Incremental-Cost Approach

| | Year | Cash Flows | 10% Factor | Present Value |
|---|---|---|---|---|
| Incremental investment | Now | $(125,000) | 1.000 | $(125,000) |
| Incremental cost of brushes | 6 | $ 30,000 | 0.564 | 16,920 |
| Increased net cash inflows | 1-10 | 15,000 | 6.145 | 92,175 |
| Salvage of old equipment | Now | 40,000 | 1.000 | 40,000 |
| Salvage of new equipment | 10 | 7,000 | 0.386 | 2,702 |
| Net present value | | | | $ 26,797 |



## Least Cost Decisions

In decisions where revenues are not directly involved, managers should choose the alternative that has the least total cost from a present value perspective.

Let's look at the Home Furniture Company example.

## Least Cost Decisions

- Home Furniture Company is trying to decide whether to overhaul an old delivery truck or purchase a new one.
- The company uses a discount rate of 10%.

## Least Cost Decisions

**Here is information about the trucks . . .**

| Old Truck | |
|---|---|
| Overhaul cost | $ 4,500 |
| Annual operating costs | 10,000 |
| Salvage value in 5 years | 250 |
| Salvage value now | 9,000 |

| New Truck | |
|---|---|
| Purchase price | $ 21,000 |
| Annual operating costs | 6,000 |
| Salvage value in 5 years | 3,000 |



## Least Cost Decisions

Buy the New Truck

| | Year | Cash Flows | 10% Factor | Present Value |
|---|---|---|---|---|
| Purchase price | Now | $ (21,000) | 1.000 | $ (21,000) |
| Annual operating costs | 1-5 | (6,000) | 3.791 | (22,746) |
| Salvage value of old truck | Now | 9,000 | 1.000 | 9,000 |
| Salvage value of new truck | 5 | 3,000 | 0.621 | 1,863 |
| Net present value | | | | (32,883) |

**If we invest in the new truck, the net present value of future costs is $32,883.**

## 14 Least Cost Decisions

| Keep the Old Truck | Year | Cash Flows | 10% Factor | Present Value |
|---|---|---|---|---|
| Overhaul cost | Now | $ (4,500) | 1.000 | $ (4,500) |
| Annual operating costs | 1-5 | (10,000) | 3.791 | (37,910) |
| Salvage value of old truc | 5 | 250 | 0.621 | 155 |
| Net present value | | | | (42,255) |

**If we keep the existing truck and overhaul it, the net present value of our future costs is $42,255.**



## 14 Least Cost Decisions

Home Furniture should purchase the new truck.

| | |
|---|---|
| Net present value of costs associated with purchase of new truck | $(32,883) |
| Net present value of costs associated with remodeling existing truck | (42,255) |
| Net present value in favor of purchasing the new truck | $ 9,372 |



## 14 Capital Budgeting and Nonprofit Organizations

The only real problem in the use of capital budgeting by nonprofit organizations is determining the proper discount rate to use in the analysis of data.

## Investments in Automated Equipment

- Investments in automated equipment tend to be very large in dollar amount.
- The benefits received are often indirect and intangible.

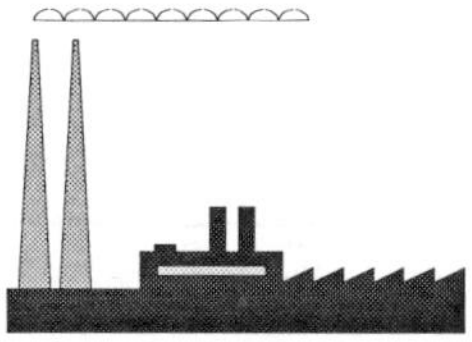



## Other Approaches to Capital Budgeting Decisions

- Other methods of making capital budgeting decisions include . . .
  1. The Payback Method.
  2. Simple Rate of Return.

## The Payback Method

The payback period is the length of time that it takes for an investment project to recover its own initial cost out of the cash receipts that it generates.

## The Payback Method

- The payback period is expressed in years.
- When the net annual cash inflow is the same every year, the following formula can be used to compute the payback period:

$$\text{Payback period} = \frac{\text{Investment required}}{\text{Net annual cash inflow}}$$

## The Payback Method

- Meyers Company wants to install an espresso bar in its restaurant.
- The espresso bar:
  - Cost $140,000 and has a 10-year life.
  - Will generate net annual cash inflows of $35,000.
- Meyers requires a payback period of 5 years or less on all investments.

Should Meyers invest in the espresso bar?



## The Payback Method

$$\text{Payback period} = \frac{\text{Investment required}}{\text{Net annual cash inflow}}$$

## The Payback Method

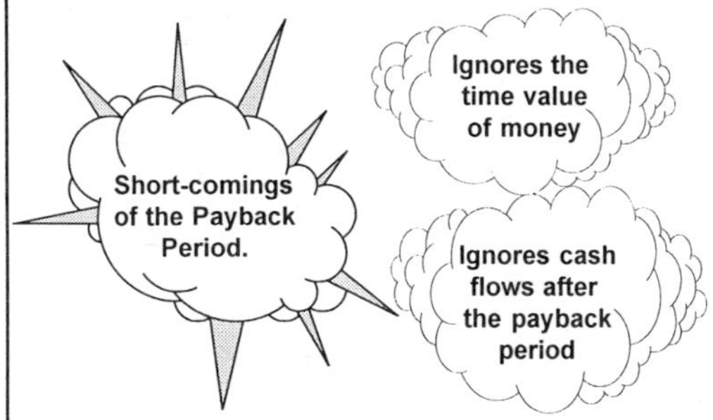
Short-comings of the Payback Period.
Ignores the time value of money
Ignores cash flows after the payback period

## The Simple Rate of Return Method

- Unlike the other capital budgeting methods, the simple rate of return does not focus on cash flows -- rather it focuses on accounting income.
- The following formula is used to calculate the simple rate of return:

$$\text{Simple rate of return} = \frac{\text{Incremental revenues} - \text{Incremental expenses, including depreciation}}{\text{Initial investment}}$$

## The Simple Rate of Return Method

- Meyers Company wants to install an espresso bar in its restaurant.
- The espresso bar:
  - Cost $140,000 and has a 10-year life.
  - Will generate incremental revenues of $100,000 and incremental expenses of $65,000 including depreciation.

What is the simple rate of return on the investment project?

## 14 Postaudit of Investment Projects

A postaudit is a follow-up after the project has been approved to see whether or not expected results are actually realized.

## 14 End of Chapter 14

GARRISON

# MANAGERIAL ACCOUNTING

Eighth Edition

NOREEN

---

15

Chapter 15

## Further Aspects of Investment Decisions



---

15

## Income Taxes and Capital Budgeting

The effects of income taxes on cash flows must be considered in capital budgeting decisions when an organization is subject to income taxes.

## 15 The Concept of After-Tax Cost

A cash expense net of its tax effect is known as after-tax cost.

Let's look at the East and West Companies example.

East & West



## 15 The Concept of After-Tax Cost

East and West Companies are identical except that East has a $40,000 annual cash expense for an employee training program.

| | East Company | West Company |
|---|---|---|
| Sales | $ 250,000 | $ 250,000 |
| Less expenses: | | |
| Salaries, insurance, etc. | 150,000 | 150,000 |
| Training program | 40,000 | - |
| Total expenses | 190,000 | 150,000 |
| Income before taxes | 60,000 | 100,000 |
| Less: income taxes (30%) | 18,000 | 30,000 |
| Net income | $ 42,000 | $ 70,000 |



## 15 The Concept of After-Tax Cost

- The following formula shows the after-tax cost of any tax-deductible cash expense:

(1 – Tax rate) × Cash expense = After-tax cost

## 15 The Concept of After-Tax Cost

North Company receives $80,000 per year from subleasing part of its office space. North is subject to a 30% tax rate.

What is the after-tax benefit from the sublease?



## 15 The Concept of After-Tax Cost

North Company receives $80,000 per year from subleasing part of its office space. North is subject to a 30% tax rate.

What is the after-tax benefit from the sublease?

(1 – Tax rate) × Cash receipt = After-tax benefit



## 15 The Concept of After-Tax Cost

South Company can invest in a project that would provide cash receipts of $400,000 per year. Cash operating expenses would be $280,000 per year. The tax rate is 30%.

What is the after-tax benefit (net cash inflow) each year from this project?

## 15 The Concept of After-Tax Cost

| | |
|---|---|
| Annual cash receipts | $400,000 |
| Annual cash operating expenses | 280,000 |
| Annual net cash inflow | 120,000 |
| Multiply by (100% - 30%) | 70% |
| Annual after-tax net cash inflows | $ 84,000 |



## 15 The Concept of Depreciation Tax Shield

Although depreciation is not a cash flow, it does have an impact on the amount of income taxes that a company will pay. Depreciation deductions shield revenues from taxation and thereby reduce tax payments.

Let's look at an example of a depreciation tax shield.



## 15 The Concept of Depreciation Tax Shield

Art and Music Companies are identical except that Art has a $60,000 annual depreciation expense:

| | Art Company | Music Company |
|---|---|---|
| Sales | $500,000 | $500,000 |
| Less expenses: | | |
| Cash operating expenses | 340,000 | 340,000 |
| Depreciation expense | 60,000 | - |
| Total expenses | 400,000 | 340,000 |
| Income before taxes | 100,000 | 160,000 |
| Less income taxes (30%) | 30,000 | 48,000 |
| Net income | $ 70,000 | $112,000 |

## The Concept of Depreciation Tax Shield

Let's look more closely at the difference in net income.

| | |
|---|---|
| Net income of Music | $112,000 |
| Net income of Art | 70,000 |
| Difference in net income | 42,000 |



## The Concept of Depreciation Tax Shield

The tax savings provided by the depreciation tax shield can be computed by the following formula:

$$\text{Tax rate} \times \text{Depreciation deduction} = \text{Tax Savings}$$



## Modified Accelerated Cost Recovery System (MACRS)

| Year | 3-Year | 5-Year |
|---|---|---|
| 1 | 33.3% | 20.0% |
| 2 | 44.5% | 32.0% |
| 3 | 14.8% | 19.2% |
| 4 | 7.4% | 11.5% * |
| 5 | | 11.5% |
| 6 | | 5.8% |
| | 100% | 100% |

*Change to straight-line

**MACRS table of 3 and 5-year assets**

## 15 Modified Accelerated Cost Recovery System

Mason Company purchased a light truck at a cost of $30,000 in March of 19X1. The truck's useful life is 5 years and it has a salvage value of $2,000.

Let's calculate MACRS depreciation.



## 15 Modified Accelerated Cost Recovery System

Mason Company purchased a light truck at a cost of $30,000 in March of 19X1. The truck's useful life is 5 years and it has a salvage value of $2,000.

| Year | Cost | MACRS % | Depr. Expense |
|---|---|---|---|
| 1 | $ 30,000 | 20.0% | $ 6,000 |
| | | 20.0% | $ 6,000 |

*Change to straight-lin



## 15 Modified Accelerated Cost Recovery System

Mason Company purchased a light truck at a cost of $30,000 in March of 19X1. The truck's useful life is 5 years and it has a salvage value of $2,000.

| Year | Cost | MACRS % | Depr. Expense |
|---|---|---|---|
| 1 | $ 30,000 | 20.0% | $ 6,000 |
| 2 | 30,000 | 32.0% | 9,600 |
| 3 | 30,000 | 19.2% | 5,760 |
| 4 | 30,000 | 11.5% * | 3,450 |
| 5 | 30,000 | 11.5% | 3,450 |
| 6 | 30,000 | 5.8% | 1,740 |
| | | 100.0% | $ 30,000 |

*Change to straight-lin

## The Choice of a Depreciation Method

- For financial reporting a company may elect to use straight-line, units of output or accelerated depreciation.
- For income tax reporting in the United States MACRS is required.
- We should use the income tax method because we are computing the tax savings from depreciation deductions.

## Capital Budgeting and Taxes

Martin Company has an investment opportunity that would involve the following cash flows:

| | |
|---|---|
| Cost of new equipment | $ 400,000 |
| Working capital required | 80,000 |
| Net annual cash receipts for 8 years | 100,000 |
| Equipment repairs in 4 years | 40,000 |
| Salvage value of equipment | 50,000 |



## Capital Budgeting and Taxes

- The equipment has an estimated useful life of 8 years.
- For tax purposes the equipment is classified in the 5-year MACRS property class.
- Martin has an after-tax cost of capital of 10% and is subject to a 30% income tax rate.

Should Martin invest in this project?

## Capital Budgeting and Taxes

| Year | Cost | MACRS % | Depr. |
|---|---|---|---|
| 1 | $400,000 | 20.0% | $ 80,000 |
| 2 | 400,000 | 32.0% | 128,000 |
| 3 | 400,000 | 19.2% | 76,800 |
| 4 | 400,000 | 11.5% | 46,000 |
| 5 | 400,000 | 11.5% | 46,000 |
| 6 | 400,000 | 5.8% | 23,200 |
| | | 100.0% | $400,000 |

Depreciation expense deducted on Martin's tax return each year.



## Capital Budgeting and Taxes

| Year | Depr. | Tax Effect | After tax cash flow |
|---|---|---|---|
| 1 | $ 80,000 | 30.0% | $ 24,000 |
| 2 | 128,000 | 30.0% | 38,400 |
| 3 | 76,800 | 30.0% | 23,040 |
| 4 | 46,000 | 30.0% | 13,800 |
| 5 | 46,000 | 30.0% | 13,800 |
| 6 | 23,200 | 30.0% | 6,960 |

The tax savings resulting from the annual depreciation deduction.



## Capital Budgeting and Taxes

| Year | After tax cash flow | 10% factor | Present value |
|---|---|---|---|
| 1 | $ 24,000 | 0.9090 | $ 21,816 |
| 2 | 38,400 | 0.8260 | 31,718 |
| 3 | 23,040 | 0.7510 | 17,303 |
| 4 | 13,800 | 0.6830 | 9,425 |
| 5 | 13,800 | 0.6210 | 8,570 |
| 6 | 6,960 | 0.5640 | 3,926 |
| Total | | | $ 92,758 |

Present value of $1 table.

## Capital Budgeting and Taxes

Cash flows other than the tax savings from depreciation

| | Year(s) | Amount | Tax effect | After tax cash flows |
|---|---|---|---|---|
| Cost of equipment | Now | $(400,000) | - | $(400,000) |
| Working capital | Now | (80,000) | - | (80,000) |
| Cash receipts | 1-8 | 100,000 | 0.70 | 70,000 |
| Equipment repairs | 4 | (40,000) | 0.70 | (28,000) |
| Salvage value | 8 | 50,000 | 0.70 | 35,000 |
| Release of working capital | 8 | 80,000 | - | 80,000 |



## Capital Budgeting and Taxes

Cash flows other than the tax savings from depreciation

| | Year(s) | Amount | Tax effect | After tax cash flows |
|---|---|---|---|---|
| Cost of equipment | Now | $(400,000) | - | $(400,000) |
| Working capital | Now | (80,000) | - | (80,000) |
| Cash receipts | 1-8 | 100,000 | 0.70 | 70,000 |
| Equipment repairs | 4 | (40,000) | 0.70 | (28,000) |
| Salvage value | 8 | 50,000 | 0.70 | 35,000 |
| Release of working capital | 8 | 80,000 | - | 80,000 |

Now, lets calculate the present value of these cash flows.



## Capital Budgeting and Taxes

| | Year(s) | After tax cash flow | 10% Factor | Present Value |
|---|---|---|---|---|
| Cost of equipment | Now | $(400,000) | 1.000 | $(400,000) |
| Working capital | Now | (80,000) | 1.000 | (80,000) |
| Cash receipts | 1-8 | 70,000 | 5.335 | 373,450 |
| Equipment repairs | 4 | (28,000) | 0.683 | (19,124) |
| Salvage value | 8 | 35,000 | 0.467 | 16,345 |
| Release of working capital | 8 | 80,000 | 0.467 | 37,360 |

Now, lets put all the present value computations together.

## Capital Budgeting and Taxes

| | Year(s) | Present Value |
|---|---|---|
| Cost of equipment | Now | $ (400,000) |
| Working capital | Now | (80,000) |
| Annual cash receipts | 1-8 | 373,450 |
| Depreciation | 1-6 | 92,758 |
| Equipment repairs | 4 | (19,124) |
| Salvage value | 8 | 16,345 |
| Release of working capital | 8 | 37,360 |
| Net Present value | | $ 20,789 |



## Capital Budgeting and Taxes

| | Year(s) | Present Value |
|---|---|---|
| Cost of equipment | Now | $ (400,000) |
| Working capital | Now | (80,000) |
| Annual cash receipts | 1-8 | 373,450 |
| Depreciation | 1-6 | 92,758 |
| Equipment repairs | 4 | (19,124) |
| Salvage value | 8 | 16,345 |
| Release of working capital | 8 | 37,360 |
| Net Present value | | $ 20,789 |

This investment project is acceptable to Martin.



## Preference Decisions – The Ranking of Investment Projects

- Next, we examine all acceptable projects to find the one that is best for our company. This is the preference decision.
- First, we screen available projects to identify those that are acceptable.

## Preference Decisions – The Ranking of Investment Projects

✦ In making the preference decision we can use the . . .

❶ Internal rate of return, or

❷ Net present value method.

## Preference Decisions – The Ranking of Investment Projects

**Internal Rate of Return**

The project with the higher rate of return is preferable to the project with a lower rate of return.

**Net Present Value**

We cannot compare net present values from two competing projects directly.

We must calculate the profitability index.



## Preference Decisions – The Ranking of Investment Projects

$$\frac{\text{Present value of cash inflows}}{\text{Investment required}} = \text{Profitability index}$$

## 15 Comparing the Preference Rules

- The profitability index is superior to the internal rate of return method of making preference decisions.
- If project lives are unequal, the internal rate of return can lead the manager to make incorrect decisions.

## 15 End of Chapter 15

GARRISON

**MANAGERIAL**

Eighth Edition

**ACCOUNTING**

NOREEN

---

16

# Service Department Costing:
An Activity Approach

*Chapter* 16



---

16

## The Need for Cost Allocations

**Operating Departments**

Carry out the central purposes of an organization

**Service Departments**

Provide support that facilitates the activities of operating departments

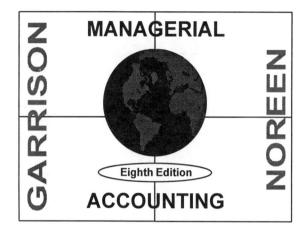

## 16 The Need for Cost Allocations

## 16 The Need for Cost Allocations

## 16 The Need for Cost Allocations

## 16 The Need for Cost Allocations

## 16 The Need for Cost Allocations

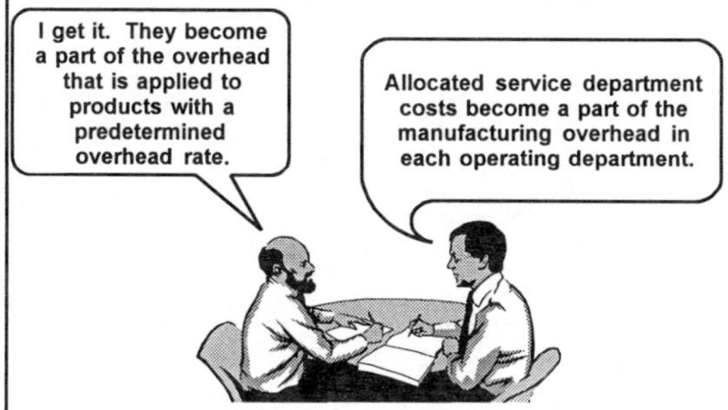




## 16 The Need for Cost Allocations

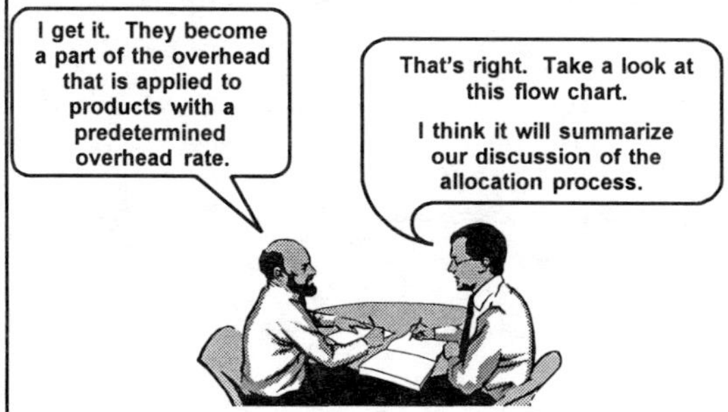

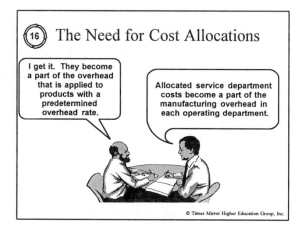

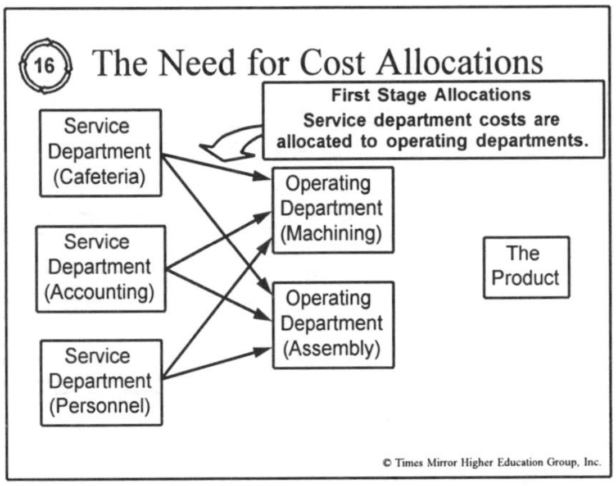
16
The Need for Cost Allocations
First Stage Allocations
Service department costs are allocated to operating departments.
Service Department (Cafeteria)
Service Department (Accounting)
Service Department (Personnel)
Operating Department (Machining)
Operating Department (Assembly)
The Product
© Times Mirror Higher Education Group, Inc.

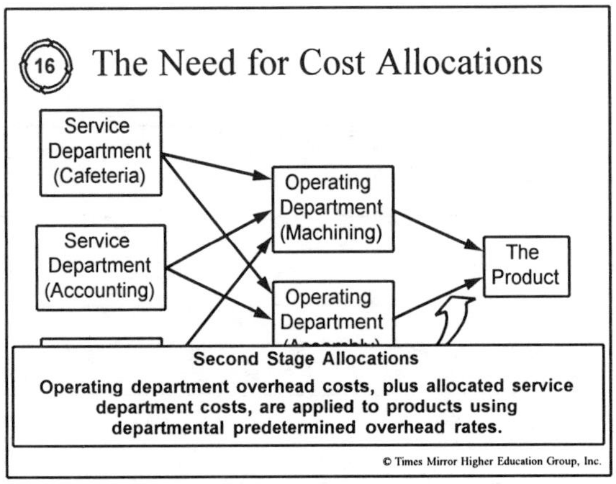
16
The Need for Cost Allocations
Service Department (Cafeteria)
Service Department (Accounting)
Operating Department (Machining)
Operating Department
The Product
Second Stage Allocations
Operating department overhead costs, plus allocated service department costs, are applied to products using departmental predetermined overhead rates.
© Times Mirror Higher Education Group, Inc.

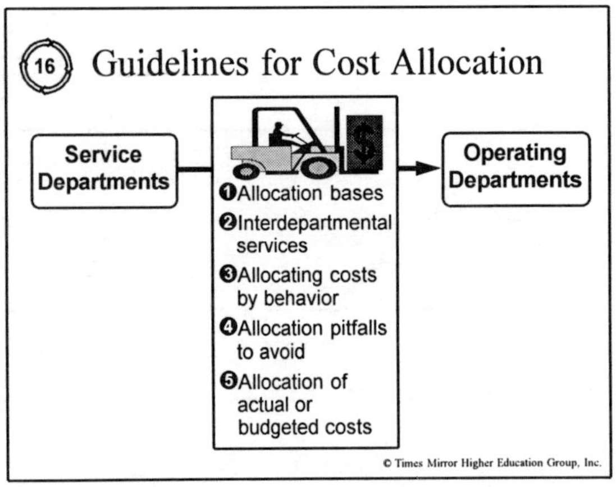
16
Guidelines for Cost Allocation
Service Departments
Operating Departments
❶Allocation bases
❷Interdepartmental services
❸Allocating costs by behavior
❹Allocation pitfalls to avoid
❺Allocation of actual or budgeted costs
© Times Mirror Higher Education Group, Inc.

## 16 Selecting Allocation Bases

**Typical Allocation Bases**

- **Personnel:** Number of employees
- **Custodial:** Square footage
- **Receiving:** Units handled
- **Cafeteria:** Number of employees
- **Security:** Square footage
- **Accounting:** Staff hours
- **Power:** Kilowatt hours



## 16 Interdepartmental Services

**Problem**

**Allocating costs when service departments provide services to each other**

**Solutions**

**Direct Method**

**Step method**

**Reciprocal method**

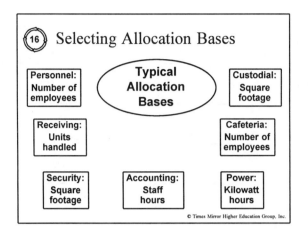

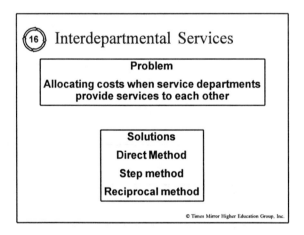

## 16 Direct Method

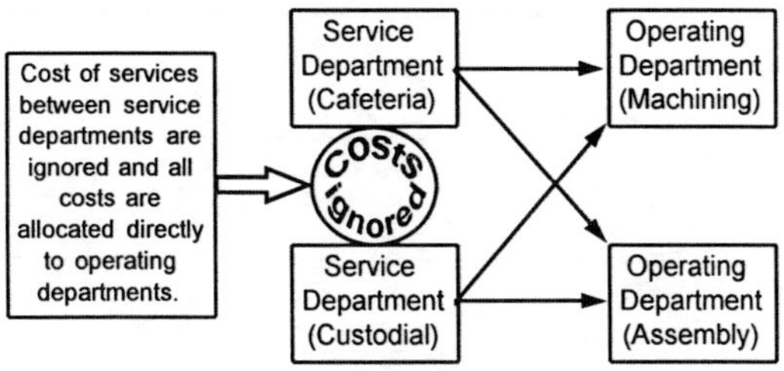

## Direct Method Example

| | Service Departments | | Operating Departments | |
|---|---|---|---|---|
| | Cafeteria | Custodial | Machining | Assembly |
| Departmental costs before allocation | $360,000 | $ 90,000 | $ 400,000 | $ 700,000 |
| Number of employees | 15 | 10 | 20 | 30 |
| Square feet occupied | 5,000 | 2,000 | 25,000 | 50,000 |

| Service Department | Allocation Base |
|---|---|
| Cafeteria | Number of employees |
| Custodial | Square feet occupied |



## Direct Method Example

| | Service Departments | | Operating Departments | |
|---|---|---|---|---|
| | Cafeteria | Custodial | Machining | Assembly |
| Departmental costs before allocation | $360,000 | $ 90,000 | $ 400,000 | $ 700,000 |
| Cafeteria allocation | | | | |
| Custodial allocation | | | | |
| Total after allocation | | | | |



## Direct Method Example

| | Service Departments | | Operating Departments | |
|---|---|---|---|---|
| | Cafeteria | Custodial | Machining | Assembly |
| Departmental costs before allocation | $360,000 | $ 90,000 | $ 400,000 | $ 700,000 |
| Cafeteria allocation | (360,000) | | 144,000 | 216,000 |
| Custodial allocation | | (90,000) | 30,000 | 60,000 |
| Total after allocation | $ 0 | $ 0 | $ 574,000 | $ 976,000 |

## 16 Step Method

Service department costs are allocated to other service departments and to operating departments, usually starting with the service department that provides the greatest amount of service to other departments.

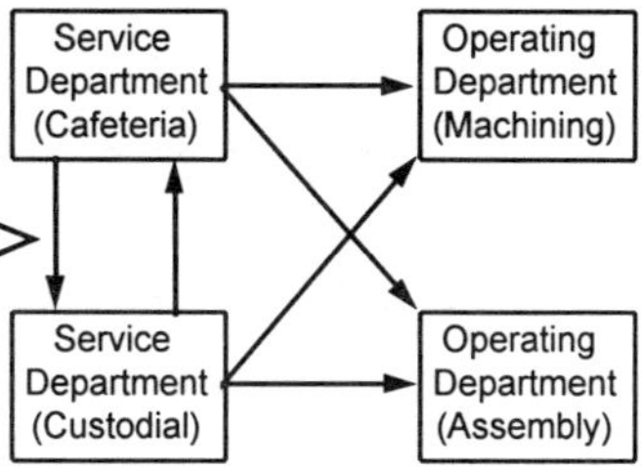




## 16 Step Method

Once a service department's costs are allocated, other service department costs are not allocated back to it.

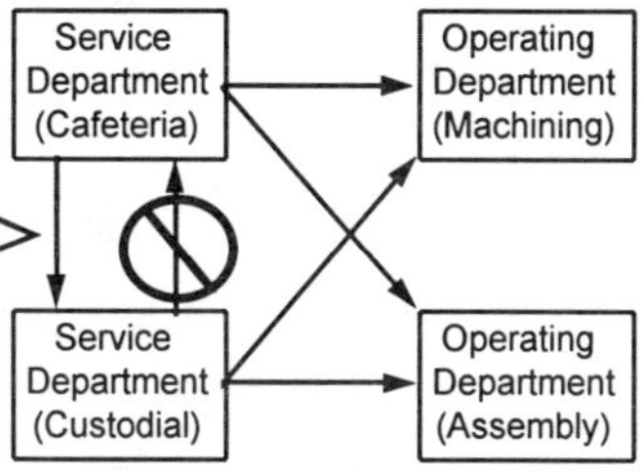




## 16 Step Method

Custodial will have a new total to allocate to operating departments: it's own costs plus those costs allocated from the cafeteria.

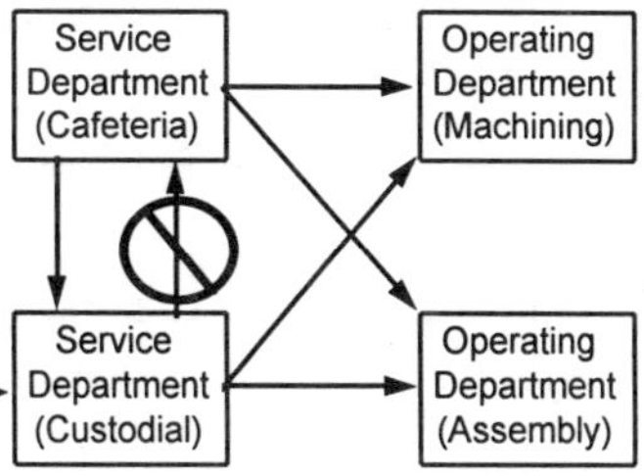

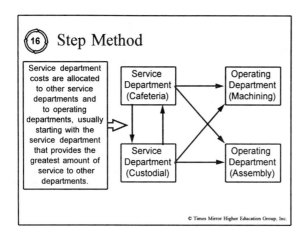

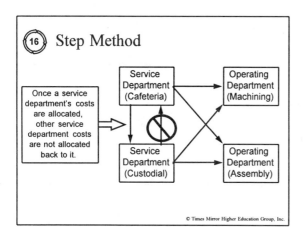

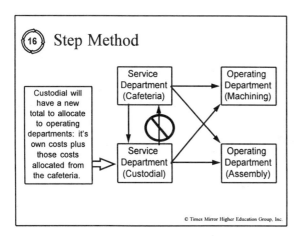

## Step Method Example

**We will use the same data used in the direct method example.**

| | Service Departments | | Operating Departments | |
|---|---|---|---|---|
| | Cafeteria | Custodial | Machining | Assembly |
| Departmental costs before allocation | $ 360,000 | $ 90,000 | $ 400,000 | $ 700,000 |
| Number of employees | 15 | 10 | 20 | 30 |
| Square feet occupied | 5,000 | 2,000 | 25,000 | 50,000 |

| Service Department | Allocation Base |
|---|---|
| Cafeteria | Number of employees |
| Custodial | Square feet occupied |



## Step Method Example

| | Service Departments | | Operating Departments | |
|---|---|---|---|---|
| | Cafeteria | Custodial | Machining | Assembly |
| Departmental costs before allocation | $ 360,000 | $ 90,000 | $ 400,000 | $ 700,000 |
| Cafeteria allocation | | | | |
| Custodial allocation | | | | |
| Total after allocation | | | | |



## Step Method Example

| | Service Departments | | Operating Departments | |
|---|---|---|---|---|
| | Cafeteria | Custodial | Machining | Assembly |
| Departmental costs before allocation | $ 360,000 | $ 90,000 | $ 400,000 | $ 700,000 |
| Cafeteria allocation | (360,000) | 60,000 | 120,000 | 180,000 |
| Custodial allocation | | (150,000) | 50,000 | 100,000 |
| Total after allocation | $ 0 | $ 0 | $ 570,000 | $ 980,000 |

## 16 Reciprocal Method

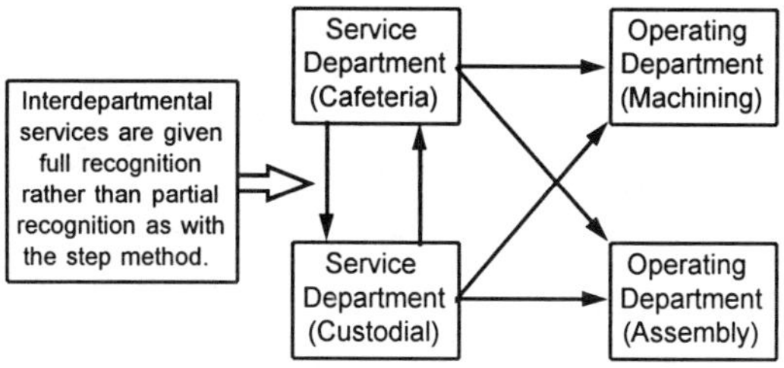




## 16 Reciprocal Method

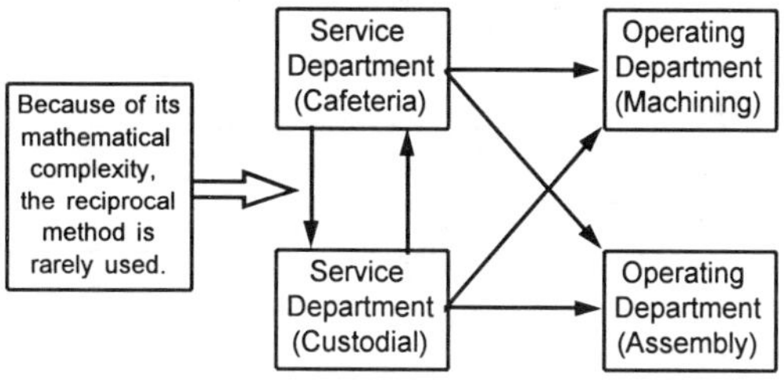




## 16 Comparison of Methods

| | Totals after allocation | |
|---|---|---|
| Method | Machining Department | Assembly Department |
| Direct | $ 574,000 | $ 976,000 |
| Step | 570,000 | 980,000 |
| Reciprocal | Results are similar to step method | |

## 16 Allocating Costs by Behavior

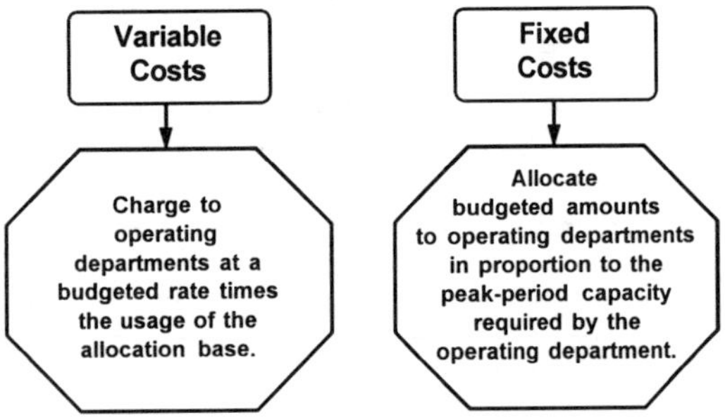

Variable Costs
Fixed Costs
Charge to operating departments at a budgeted rate times the usage of the allocation base.
Allocate budgeted amounts to operating departments in proportion to the peak-period capacity required by the operating department.

## 16 Allocating Costs by Behavior Example

SimCo has a maintenance department and two operating departments: cutting and assembly. Variable maintenance costs are budgeted at $0.60 per machine hour. Fixed maintenance costs are budgeted at $200,000 per year. Data relating to the current year are:

| Operating Departments | Percent of Peak-Period Capacity Required | Hours Used |
|---|---|---|
| Cutting | 60% | 80,000 |
| Assembly | 40% | 40,000 |
| Total hours | 100% | 120,000 |

Allocate maintenance costs to the two operating departments.



## 16 Allocating Costs by Behavior Example

| | Cutting Department | Assembly Department |
|---|---|---|
| Variable cost allocation: | | |
| $0.60 × 80,000 hours used | $ 48,000 | |
| $0.60 × 40,000 hours used | | $ 24,000 |
| Fixed cost allocation | | |
| 60% of $200,000 | 120,000 | |
| 40% of $200,000 | | 80,000 |
| Total allocated cost | $ 168,000 | $ 104,000 |

**Variable costs are allocated based on hours used. Fixed costs are allocated based on peak-period capacity required.**

## 16 Allocation Pitfalls to Avoid

**Pitfall 1**

Using sales dollars as an allocation base

**Result**

Departments that increase revenues are penalized by receiving more allocated costs.



## 16 Allocation Pitfalls to Avoid

**Pitfall 2**

Allocating fixed costs using a variable activity allocation base

**Result**

Total fixed costs do not change, but departments that increase activities to support increased revenues are penalized by receiving more allocated costs.



## 16 Should All Costs Be Allocated?

My performance looked good until they allocated those service department costs, so I'm not going to use the service again.
But that would not be beneficial to the company.
What if we charged a flat annual fee for the service?

## 16 Should All Costs Be Allocated?

## 16 End of Chapter 16

# "How Well Am I Doing?" Statement of Cash Flows

Chapter 17



## Purpose of the Statement of Cash Flows

- Highlights the major activities that impact cash flows
- Serves as a valuable analytical tool for managers
- Answers questions such as:

?

## Cash

The term ***cash*** on the statement of cash flows refers broadly to both currency and cash equivalents.

## Constructing the Statement of Cash Flows

- Increases in noncash asset accounts imply uses of cash.

**Example:** **Inventory is purchased on credit from a supplier.**



## Constructing the Statement of Cash Flows

- Decreases in noncash assets accounts imply sources of cash.

**Example:** **A customer paid his bill.**



## Constructing the Statement of Cash Flows

- Decreases in liability accounts imply uses of cash.

**Example:** **The company made a payment on a note payable held by a creditor.**

## Organizing a Full-Fledged Statement of Cash Flows

The FASB requires cash flows to be divided into three categories.

XYZ Company
Cash Flow Statement
For the Period Ending MM/DD/YY

| | | |
|---|---|---|
| I. | Operating Activities | $ XXX |
| II. | Investing Activities | XXX |
| III. | Financing Activities | XXX |
| Net Cash Flows for the Period | | $ XXX |
| Add: Beg. Cash Balance | | XXX |
| Ending Cash Balance | | $ XXX |



## Organizing a Full-Fledged Statement of Cash Flows

A reconciliation of beginning cash to ending cash is also included.

XYZ Company
Cash Flow Statement
For the Period Ending MM/DD/YY

| | | |
|---|---|---|
| I. | Operating Activities | $ XXX |
| II. | Investing Activities | XXX |
| III. | Financing Activities | XXX |
| Net Cash Flows for the Period | | $ XXX |
| Add: Beg. Cash Balance | | XXX |
| Ending Cash Balance | | $ XXX |



## Operating Activities

Includes those activities that enter into the determination of net income

**Operating Activities**

| | |
|---|---|
| Net Income | $ XXX |
| Add: Decr. in Current Noncash Assets | XXX |
| Incr. in Current Liabilities | XXX |
| Depreciation Exp. | XXX |
| Losses | XXX |
| Less: Incr. in Current Noncash Assets | XXX |
| Decr. in Current Liabilities | XXX |
| Gains | XXX |
| Net Cash Flows from Operating Activities | $ XXX |

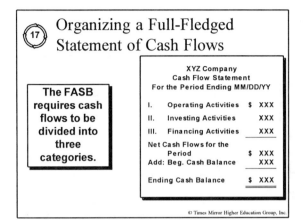

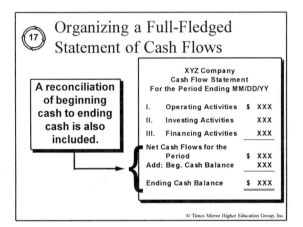

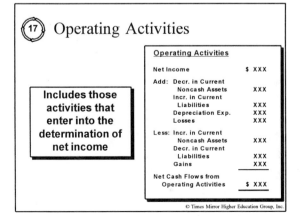

## Operating Activities

- Changes in current assets and current liabilities imply changes in cash.
- Changes in current assets and current liabilities are treated as indicated below:

| | Change in Account Balance during Period | |
|---|---|---|
| | Increase | Decrease |
| Current Noncash Assets | Subtract from net income | Add to net income |
| Current Liabilities | Add to net income | Subtract from net income |



## Operating Activities

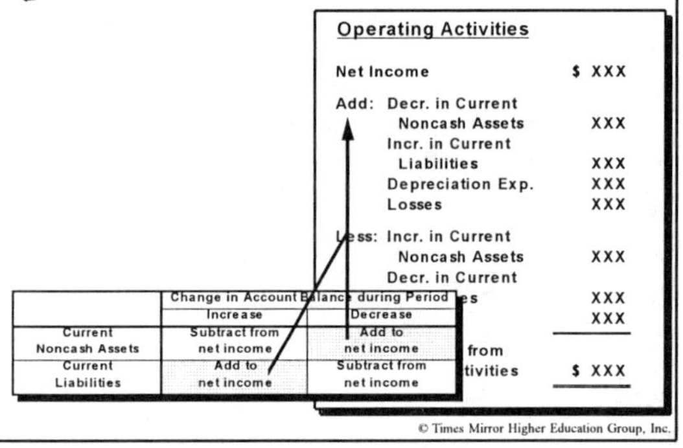




## Operating Activities

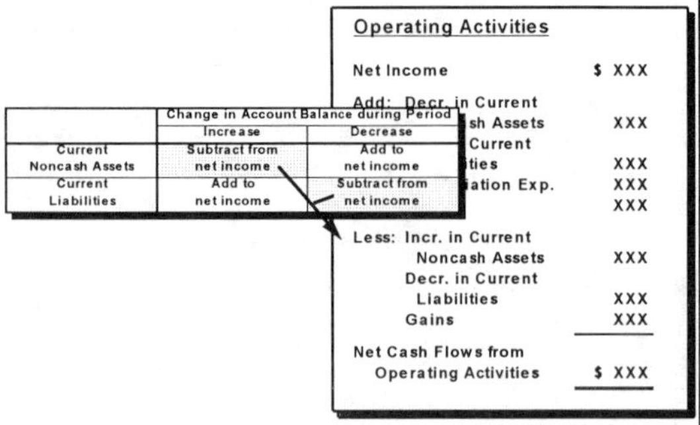

## Investing Activities

Includes transactions that involve the acquisition or disposal of noncurrent assets

| Investing Activities | |
|---|---|
| Add: Proceeds from sale of land, buildings, equipment, or other noncurrent assets | $ XXX |
| Receipt of principal from investments | XXX |
| Less: Payments to acquire land, buildings, equipment or other noncurrent assets | XXX |
| Payments to acquire investments | XXX |
| Net Cash Flows from Investing Activities | $ XXX |



## Financing Activities

Includes transactions involving receipts from or payments to creditors and owners

| Financing Activities | |
|---|---|
| Add: Proceeds from borrowings | $ XXX |
| Proceeds from issuing capital stock | XXX |
| Proceeds from sale of bonds | XXX |
| Less: Principal payments on borrowed funds | XXX |
| Payments related to bond maturities | XXX |
| Dividend payments | XXX |
| Net Cash Flows from Financing Activities | $ XXX |



## Other Cash Flow Issues

- **For investing activities and financing activities, like-kind inflows and outflows of cash must be shown separately on the statement of cash flows.**

**Example:**

- **XYZ sells an old building for $700,000 and purchases a new building for $1,000,000.**
- **The $700,000 inflow of cash and the $1,000,000 outflow of cash must be shown separately.**

## Other Cash Flow Issues

- Direct exchange transactions occur when noncurrent balance sheet items are swapped.
- Such exchanges must be disclosed.

**Example:**

- Bobo, Inc. acquires a building in exchange for 2,000 shares of common stock.
- This is reported in a separate supplemental schedule attached to the statement of cash flows.



## Direct Method or Indirect Method?

| Direct Method | Indirect Method |
| --- | --- |
| Net income is reconstructed on a cash basis. | Net income is reconciled to cash flow from operating activities. |
| Requires a supplemental reconciliation of net income to cash flow from operating activities. | No supplemental schedule is required. |
| Used by 2.5% of companies. | Used by 97.5% of companies. |



## Interpretation of the Statement of Cash Flows

- Examine the operating activities section carefully.
  - Negative cash flow is usually a sign of fundamental difficulties.
  - Ultimately, a positive cash flow is necessary to avoid liquidating assets or borrowing money to pay for day-to-day activities.

# Example - Indirect Method

Ed's Hut is a local pizza restaurant. Ed has prepared an adjusted trial balance as of 3/31/X7. Ed needs help preparing the Statement of Cash Flows.

Examine the information provided and prepare a Statement of Cash Flows using the indirect method.

# Example - Indirect Method

Ed's Hut
Comparative Trial Balances

| | 3/31/X7 DR (CR) | 3/31/X6 DR (CR) | Change Incr. (Decr.) |
|---|---|---|---|
| Cash | $ 54,000 | $ 90,000 | $ (36,000) |
| Accounts Receivable | 23,000 | 40,000 | (17,000) |
| Inventory | 350,000 | 300,000 | 50,000 |
| Land | 68,000 | 100,000 | (32,000) |
| Equipment, net | 39,000 | 45,000 | (6,000) |
| Accounts Payable | (38,000) | (27,000) | 11,000 |
| Salaries Payable | (9,000) | (14,000) | (5,000) |
| Note Payable - Joe Doe | - | (50,000) | (50,000) |
| Common Stock | (500,000) | (450,000) | 50,000 |
| Retained Earnings, Beg. | (34,000) | (2,500) | 31,500 |
| Dividends | 20,000 | - | 20,000 |
| Sales Revenues | (727,000) | (645,000) | 82,000 |
| Operating Expenses | 748,000 | 608,500 | 139,500 |
| Depreciation Expense | 6,000 | 5,000 | 1,000 |
| | $ - | $ - | |



# Example - Indirect Method

- Additional Information:
  - During the year, Ed sold land originally costing $32,000 for $32,000.
  - During the year, Ed paid dividends of $20,000 to the stockholders.
  - Ed issued $50,000 of common stock to settle the note due to Joe Doe.

GARRISON

# MANAGERIAL ACCOUNTING

Eighth Edition

NOREEN

---

18

# "How Well Am I Doing?" Financial Statement Analysis

*Chapter* 18



---

18

## Limitations of Financial Statement Analysis

Differences in accounting methods between companies sometimes make comparisons difficult.

**We use the LIFO method to value inventory.**

**We use the FIFO method to value inventory.**

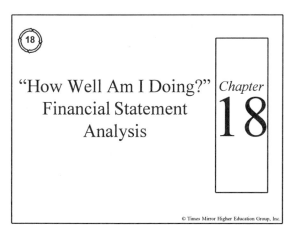

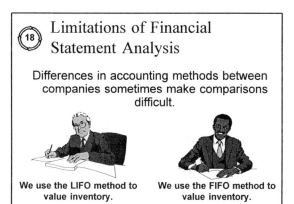

## 18 The Need to Look Beyond Ratios

- Changes within the firm
- Industry trends
- Consumer tastes
- Technological changes
- Economic factors

In addition to ratios, an analyst should consider . . .



## 18 Statements in Comparative and Common-Size Form

Analytical techniques used to examine relationships among financial statement items

❶ Dollar and percentage changes on statements

❷ Common-size statements

❸ Ratios



## 18 Dollar and Percentage Changes on Statements

**Comparing statements underscores movements and trends and may provide valuable clues about what to expect in the future.**

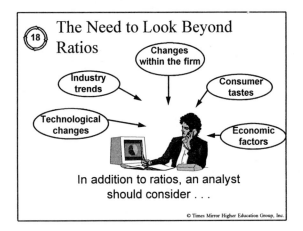

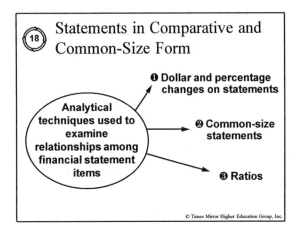

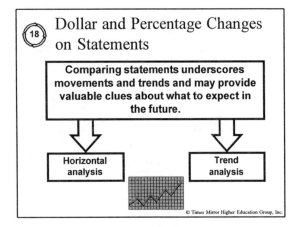

- Horizontal analysis
- Trend analysis

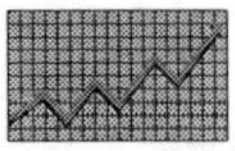

## (18) Horizontal Analysis

Horizontal analysis shows the changes between years in the financial data in both dollar and percentage form.

## (18) Horizontal Analysis

Example

The following slides illustrate a horizontal analysis of Clover Corporation's December 31, 19X5 and 19X4 comparative balance sheets and comparative income statements.



## (18) Horizontal Analysis

CLOVER CORPORATION
Comparative Balance Sheets
December 31, 19X5 and 19X4

| | | | Increase (Decrease) | |
|---|---|---|---|---|
| | 19X5 | 19X4 | Amount | % |
| Assets | | | | |
| Current assets: | | | | |
| Cash | $ 12,000 | $ 23,500 | | |
| Accounts receivable, net | 60,000 | 40,000 | | |
| Inventory | 80,000 | 100,000 | | |
| Prepaid expenses | 3,000 | 1,200 | | |
| Total current assets | 155,000 | 164,700 | | |
| Property and equipment: | | | | |
| Land | 40,000 | 40,000 | | |
| Buildings and equipment, net | 120,000 | 85,000 | | |
| Total property and equipment | 160,000 | 125,000 | | |
| Total assets | $ 315,000 | $ 289,700 | | |

## 18 Horizontal Analysis

Calculating Change in Dollar Amounts

| Dollar Change | = | Current Year Figure | – | Base Year Figure |

$



## 18 Horizontal Analysis

Calculating Change in Dollar Amounts

| Dollar Change | = | Current Year Figure | – | Base Year Figure |

**Since we are measuring the amount of the change between 19X4 and 19X5, the dollar amounts for 19X4 become the "base" year figures.**



## 18 Horizontal Analysis

Calculating Change as a Percentage

$$\text{Percentage Change} = \frac{\text{Dollar Change}}{\text{Base Year Figure}} \times 100\%$$

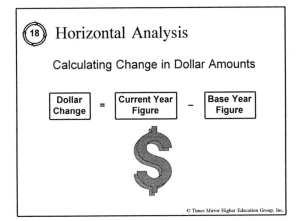

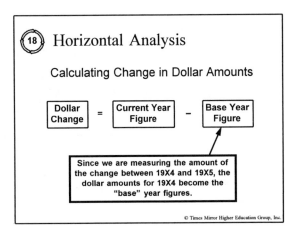

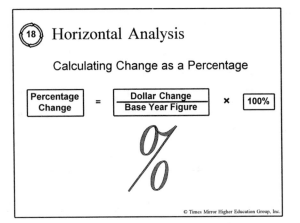

%

## Horizontal Analysis

**CLOVER CORPORATION**
**Comparative Balance Sheets**
**December 31, 19X5 and 19X4**

| | 19X5 | 19X4 | Increase (Decrease) Amount | Increase (Decrease) % |
|---|---|---|---|---|
| Assets | | | | |
| Current assets: | | | | |
| Cash | $ 12,000 | $ 23,500 | $ | |
| Accounts receivable, net | 60,000 | 40,000 | 20,000 | 50.0 |
| Inventory | 80,000 | 100,000 | (20,000) | (20.0) |
| Prepaid expenses | 3,000 | 1,200 | 1,800 | 150.0 |
| Total current assets | 155,000 | 164,700 | (9,700) | (5.9) |
| Property and equipment: | | | | |
| Land | 40,000 | 40,000 | - | 0.0 |
| Buildings and equipment, net | 120,000 | 85,000 | 35,000 | 41.2 |
| Total property and equipment | 160,000 | 125,000 | 35,000 | 28.0 |
| Total assets | $ 315,000 | $ 289,700 | $ 25,300 | 8.7 |



## Horizontal Analysis

Let's use the same procedures and calculate the dollar and percentage changes for the liabilities, stockholders' equity, and income statement accounts.



## Horizontal Analysis

**CLOVER CORPORATION**
**Comparative Balance Sheets**
**December 31, 19X5 and 19X4**

| | 19X5 | 19X4 | Increase (Decrease) Amount | Increase (Decrease) % |
|---|---|---|---|---|
| Liabilities and Stockholders' Equity | | | | |
| Current liabilities: | | | | |
| Accounts payable | $ 67,000 | $ 44,000 | $ 23,000 | 52.3 |
| Notes payable | 3,000 | 6,000 | (3,000) | (50.0) |
| Total current liabilities | 70,000 | 50,000 | 20,000 | 40.0 |
| Long-term liabilities: | | | | |
| Bonds payable, 8% | 75,000 | 80,000 | (5,000) | (6.3) |
| Total liabilities | 145,000 | 130,000 | 15,000 | 11.5 |
| Stockholders' equity: | | | | |
| Preferred stock | 20,000 | 20,000 | - | 0.0 |
| Common stock | 60,000 | 60,000 | - | 0.0 |
| Additional paid-in capital | 10,000 | 10,000 | - | 0.0 |
| Total paid-in capital | 90,000 | 90,000 | - | 0.0 |
| Retained earnings | 80,000 | 69,700 | 10,300 | 14.8 |
| Total stockholders' equity | 170,000 | 159,700 | 10,300 | 6.4 |
| Total liabilities and stockholders' equity | $ 315,000 | $ 289,700 | $ 25,300 | 8.7 |

## 18 Horizontal Analysis

**CLOVER CORPORATION**
**Comparative Income Statements**
**For the Years Ended December 31, 19X5 and 19X4**

| | | | Increase (Decrease) | |
|---|---|---|---|---|
| | 19X5 | 19X4 | Amount | % |
| Net sales | $520,000 | $480,000 | $ 40,000 | 8.3 |
| Cost of goods sold | 360,000 | 315,000 | 45,000 | 14.3 |
| Gross margin | 160,000 | 165,000 | (5,000) | (3.0) |
| Operating expenses | 128,600 | 126,000 | 2,600 | 2.1 |
| Net operating income | 31,400 | 39,000 | (7,600) | (19.5) |
| Interest expense | 6,400 | 7,000 | (600) | (8.6) |
| Net income before taxes | 25,000 | 32,000 | (7,000) | (21.9) |
| Less income taxes (30%) | 7,500 | 9,600 | (2,100) | (21.9) |
| Net income | $ 17,500 | $ 22,400 | $ (4,900) | (21.9) |



## 18 Trend Percentages

**Trend percentages state several years' financial data in terms of a base year, which equals 100 percent.**

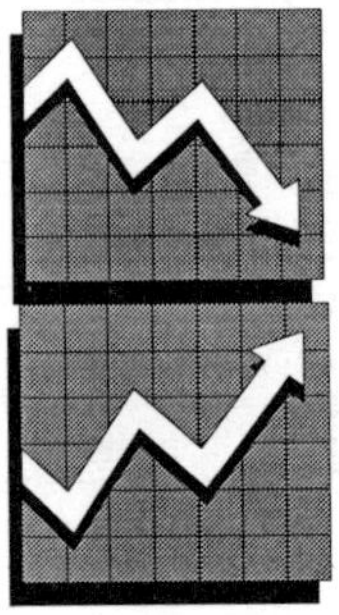



## 18 Trend Analysis

$$\text{Trend Percentage} = \frac{\text{Current Year Amount}}{\text{Base Year Amount}} \times 100\%$$

## 18 Trend Analysis

### Example

Look at the income information for Berry Products for the years 19X1 through 19X5. We will do a trend analysis on these amounts to see what we can learn about the company.



## 18 Trend Analysis

Berry Products
Income Information
For the Years Ended December 31,

| Item | Year | | | | |
|---|---|---|---|---|---|
| | 19X5 | 19X4 | 19X3 | 19X2 | 19X1 |
| Sales | $ 400,000 | $ 355,000 | $ 320,000 | $ 290,000 | $ 275,000 |
| Cost of goods sold | 285,000 | 250,000 | 225,000 | 198,000 | 190,000 |
| Gross margin | 115,000 | 105,000 | 95,000 | 92,000 | 85,000 |

**The base year is 19X1, and its amounts will equal 100%.**



## 18 Trend Analysis

Berry Products
Income Information
For the Years Ended December 31,

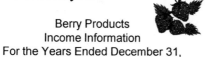

| Item | Year | | | | |
|---|---|---|---|---|---|
| | 19X5 | 19X4 | 19X3 | 19X2 | 19X1 |
| Sales | 145% | 129% | 116% | | 100% |
| Cost of goods sold | 150% | 132% | 118% | | 100% |
| Gross margin | 135% | 124% | 112% | | 100% |

**By analyzing the trends for Berry Products, we can see that cost of goods sold is increasing faster than sales, which is slowing the increase in gross margin.**

## Trend Analysis

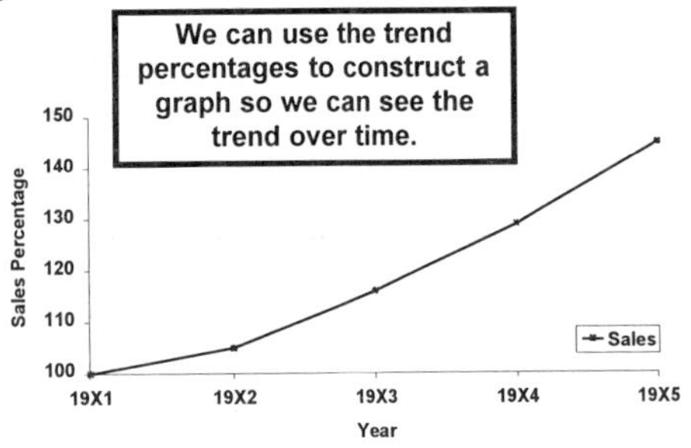




## Common-Size Statements

Example

Let's take another look at the information from the comparative income statements of Clover Corporation for 19X5 and 19X4.

This time let's prepare common-size statements.



## Common-Size Statements

CLOVER CORPORATION
Comparative Income Statements
For the Years Ended December 31, 19X5 and 19X4

| | Common-Size Percentages | |
|---|---|---|
| | 19X5 | 19X4 |

Common-size statements use percentages to express the relationship of individual components to a total within a single period. This is also known as vertical analysis.

18

# Common-Size Statements

CLOVER CORPORATION
Comparative Income Statements
For the Years Ended December 31, 19X5 and 19X4

| | | | Common-Size Percentages | |
|---|---|---|---|---|
| | 19X5 | 19X4 | 19X5 | 19X4 |
| Net sales | $ 520,000 | $ 480,000 | | |
| Cost of goods sold | 360,000 | 315,000 | | |
| Gross margin | 160,000 | 165,000 | | |
| Operating expenses | 128,600 | 126,000 | 24.8 | 26.2 |
| Net operating income | 31,400 | 39,000 | 6.0 | 8.2 |
| Interest expense | 6,400 | 7,000 | 1.2 | 1.5 |
| Net income before taxes | 25,000 | 32,000 | 4.8 | 6.7 |
| Less income taxes (30%) | 7,500 | 9,600 | 1.4 | 2.0 |
| Net income | $ 17,500 | $ 22,400 | 3.4 | 4.7 |

18

Now, let's look at Norton Corporation's 19X5 and 19X4 financial statements.




18

NORTON CORPORATION
Balance Sheets
December 31, 19X5 and 19X4

| | 19X5 | 19X4 |
|---|---|---|
| Assets | | |
| Current assets: | | |
| Cash | $ 30,000 | $ 20,000 |
| Accounts receivable, net | 20,000 | 17,000 |
| Inventory | 12,000 | 10,000 |
| Prepaid expenses | 3,000 | 2,000 |
| Total current assets | 65,000 | 49,000 |
| Property and equipment: | | |
| Land | 165,000 | 123,000 |
| Buildings and equipment, net | 116,390 | 128,000 |
| Total property and equipment | 281,390 | 251,000 |
| Total assets | $ 346,390 | $ 300,000 |

18

**NORTON CORPORATION**
**Balance Sheets**
**December 31, 19X5 and 19X4**

| | 19X5 | 19X4 |
|---|---|---|
| Liabilities and Stockholders' Equity | | |
| Current liabilities: | | |
| Accounts payable | $ 39,000 | $ 40,000 |
| Notes payable, short-term | 3,000 | 2,000 |
| Total current liabilities | 42,000 | 42,000 |
| Long-term liabilities: | | |
| Notes payable, long-term | 70,000 | 78,000 |
| Total liabilities | 112,000 | 120,000 |
| Stockholders' equity: | | |
| Common stock, $1 par value | 27,400 | 17,000 |
| Additional paid-in capital | 158,100 | 113,000 |
| Total paid-in capital | 185,500 | 130,000 |
| Retained earnings | 48,890 | 50,000 |
| Total stockholders' equity | 234,390 | 180,000 |
| Total liabilities and stockholders' equity | $ 346,390 | $ 300,000 |



18

NORTON CORPORATION
Income Statements
For the Years Ended December 31, 19X5 and 19X4

| | 19X5 | 19X4 |
|---|---|---|
| Net sales | $ 494,000 | $ 450,000 |
| Cost of goods sold | 140,000 | 127,000 |
| Gross margin | 354,000 | 323,000 |
| Operating expenses | 270,000 | 249,000 |
| Net operating income | 84,000 | 74,000 |
| Interest expense | 7,300 | 8,000 |
| Net income before taxes | 76,700 | 66,000 |
| Less income taxes (30%) | 23,010 | 19,800 |
| Net income | $ 53,690 | $ 46,200 |



18

Now, let's calculate some ratios based on Norton Corporation's financial statements.

## Ratio Analysis – The Common Stockholder

**Use this information to calculate ratios to measure the well-being of the common stockholders of Norton Corporation.**

| NORTON CORPORATION 19X5 | |
|---|---|
| Number of common shares outstanding | |
| Beginning of year | 17,000 |
| End of year | 27,400 |
| Net income | $ 53,690 |
| Stockholders' equity | |
| Beginning of year | 180,000 |
| End of year | 234,390 |
| Dividends per share | 2 |
| Dec. 31 market price per share | 20 |
| Interest expense | 7,300 |
| Total assets | |
| Beginning of year | 300,000 |
| End of year | 346,390 |



## Ratio Analysis – The Common Stockholder

- Earnings per Share

$$\text{Earnings per Share} = \frac{\text{Net Income} - \text{Preferred Dividends}}{\text{Average Number of Common Shares Outstanding}}$$

**This measure indicates how much income was earned for each share of common stock outstanding.**



## Ratio Analysis – The Common Stockholder

- When extraordinary gains or losses appear on the income statement, two earnings per share figures must be computed.
  1. One calculation must show earnings per share from the normal operations.
  2. Another calculation must show earnings per share from the extraordinary items, net of tax effects.

## Ratio Analysis – The Common Stockholder

- When convertible securities exist, two earnings per share figures must be computed.
  - ❶One calculation must show earnings per share assuming no conversion into common stock is made.
  - ❷Another calculation must show fully diluted earnings per share assuming a full conversion into common stock is made.



## Ratio Analysis – The Common Stockholder

- Price-Earnings Ratio

$$\text{Price-Earnings Ratio} = \frac{\text{Market Price Per Share}}{\text{Earnings Per Share}}$$

**This measure is often used by investors as a general guideline in gauging stock values. Generally, the higher the price-earnings ratio, the more opportunity a company has for growth.**



## Ratio Analysis – The Common Stockholder

- Dividend Payout Ratio

$$\text{Dividend Payout Ratio} = \frac{\text{Dividends Per Share}}{\text{Earnings Per Share}}$$

**This ratio gauges the portion of current earnings being paid out in dividends. Investors seeking current income would like this ratio to be large.**

## Ratio Analysis – The Common Stockholder

✦ Dividend Yield

$$\text{Dividend Yield} = \frac{\text{Dividends Per Share}}{\text{Market Price Per Share}}$$

This ratio identifies the return, in terms of cash dividends, on the current market price of the stock.



## Ratio Analysis – The Common Stockholder

✦ Return on Total Assets

$$\text{Return on Total Assets} = \frac{\text{Net Income} + [\text{Interest Expense} \times (1 - \text{Tax Rate})]}{\text{Average Total Assets}}$$

Whenever a ratio divides an income statement balance by a balance sheet balance, the average for the year is used in the denominator.



## Ratio Analysis – The Common Stockholder

✦ Return on Total Assets

$$\text{Return on Total Assets} = \frac{\text{Net Income} + [\text{Interest Expense} \times (1 - \text{Tax Rate})]}{\text{Average Total Assets}}$$

This ratio measures how well assets have been employed.

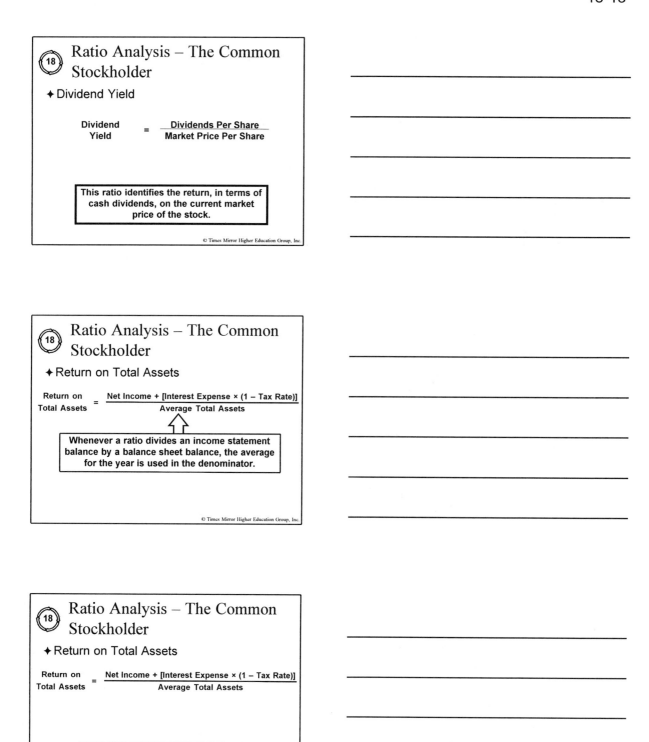

## Ratio Analysis – The Common Stockholder

✦ Return on Common Stockholders' Equity

$$\text{Return on Common Stockholders' Equity} = \frac{\text{Net Income} - \text{Preferred Dividends}}{\text{Average Stockholders' Equity}}$$

**This measure indicates how well the company employed the owners' investments to earn income.**



## Ratio Analysis – The Common Stockholder

Financial leverage involves acquiring assets with funds at a fixed rate of interest.

| | | | | |
|---|---|---|---|---|
| **Return on investment in assets** | **>** | **Fixed rate of of return on borrowed funds** | **=** | **Positive financial leverage** |

| | | | | |
|---|---|---|---|---|
| **Return on investment in assets** | **<** | **Fixed rate of of return on borrowed funds** | **=** | **Negative financial leverage** |



## Ratio Analysis – The Common Stockholder

Because interest on debt is tax deductible and dividends paid to preferred stockholders are not tax deductible, debt is more efficient in generating positive financial leverage than preferred stock.

## Ratio Analysis – The Common Stockholder

- Book Value per Share

$$\text{Book Value per Share} = \frac{\text{Common Stockholders' Equity}}{\text{Number of Common Shares Outstanding}}$$

**This ratio measures the amount that would be distributed to holders of each share of common stock if all assets were sold at their balance sheet carrying amounts and if all creditors were paid off.**



## Ratio Analysis – The Short-Term Creditor

**Use this information to calculate ratios to measure the well-being of the short-term creditors for Norton Corporation.**

| NORTON CORPORATION 19X5 | |
|---|---|
| Cash | $ 30,000 |
| Accounts receivable, net | |
| Beginning of year | 17,000 |
| End of year | 20,000 |
| Inventory | |
| Beginning of year | 10,000 |
| End of year | 12,000 |
| Total current assets | 65,000 |
| Total current liabilities | 42,000 |
| Sales on account | 500,000 |
| Cost of goods sold | 140,000 |



## Ratio Analysis – The Short-Term Creditor

Working capital is the excess of current assets over current liabilities.

This measure represents current assets financed from long-term capital sources that do not require near-term repayment.

| | December 31, 19X5 |
|---|---|
| Current assets | $ 65,000 |
| Current liabilities | (42,000) |
| Working capital | $ 23,000 |

## Ratio Analysis – The Short–Term Creditor

✦ Current Ratio

$$\text{Current Ratio} = \frac{\text{Current Assets}}{\text{Current Liabilities}}$$

This ratio measures the ability of the company to pay current debts as they become due.



## Ratio Analysis – The Short–Term Creditor

✦ Acid-Test Ratio (or Quick Ratio)

$$\text{Acid-Test Ratio} = \frac{\text{Quick Assets}}{\text{Current Liabilities}}$$

Quick assets are Cash, Marketable Securities, Accounts Receivable and current Notes Receivable.



## Ratio Analysis – The Short–Term Creditor

✦ Acid-Test Ratio (or Quick Ratio)

$$\text{Acid-Test Ratio} = \frac{\text{Quick Assets}}{\text{Current Liabilities}}$$

This ratio is like the current ratio but excludes current assets such as inventories that may be difficult to quickly convert into cash.

## Ratio Analysis – The Short-Term Creditor

- Accounts Receivable Turnover

$$\text{Accounts Receivable Turnover} = \frac{\text{Sales on Account}}{\text{Average Accounts Receivable}}$$

This ratio measures how many times a company converts its receivables into cash each year.



## Ratio Analysis – The Short-Term Creditor

- Average Collection Period

$$\text{Average Collection Period} = \frac{\text{365 Days}}{\text{Accounts Receivable Turnover}}$$

This ratio measures, on average, how many days it takes to collect an account receivable.



## Ratio Analysis – The Short-Term Creditor

- Inventory Turnover

$$\text{Inventory Turnover} = \frac{\text{Cost of Goods Sold}}{\text{Average Inventory}}$$

This ratio measures the number of times merchandise inventory is sold and replaced during the year.

# Ratio Analysis – The Short–Term Creditor

✦ Average Sale Period

$$\text{Average Sale Period} = \frac{\text{365 Days}}{\text{Inventory Turnover}}$$

This ratio measures how many days, on average, it takes to sell the inventory.



# Ratio Analysis – The Long–Term Creditor

**Use this information to calculate ratios to measure the well-being of the long-term creditors for Norton Corporation.**

| NORTON CORPORATION 19X5 | |
|---|---|
| Earnings before interest expense and income taxes | $ 84,000 |
| Interest expense | 7,300 |
| Total stockholders' equity | 234,390 |
| Total liabilities | 112,000 |



# Ratio Analysis – The Long–Term Creditor

✦ Times Interest Earned Ratio

$$\text{Times Interest Earned} = \frac{\text{Earnings before Interest Expense and Income Taxes}}{\text{Interest Expense}}$$

This is the most common measure of the ability of a firm's operations to provide protection to the long-term creditor.

## Ratio Analysis – The Long–Term Creditor

- Debt–to–Equity Ratio

$$\text{Debt–to–Equity Ratio} = \frac{\text{Total Liabilities}}{\text{Stockholders' Equity}}$$

**This ratio measures the amount of assets being provided by creditors for each dollar of assets being provided by the owners of the company.**



## End of Chapter 18

## GENERAL JOURNAL

Page 42

| Date | | Description | Post. Ref. | Debit | Credit |
|---|---|---|---|---|---|
| | | | | | |
| | | | | | |
| | | | | | |
| | | | | | |
| | | | | | |
| | | | | | |
| | | | | | |
| | | | | | |
| | | | | | |
| | | | | | |
| | | | | | |
| | | | | | |

## GENERAL JOURNAL

Page 42

| Date | | Description | Post. Ref. | Debit | Credit |
|---|---|---|---|---|---|
| | | | | | |
| | | | | | |
| | | | | | |
| | | | | | |
| | | | | | |
| | | | | | |
| | | | | | |
| | | | | | |
| | | | | | |
| | | | | | |
| | | | | | |
| | | | | | |

# GENERAL JOURNAL

Page 42

| Date | | Description | Post. Ref. | Debit | Credit |
|---|---|---|---|---|---|
| | | | | | |
| | | | | | |
| | | | | | |
| | | | | | |
| | | | | | |
| | | | | | |
| | | | | | |
| | | | | | |
| | | | | | |
| | | | | | |
| | | | | | |
| | | | | | |

## GENERAL JOURNAL

Page 42

| Date | | Description | Post. Ref. | Debit | Credit |
|---|---|---|---|---|---|
| | | | | | |
| | | | | | |
| | | | | | |
| | | | | | |
| | | | | | |
| | | | | | |
| | | | | | |
| | | | | | |
| | | | | | |
| | | | | | |
| | | | | | |
| | | | | | |

## GENERAL JOURNAL

Page 42

| Date | | Description | Post. Ref. | Debit | Credit |
|---|---|---|---|---|---|
| | | | | | |
| | | | | | |
| | | | | | |
| | | | | | |
| | | | | | |
| | | | | | |
| | | | | | |
| | | | | | |
| | | | | | |
| | | | | | |
| | | | | | |
| | | | | | |

## GENERAL JOURNAL

Page 42

| Date | | Description | Post. Ref. | Debit | Credit |
|---|---|---|---|---|---|
| | | | | | |
| | | | | | |
| | | | | | |
| | | | | | |
| | | | | | |
| | | | | | |
| | | | | | |
| | | | | | |
| | | | | | |
| | | | | | |
| | | | | | |
| | | | | | |

## GENERAL LEDGER

Account                                                    Account No.

| | | | | | Balance | |
|---|---|---|---|---|---|---|
| Date | Item | Post. Ref. | Debit | Credit | Debit | Credit |
| | | | | | | |
| | | | | | | |
| | | | | | | |
| | | | | | | |
| | | | | | | |
| | | | | | | |
| | | | | | | |
| | | | | | | |
| | | | | | | |

## GENERAL LEDGER

Account                                                    Account No.

| | | | | | Balance | |
|---|---|---|---|---|---|---|
| Date | Item | Post. Ref. | Debit | Credit | Debit | Credit |
| | | | | | | |
| | | | | | | |
| | | | | | | |
| | | | | | | |
| | | | | | | |
| | | | | | | |
| | | | | | | |
| | | | | | | |
| | | | | | | |

## GENERAL LEDGER

Account | Account No.

| Date | Item | Post. Ref. | Debit | Credit | Balance Debit | Balance Credit |
|---|---|---|---|---|---|---|
| | | | | | | |
| | | | | | | |
| | | | | | | |
| | | | | | | |
| | | | | | | |
| | | | | | | |
| | | | | | | |
| | | | | | | |
| | | | | | | |

## GENERAL LEDGER

Account | Account No.

| Date | Item | Post. Ref. | Debit | Credit | Balance Debit | Balance Credit |
|---|---|---|---|---|---|---|
| | | | | | | |
| | | | | | | |
| | | | | | | |
| | | | | | | |
| | | | | | | |
| | | | | | | |
| | | | | | | |
| | | | | | | |
| | | | | | | |

## GENERAL LEDGER

Account | Account No.

| | | | | | Balance | |
|---|---|---|---|---|---|---|
| Date | Item | Post. Ref. | Debit | Credit | Debit | Credit |
| | | | | | | |
| | | | | | | |
| | | | | | | |
| | | | | | | |
| | | | | | | |
| | | | | | | |
| | | | | | | |
| | | | | | | |
| | | | | | | |

## GENERAL LEDGER

Account | Account No.

| | | | | | Balance | |
|---|---|---|---|---|---|---|
| Date | Item | Post. Ref. | Debit | Credit | Debit | Credit |
| | | | | | | |
| | | | | | | |
| | | | | | | |
| | | | | | | |
| | | | | | | |
| | | | | | | |
| | | | | | | |
| | | | | | | |
| | | | | | | |

## GENERAL LEDGER

Account　　　　　　　　　　Account No.

| Date | Item | Post. Ref. | Debit | Credit | Balance Debit | Balance Credit |
|---|---|---|---|---|---|---|
| | | | | | | |

## GENERAL LEDGER

Account　　　　　　　　　　Account No.

| Date | Item | Post. Ref. | Debit | Credit | Balance Debit | Balance Credit |
|---|---|---|---|---|---|---|
| | | | | | | |

## GENERAL LEDGER

Account ________ Account No. ________

| Date | Item | Post. Ref. | Debit | Credit | Balance Debit | Balance Credit |
|---|---|---|---|---|---|---|
| | | | | | | |
| | | | | | | |
| | | | | | | |
| | | | | | | |
| | | | | | | |
| | | | | | | |
| | | | | | | |
| | | | | | | |
| | | | | | | |

## GENERAL LEDGER

Account ________ Account No. ________

| Date | Item | Post. Ref. | Debit | Credit | Balance Debit | Balance Credit |
|---|---|---|---|---|---|---|
| | | | | | | |
| | | | | | | |
| | | | | | | |
| | | | | | | |
| | | | | | | |
| | | | | | | |
| | | | | | | |
| | | | | | | |
| | | | | | | |

## GENERAL LEDGER

Account | Account No.

| Date | Item | Post. Ref. | Debit | Credit | Balance Debit | Balance Credit |
|---|---|---|---|---|---|---|
| | | | | | | |
| | | | | | | |
| | | | | | | |
| | | | | | | |
| | | | | | | |
| | | | | | | |
| | | | | | | |
| | | | | | | |
| | | | | | | |

## GENERAL LEDGER

Account | Account No.

| Date | Item | Post. Ref. | Debit | Credit | Balance Debit | Balance Credit |
|---|---|---|---|---|---|---|
| | | | | | | |
| | | | | | | |
| | | | | | | |
| | | | | | | |
| | | | | | | |
| | | | | | | |
| | | | | | | |
| | | | | | | |
| | | | | | | |